Praise for *I've N...*
Vegas, but My Luggage Has

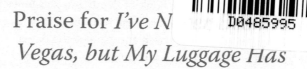

You love Mandy from page one. It's rare to be this sweet, compelling, and funny all the way through while also being this insightful about life. We are in love, Mandy Hale—but we're seeing someone at the moment.

—GREG BEHRENDT, *NEW YORK TIMES* BEST-SELLING
AUTHOR, *HE'S JUST NOT THAT INTO YOU* AND *IT'S CALLED
A BREAKUP BECAUSE IT'S BROKEN* AND FORMER SCRIPT
CONSULTANT FOR *SEX & THE CITY*; AND AMIIRA RUOTOLA-
BEHRENDT, CO-AUTHOR, *IT'S CALLED A BREAKUP BECAUSE
IT'S BROKEN* (AND FABULOUS WIFE TO GREG)

Your story is such a Romans 8:28 story—"And we know all things work together for the good of them that love the Lord." He took your pain and used it to inspire, encourage, and lead others to walk in their purposes, as you are walking in yours!

—SHERRI SHEPHERD, ACTRESS,
COMEDIAN, AND HOST, ABC'S *THE VIEW*

Move over Carrie Bradshaw. Here comes Mandy Hale! *I've Never Been to Vegas, but My Luggage Has* is a wonderfully-crafted "coming of singleness story" that will entertain and inspire all seekers of true love and faith.

—DANIEL GODDARD, ACTOR,
THE YOUNG AND THE RESTLESS

The Single Woman message has been a blessing! Mandy lets you know that it's okay to be single and to work on YOU! Empowering! Encouraging!

—MICHELLE WILLIAMS, SINGER/SONGWRITER,
PRODUCER, ACTRESS, AND MEMBER OF
GRAMMY-WINNING DESTINY'S CHILD

Mandy Hale's wit and southern-girl charm will disarm you, but don't let it fool you! She's got a mean left hook of depth and substance that will quickly get your attention. She is a fresh and relevant voice whose message to her generation is beautifully woven throughout the pages of her own life, a product of her own adventures, triumphs, failures, fresh starts, false starts, tears, and laughs."

—JON ACUFF, NEW YORK TIMES BEST-
SELLING AUTHOR OF START AND QUITTER

The Single Woman message isn't just about being solo and loving it. It's about being a better human all around—something we should all aspire to!

—ESTELLE, GRAMMY-WINNING SINGER/
SONGWRITER, RAPPER, AND PRODUCER

Reading Mandy Hale's story feels like riding shotgun with a close girlfriend who is on the ride of her life, discovering and growing from the purpose in every twist, turn, and bump in the road. I love the vulnerability Mandy shares from her own life. The journey truly is the destination.

—NATALIE GRANT, GRAMMY-NOMINATED SINGER/
SONGWRITER AND FOUNDER OF ABOLITION INTERNATIONAL

With this book, Mandy gives the most amazing perspective on the ups and downs of life. And in an often hilarious way, she lets us know we are not on this journey alone. This is, hands down, on my short list of favorite books!

—MELINDA DOOLITTLE, RECORDING ARTIST, AUTHOR,
AND FINALIST ON SEASON 6 OF AMERICAN IDOL

As a pastor of a church with a lot of singles, I can say that Mandy Hale is a brilliant storyteller who adds a fresh and energetic voice to the needs and wants of single women. When you read this book, you will laugh, be encouraged, and learn that God's love is woven into the tapestry of every great story, including yours and mine.

—PETE WILSON, SENIOR PASTOR, CROSS POINT
CHURCH, AND AUTHOR, PLAN B AND LET HOPE IN

It is such a great adventure and pleasure to be part of Mandy Hale's world. Her book provides comfort and hope that in the midst life's ups and downs there are giggles and redemption. A memoir that is also a great self-help book for anyone who needs uplifting!

—DODINSKY, NEW YORK TIMES BEST-SELLING
AUTHOR, IN THE GARDEN OF THOUGHTS

If you're ready for an adventure into your own heart and soul and if you're ready to be challenged, become more courageous, and realize that the journey—not the destination—is the best part of life, you need to read Mandy Hale's *I've Never Been to Vegas, but My Luggage Has*. Simply put, this is one of the best books I've read in a long time.

—WENDY GRIFFITH, CO-HOST, *THE 700 CLUB*

What I love about The Single Woman message is it empowers single sisters (such as myself) to embrace, appreciate, and grow during our single times. Mandy's wisdom and sense of humor make her nuggets of truth both life-changing and easy to digest! I am so thankful for the role she has played in my life!

—MANDISA, GRAMMY-NOMINATED
CHRISTIAN RECORDING ARTIST

If you've ever felt too flawed, too weak, or too inadequate to be used by God, Mandy's story is for you. Her journey is proof that you don't have to be perfect—you just have to be available. A wonderful reminder for any single woman (or man) that there is more than one way to Happily Ever After, and if you are willing to hand the pen over to God, He'll write an infinitely more beautiful story for your life than you could ever imagine.

—LISA OSTEEN COMES, AUTHOR,
YOU ARE MADE FOR MORE!

Strong, grounded, on point and real! A must-read for every sister who wants to walk this walk victoriously!

—MICHELLE MCKINNEY-HAMMOND, EMMY AWARD–
WINNING TALK SHOW HOST AND BEST-SELLING AUTHOR

I love The Single Woman message because it gives you permission to feel okay about being single. And not just okay—confident! Mandy inspires me to take care of me, to not settle, and to expect the best from love and life. As a single woman, it's vital to embrace and love yourself, and Mandy's books inspire you and challenge you to do just that!

—LISA VALASTRO, REALITY STAR, TLC's *CAKE BOSS*

I started out reading Mandy's memoir feeling like I was looking through a window, watching her every move, and empathizing with her. It didn't take long before that window somehow turned into a mirror, and then it felt like I was reading about myself. Mandy's truth is hers, but I think everyone will find a piece of themselves in it as well. Heartfelt, honest, and entertaining.

—CAROLYN DAWN JOHNSON, AWARD-WINNING COUNTRY
MUSIC SINGER/SONGWRITER AND PRODUCER

As a professional matchmaker, a key ingredient to building a successful partnership is starting with two whole, complete, healthy people. Mandy's message is all about empowering and motivating single women to become all that they're meant to become, independent from a relationship so that they invite love into their lives to complement rather than complete them. This book gives women permission to enjoy the journey to Happily Ever After, even as they look forward to the destination. Perfect for the woman (or man) who needs a reminder that happy single life helps create the foundation of a happy married life.

—PAUL CARRICK BRUNSON, CO-
HOST, OWN'S *LOVE TOWN* AND
PROFESSIONAL MATCHMAKER

I've Never Been to Vegas, but My Luggage Has is an inspiring story about growth, self-acceptance, faith, and redemption that's relatable to women of all walks and stages of life. Anyone who reads it will come away with a better understanding of where she's been, comfort for where she's going, and contentment in knowing she's where God wants her to be. You'll want to give this book to every woman you love!

—NIKKI WOODS, SENIOR PRODUCER, *TOM JOYNER
MORNING SHOW* AND CEO, NIKKI WOODS MEDIA

Mandy's real-life story of her stumbles, disappointments, and mountain-top moments are beautifully transparent and filled with hope and humor. Combine the warm coffee talk of *Friends* with the zany moments of *I Love Lucy,* all laced with non-judgmental, godly wisdom, and you have Mandy's new book. I was so caught up in her story; I began reading it during stop lights! When I finished, I felt encouraged that I was *not* the only one still struggling to "get it right," and that God does indeed have endless grace for His children!

—ELISA JONES, MANAGER OF PHILANTHROPY,
EASTERN TERRITORIES—K-LOVE RADIO

I'VE NEVER BEEN
TO VEGAS
but My Luggage Has

MISHAPS AND MIRACLES ON THE
ROAD TO HAPPILY EVER AFTER

MANDY HALE

NELSON
BOOKS

An Imprint of Thomas Nelson

Published in Nashville, Tennessee, by Nelson Books, an imprint of Thomas Nelson. Nelson Books and Thomas Nelson are registered trademarks of HarperCollins Christian Publishing, Inc.

Thomas Nelson, Inc., titles may be purchased in bulk for educational, business, fund-raising, or sales promotional use. For information, please e-mail SpecialMarkets@ThomasNelson.com.

Cataloging-in-Publication Data available through the Library of Congress

ISBN: 978-1-40020-525-7

Printed in the United States of America

14 15 16 17 18 RRD 6 5 4 3 2 1

To the current love of my life, my precious Lord Jesus, thank You for taking my colorful, funny, imperfect, and wildly unexpected journey and turning it into something beautiful. I once heard it said that a perfect life makes a boring book. If that's the case, this should be the most entertaining book to hit shelves in years! For loving me, for redeeming me, for carrying me, for guiding me, for making sure I always get where I'm meant to be in life (even if my luggage doesn't), and for so many other reasons: thank You. This book is my humble offering to You.

And to the future love of my life—whoever and wherever he may be—may the stories contained in this book be merely a prologue to the epic love story we will write together.

Contents

Chapter 1

Once Upon a Flight

$\mathcal{I}$'ve never been to Vegas, but my luggage has.

Allow me to explain.

Eight years ago I was living the dream. Working as an associate producer in Country Music Television's news department, I had been bumped up from production assistant in a record three months without having to step on anyone to get there. For the first couple of months, the producers tossed me menial tasks like transcribing tapes and running errands, but I caught my big break one September day when one of the senior staff members called in sick, leaving us short-staffed. With an up-and-coming country music singer due in the CMT studios later that day to record a piece about his workout habits, and no one available to do the interview, I was assigned to the task at the last minute. Nervous and shaky but feigning confidence, I completed the interview with ease and even managed to vibe with the country cutie. Having proven my ability to rise to the occasion, I found that my responsibilities continued to increase, and a few months later I was handed the plum assignment of interviewing the stars on the red carpet at the CMT Music Awards! I could barely contain my excitement. Dierks and Kenny and Keith—oh my! After a mildly unpleasant run-in with an older actor who seemed exceedingly grouchy for someone at an awards show (let's just say he must have been on leave from the Starship *Enterprise* and wasn't happy about it), I looked up to see a vision in brown making his way toward me. Keith Urban, in all his still-single, pre–Nicole Kidman glory, was standing in front of my microphone with an expectant look on his face. I managed to snap to attention and point the microphone at Keith, ready to get down to the business of talking clothes.

"So, Keith," I said brightly, pretending I was chatting with an average Joe, "tell me about your outfit!"

Keith looked at me with a bit of hesitation. In the midst of the awkward pause, with me shifting around nervously, he reached over to grab the hand of the woman standing beside him. Much to my mortification, the hand just happened to be attached to Ms. Loretta Lynn—one of country music's biggest legends, decked out in a gigantic ball gown that rivaled Cinderella's—and I had completely overlooked her. The associate producer there to talk about fashion—me—had slighted a country music icon who also happened to be wearing possibly the most ornate, sparkly, and grand outfit of the entire evening.

"Why don't we talk about Ms. Loretta's outfit first?" Keith said in his adorable Aussie twang, showing me incredible amounts of grace, considering I had basically just snubbed one of country music's most beloved divas.

Wanting very much to crawl under the red carpet and disappear, I turned to Loretta Lynn, who gazed compassionately back at this completely clueless and inexperienced twenty-five-year-old associate producer who was just trying to make her way in a world that Ms. Lynn had long ago taken by storm. Not an ounce of indignation or attitude or impatience on her face, the beautiful, graceful woman answered all my questions humbly and kindly, not at all ruffled by the fact that a punk kid had completely disregarded her in order to drool over the much younger, and at the time much less established, Keith Urban. I was taught something about true humility and grace that night—in a much gentler way than I probably deserved and by a woman who was lighting fires and blazing trails through the world before I was even a gleam in my daddy's eye.

That *gigantic* snafu aside, the rest of the evening went by in a flash of sparkly belt buckles, gleaming white teeth, and shiny cowboy boots. And the news package I put together about the colorful and boisterous fashion of the 2004 CMT Music Awards went over so well, I was given even more responsibility at work. Before I knew it, I was chosen to be a part of the team that flew to Las Vegas for the Academy of Country Music Awards in April 2005, where I would once again be producing the fashion piece of the show. I was, obviously, ecstatic and overjoyed, and I felt like, at the tender age of twenty-five, I had *arrived.* My career was on the fast track! I was flying high for weeks, until one day the sober realization hit me—I don't like to fly high. Actually, I don't like to fly at all. Nothing appealed to me about climbing into a long metal cylinder and skyrocketing thousands of feet off the ground, putting my life into the hands of pilots whom I didn't know; and though I had flown three times before, the last time I had become so unglued, I had screeched, "I want *off!*" at the top of my lungs just as the jet started taxiing full steam ahead down the runway. (I did, however, somehow manage to suck it up and hold it together for the duration of that flight.) But that flight had been pre-9/11. In the post-9/11 world of uncertainty, orange flags, and raised threat levels, I wanted no part of flying the seemingly not-so-friendly skies. But how to explain that to my bosses? And how could I turn down a hotly sought-after assignment that was guaranteed to solidify my status as a valued member of the team, possibly even nabbing myself a "producer" title instead of AP? I decided I would just have to look at it as mind over matter, get over myself, and make that flight, come hail or high water.

On the day of departure, I couldn't eat all morning. I had barely slept the night before and was a gigantic ball of nerves. I'm fairly certain I was also wild-eyed and disheveled looking as a result of my overall terror and lack of sleep. Basically, I looked like Nick Nolte in that very memorable mug shot. When I showed up at the airport, my boss looked sincerely concerned. As I fumbled to get my shoes off and go through security, the security guards peered at me a little suspiciously. I somehow managed to make it onto the plane and into my seat without passing out, noticing as I filed back to coach that the members of one of country music's biggest bands were seated with their wives in first class.

Once in my seat, I pulled out *People* magazine to distract myself. It didn't work. I went for the *Us Weekly*. Nope, that didn't work either. The girl in the seat to my left looked increasingly alarmed as I continued to dig through my purse as if I were digging my way off of this plane and to China. I took two very mild anxiety pills that my doctor had prescribed, praying that they would transport me to my happy place—or even just a slightly tolerable place. No such luck. I took several deep, calming breaths and tried to close my eyes tight to shut out the world. All around me, I could hear plane sounds, fellow passengers, and overhead luggage compartment doors slamming. Somewhere in the midst of all this, I leapt to my feet, bashing my head into the plane ceiling so hard I saw stars—and not of the country music variety. So much adrenaline was coursing through my veins from the rising panic in my stomach, I barely even registered the pain. I frantically made my way to the front of the plane, well aware that the other passengers were staring at me curiously, wondering who the Nick Nolte look-alike with the shaky hands was and if they should start trying to call 9-1-1 from their in-flight phones.

"Excuse me, ma'am," I hissed urgently at the nearest flight attendant. "I need to get off the plane!"

The young, blond flight attendant whipped around in confusion to see who was causing the commotion and seemed relieved to find me, in all my skinny, twitching glory (which I guess was preferable to a bona fide terrorist with dynamite strapped to her shoes). She immediately launched into soothing, crisis-averting mode. "Now, ma'am, it's okay. People fly every single day with no problems at all. Is there anything we can do to make your experience more enjoyable?" *Yes*, I thought. *You can knock me in the head with a blunt object and wake me up* only *once we arrive in Vegas.*

"No, I don't think so. I think I just need to get off the plane."

The country music group sitting at the front of the plane in first class was, much to my chagrin, witnessing this entire humiliating episode. Should I actually make it to Vegas and wind up interviewing them on the red carpet, at least maybe we could use this as an icebreaker. "Hey, remember the crazy girl who delayed your flight and scared everyone into thinking they were being hijacked by a washed-up eighties actor having a really bad hair day? That was me! Ha, ha, ha!"

A moment or two passed with me insisting to the flight

attendant that I must be allowed to exit the plane before one of the country stars' wives discreetly made her way up to the front of the cabin and to my side.

"Honey," she said in her sweet Southern drawl, "I deal with this same thing all the time. I had to make them let me off a flight to LA once. I hate to fly with a passion!" She put her arm around me and winked at me reassuringly. "Come sit by me, and I'll introduce you to my little friend, Valium. You'll be cleared for takeoff in no time!"

"Um, ma'am," the flustered flight attendant interrupted, looking alarmed. "Passengers aren't allowed to share medication with other passengers. It goes against our security policy."

Mrs. Star Wife looked a little miffed, but continued to pat me on the back in a very mother hen sort of way, her kindness bringing tears to my eyes. She gazed at the flight attendant imploringly. "Well, isn't there anything you can do for this young lady? Perhaps offer her a better seat, closer to the front of the plane?"

After a little shuffling around, a passenger at the front of coach agreed to trade seats with me so I could have an aisle and a wall in front of me, rather than being packed in like a sardine toward the back. *Okay, here we go*, I thought. *Take two. You can do this!* I glanced over my shoulder at my boss, who by this point was looking more than a little annoyed. Turning back to the front, I closed my eyes and began to say the Lord's Prayer to myself. I was just entering the zone when I felt the ground start to move beneath me. We were starting to taxi down the runway, and my body was going into *major* fight-or-flight response mode. Fight won that coin toss as I jumped to my feet once again and pushed my way to the front of the plane.

"Ma'am, you're going to have to sit down! The plane has

started to pull away from the terminal!" the blond flight attendant insisted, her calm exterior starting to crack a bit.

"No! I can't. I have to be let off this plane. *Now*," I asserted. "I
can't do this. I have to get off."

The flight attendant, perhaps seeing the look on my face and
realizing she was either going to have to issue me a straight jacket
or find a way to get me off that plane, turned to her little phone and
began punching buttons. After a hushed conversation, she turned
back to me. "Okay, we're going to pull back to the gate," she said.
"But you have to be seated in order for us to be able to do so."

I walked the walk of shame back to my new and improved
front-row seat, my face no doubt turning fifty shades of magenta
as the flight attendant came over the loudspeaker. "Ladies and
gentlemen, if you will remain seated and bear with us for just a
moment, we are going to have to return to the gate momentarily."

A few minutes later, as I was exiting that plane bound for
Vegas, I glanced back over my shoulder once more at Mrs. Star
Wife. She nodded back at me, her eyes filled with compassion
and understanding, tempering the sting of humiliation and
embarrassment just a tiny bit. She gave me a reassuring smile
that would stick with me over the coming weeks and months as
things got more difficult at work based on my inability to complete that flight and take my assigned spot on the red carpet. She,
like Ms. Loretta Lynn who came before her, was another guide-
post I would meet along my path to becoming the woman I was
meant to be. Even in the face of inconvenience, she was patient,
kind, and protective of a young girl she had never even met. Her
offer of Valium was less about trying to sedate me and more
about trying to do anything she could think of to help out a fellow sojourner in need. Her big heart jumped to my defense even

as my boss shot daggers at me from the back of the plane—and that was something that I have never forgotten, even all these years later.

After slinking off the plane in a cloud of humiliation, it occurred to me that I had packed everything but the kitchen sink in my luggage, which was now footloose, fancy-free, and Vegas bound. The extent of my wardrobe left behind consisted of the clothes on my back, a few other grungy T-shirts, and one holey pair of jeans. I had no toiletries, no makeup, no shoes, not even any clean underwear. (Let's just say packing lightly has never been my specialty.)

Over the next three days, while the rest of my coworkers partied with my luggage in Vegas, I went by the airport every morning to check on the status of my bags. Each day the situation seemed more and more hopeless, as now the airport couldn't even tell me that my luggage had, in fact, made it to Vegas. This only stood to reason. I mean, if the *owner* of the luggage couldn't get over her fear and make it there, why should her luggage be held to a higher standard?

On day four, when the airport representative came rolling out my two gigantic suitcases, I wept with joy and relief, not even caring that my luggage had evidently eloped with two other suitcases while on its brief sabbatical to Las Vegas. And even though what happens in Vegas usually stays in Vegas, my suitcases (and my entire wardrobe) somehow found their way home from Sin City to Music City in one piece.

Most people get on a plane to arrive at a destination. I got on a plane to arrive at the undeniable conclusion that the journey is, in fact, the destination.

Yep. I've never been to Vegas—but my luggage has.

I tell this story because it is a metaphor for my entire life.

Over the past thirty-four years, my journey through life has been much like that infamous plane ride to Vegas that puttered its way down the runway but quickly turned back before it could really get off the ground. It has been complete with a cast of colorful characters who have each revealed a new layer of myself to me; some have built me up, some have torn me down, but all have pushed me, challenged me, and molded me into the woman I am today. With as much excitement, anticipation, and fire as a jet hurtling down the runway, the relationships and significant milestones of my life have all been no-holds-barred, full steam ahead—until something came along and threw a wrench in the plan and the plane abruptly stopped midcourse. Sometimes the plane stopped to avoid certain disaster. Sometimes the plane stopped to allow my path to collide with someone else's who was meant to have an impact on my life. And sometimes the plane stopped to teach me a lesson that I never could have learned had it actually taken flight. Whatever the detour, roadblock, or stop sign, my life always finds a way to come magically full circle in the most beautiful, entertaining, and sometimes downright hilarious ways. And though many of my adventures have found a way to go horribly awry—often taking me places I never intended to go—I have never lost sight of the fact that the journey *is* the destination.

Does this cause me to lose hope? Absolutely not. Because in all their anticlimactic glory, my foibles, missteps, and wrong turns have pushed me ever closer to my destiny, just as your own fiascos and flaws are meant to point you to your cause. The people, experiences, and lessons I have met along the way have all been guideposts, pointing me in the direction of my own North

Star. Most people's stories resemble those of a popular "chick lit" book: Girl meets boy, girl marries boy. Girl has 2.5 kids, buys a minivan, and lives happily ever after. My journey, however, has followed a far less predictable story: stalled chapters, unexpected plot twists, and dozens of rewrites that have left the ending more than a little uncertain. But this much I know: had I never met these people and lived these wild and crazy moments of highs and lows, pleasures and pains, I would have never met myself. Without more than a few bad dates, I would have never met my fate. Am I the perfect heroine of a modern-day fairy tale? No. I've stumbled and fallen, made a fool of myself, given in to fear, acted out of insecurity, made bad decisions, battled my control issues, and broken my own glass slippers a million times. But even in the midst of my biggest, most explosive crash landings, I've never given up hope for a happy ending.

So this is my story. Imperfect and zany and disjointed as it may be, it is my fairy tale. Maybe I haven't met my Prince Charming, but I have met dozens of toads who have taught me how to rescue myself, dozens of fairy godmothers who taught me how to believe in myself, and dozens of magical moments that taught me never to give up on myself. And along the way, quite accidentally, through my blog, social media persona, and first book, *The Single Woman*, I became the voice for hundreds of thousands of women across the world who are also boldly and courageously living out their Once Upon a Time, going on nothing but faith that the road less traveled will eventually lead to Happily Ever After.

Along the way, I also met God. That has been the most significant meeting of all. And though my walk with Him has at times been just as disjointed as the rest of my story, He is the common thread that connects all the dots. Walking with God is not an easy, tidy, no-muss, no-fuss little journey as some would have you believe. It's messy and often confusing and one of the hardest things you'll ever do. It's not the wide path or the easy path; it's the narrow path—one I have strayed from many times. The really amazing, beautiful, and miraculous thing about walking with God, however, is that even when you stray, He manages to find you. He uses the ugly, dirty things you do while running from Him to draw you back to Himself. He finds the one tiny diamond in the mountains of ashes that we sometimes allow our lives to become, from burning through the wrong people, wrong relationships, and wrong experiences.

Before you throw this book aside and discount it as "just another Christian story," hang on. I'm not preaching *at* you, I'm talking *with* you. My story is not a "faith-based" story; it is a story of faith, one I feel confident you will be able to relate to and learn from, regardless of your particular spiritual beliefs. And if along the way you come to know the God I know and love, we'll count it as a bonus.

It is my hope that you will see a little glimmer of yourself in my heartbreaks, in my victories, and in my defeats. It is my hope that my story will inspire you to go out and live your own story a little more boldly and fearlessly. May my lessons become your blessings, and my mistakes chart a path for you to realize your miracles. I hope you chuckle along with me as I unapologetically follow my heart wherever it leads—even when it leads to unbelievably awkward, uncomfortable, and hilarious hijinks. And perhaps my many, many falls will help you find the courage to get back up, time and time and time again.

It is my hope that you will begin to see that every sentence, every chapter of your own story is all leading up to the bigger book, the bigger picture. Even though my story is still being told, I can look back at my journey so far and see how a heartbreak led to a breakthrough, which led to a new beginning, which then led to another piece of my destiny falling into place. I hope that after reading this book you will be able to look back at your own life with new eyes and see how every thread is connected to a bigger tapestry. It all matters. Nothing, no matter how small or seemingly insignificant, happens to you without serving a greater purpose. Call it synchronicity or fate or, as I call it, divine order; every moment of your life pushes you toward your greater calling. I know this to be true because I've lived it. For my entire life leading up to the moment when I began to step into my greater calling, God dropped little clues, hints, and breadcrumbs along the way. Sometimes He did it to draw me back to the path I needed to be on. Sometimes He did it to detour me away from a path I didn't need to be on. And sometimes He did it for no other reason, I am convinced, than to make me laugh. But whatever His reason for intervening at integral moments along the way, this is what I have learned from cowriting my story with Him: every character, every chapter, every page, and every word has meaning.

You will find loss and love and laughter and tears on these pages. You will find a much-flawed princess who has hurt people, broken hearts, made shockingly bad decisions, fallen in love with the wrong guys, and been a victim of her own bad judgment. You will find an imperfect person who has let God down as many or more times as I have pleased Him. But even taking all that into account, I wouldn't have missed any of it for the world. Because all these experiences, these people, and these divine appointments helped create *me*. These circumstances didn't define me;

they helped refine me. The ashes of the girl I used to be turned me into the diamond of the woman I am today.

And that's how, once upon a time, not so long ago and far away, a single woman became The Single Woman.

Chapter 2

Love Is in the Air

Even before I became The Single Woman, I lived up to my future moniker all the way up until I was a senior in high school. I didn't have my first real love until I was eighteen. I had carried my shyness right into my teenage years, and though I was always on the fringes of the "popular crowd," sat at the right table in the cafeteria, and was included in most of the parties, football games, and pep rallies, I still never quite felt like a card-carrying member of the cool kids' club.

Though I had a few minor crushes and a few dates here and there, I largely felt invisible to the opposite sex in high school. I can remember feeling like I never quite fit in with anyone. Now I can look back on it and see that I never quite fit in because I was never meant to. I never knew how to be a follower, and I never succumbed to the temptations of cigarettes or alcohol or drugs in high school like so many teenagers do. I was far from perfect, but I think I felt God tugging on my heart, even then, to live my life by a different standard than most. Hindsight is twenty-twenty, and I can look back at those days now and see that I was being prepared for a different sort of journey than the majority of my counterparts. At the time, though, more often than not, it just felt lonely.

After three years of high school passed by without a single steady boyfriend, one day during senior year I happened to spot a boy I had never noticed before working in the bookstore in the lunchroom. While I was standing in the candy aisle, trying to decide between the Reese's and the Snickers, I looked up and caught the boy staring at me. He smiled. I smiled. I continued to casually browse. The minute he got busy with his cash register and line of customers, I elbowed my best friend, Sherry, sharply in the ribs.

"Who's that guy?" I asked her, trying to discreetly nod his way without calling attention to myself.

Sherry looked up from her rack of magazines. "Who?" she asked, following my gaze. "Oh, that's Matt. Matt Wilson. Why?" She paused and then exclaimed, "Oh my gosh! You like him! Do you want me to say something to him? His best friend, Brad, is in my economics class. I could get him to say something to Matt!"

"*No!* Don't say anything. I don't like him. I just thought he was, you know, kinda cute. That's all."

Little did I know Matt had been eyeballing me for some time too. It turns out we had biology together junior year, and he was the guy two rows back whom I always bummed notebook paper from—though I had no recollection of this. And although Sherry swore she never said anything to Brad to say to Matt, from that day on, I started to notice Matt walking past my locker regularly. Then it became a routine, every day, like clockwork. I would dart to my locker immediately after second period and swipe on some powder and lip gloss, just in time for Matt's approach. After a week or two, his sideways glance and half grin became a "hey." I would return his "hey" with a "hey" of my own, but after a solid month, we were still just "heying" and hadn't made any progress.

Until the homecoming dance rolled around.

Most years I just went with my friends, but in fall 1996, something major happened. Matt asked me to be his date to homecoming!

Sherry and I went into a frenzy of preparations for the big night. She and her boyfriend, David, would be doubling with me and Matt to the dance. I can still recall the new outfit I purchased just for the occasion: a lavender angora sweater and matching plaid skirt (It was the Cher Horowitz, *Clueless* era after all.) I went with my mom to buy a boutonniere for Matt and picked the biggest, healthiest-looking rose I could find. It had a ton of baby's breath around it, and when I picked it up, it felt like it weighed at least a pound. Little did I know that it would wind up taking up half of Matt's chest and being more of an albatross than a decorative addition to his outfit. I also didn't realize that my supersoft angora sweater would shed throughout the evening, and as we danced, purple fuzz would wind up all over Matt's entire person until he resembled Barney the dinosaur.

The four of us went out to dinner before the dance. I remember looking over at him during dinner and thinking, *I could really like this guy.* He was so sweet and unassuming and just . . . decent. Even from that first night, I could see what a good soul he had.

We wound up having a blast at the dance, the four of us rarely sitting out a dance, even when most of our counterparts were standing by the wall in awkward embarrassment. Despite my shyness and quiet nature in high school, I never met a dance floor I didn't like, and this dance was no exception. It was during "Oh What a Night" that I looked up and realized that Matt's boutonniere was gone. The weight of the ginormous flower had finally broken it free, and, as I noticed in horror, it had taken a little scrap of Matt's sweater with it.

"Oh no!" I exclaimed, causing Matt to jump, despite the volume of the music thumping in our ears.

"What's wrong?" he asked.

"Your flower! It's gone," I said in dismay, pulling back and starting to scan the floor for the massive rose. "I don't see it anywhere."

"Well, it can't be too hard to find!" Matt said with a grin. "It's not like it's hard to miss!"

The two of us searched high and low for the rose, pushing our way through a conga line, past a couple making out, and under the giant cheesy cardboard arch where our classmates were taking their official pictures to commemorate the night. We were just about to give up when something caught my eye. There, in the middle of a circle of break dancers, being stepped on, danced on, and kicked around, was the runaway boutonniere! I grabbed Matt's hand, and we inched our way through the throng of guys, who were cheering, whooping, clapping, and fist thrusting, until Matt was able to dash in to the middle of the fray and retrieve the flower. And somehow, despite the pounding feet, the thrashing break dancers, and the gyrating bodies, the rose remained completely unscathed. Matt held it up in the light of the disco ball, and like the great Phoenix, that boutonniere stretched toward the ceiling, mighty and proud and, if possible, bigger than ever! Simultaneously, we looked at each other and broke into hysterical laughter.

"It's like the Jason or Freddy Krueger of flowers!" Matt crowed, doubled up in laughter. "This thing cannot be destroyed!"

It was in a moment of uncontrollable giggling at the Bionic Boutonniere that I think I first started to fall in love with Matt. It was an unfamiliar feeling to me—one that reached out and squeezed my heart in a way that was both painful and wonderful, all at once. And the fact that he had enough fuzz from my sweater on his face to knit another sweater made me fall for him even more. He didn't care about the monstrously embarrassing boutonniere. He pinned it proudly back on his chest. He didn't care about making a fool out of himself dancing if that's what made me happy. He was too rooted in who he was, even at age eighteen, to be swayed or dismayed by looking silly or embarrassing or wrong. He simply didn't care. That kind of solid confidence and steadiness is hard to come by, particularly in high school.

And he was also a perfect gentleman. When he took me back to my car that night and we were saying our good nights, he looked me deep in the eyes for a moment before asking, "Would it be okay if I give you a kiss?" Now, at that point in my life, I hadn't been kissed a lot, and I had certainly never kissed a guy who asked for my permission first. My heart pounding a mile a minute, I nodded a tentative yes. He gave me the sweetest, softest, briefest of kisses before pulling back and smiling at me.

"Okay, well, I had a wonderful time tonight," he said, opening my car door and waiting for me to climb in. "Drive safe. I'll see you later."

"You too," I replied, my heart in my throat. "I'll see you later." As I pulled away, I glanced in my rearview mirror and saw him still standing there, leaning against his old beat-up car, purple fuzz from my sweater clinging to his cheeks and a smile on his face bigger than the giant rose still pinned to his chest.

―――――

It was seamless how quickly Matt and I became "Matt and I" after that.

I had a boyfriend. And not just a boyfriend, but a wonderful boyfriend. A boyfriend who respected me and treated me like a princess and was on the wrestling team and gave me his class ring.

For the rest of senior year, Matt and I were inseparable. He met my parents; I met his parents. He taught me how to drive a stick shift when my old gray Sentra, which I had nicknamed "Frog," finally died and my dad bought me a car with a manual transmission. He cheered me on that spring in the senior class play as I proudly took the stage as annoying cheerleader Patty Simcox in the drama club's production of *Grease*. I can remember one moment so clearly at the end of the play when we were all sitting on the edge of the stage with our arms around one another, swaying back and forth as we sang the refrain of "We Go Together": "We'll always be together! We'll always be together!" I looked out into the audience at Matt and looked around to my right and my left at my friends and their smiling faces, and I remember thinking to myself, *If only this were true. If only we would always be together, just like this, in this happy moment right before we become grown-ups and everything we know changes.*

Little did I know, the changes were only just beginning.

———

I was at work one day in late spring at the clothing store Cato, where I worked for much of senior year. I'll never forget that day in spring 1997, standing in the front of Cato, greeting customers with absolutely no idea about the curveball I was going to be thrown. I couldn't have been more on top of the world than I was at that moment.

But my world was about to tilt on its axis.

Sometime in the afternoon Matt came bursting in to the store with a look on his face I couldn't quite place. Assuming he was just there to meet me for lunch, I grinned, excited to see him, and ran to give him a hug. He stopped me.

"We need to talk," he said earnestly.

Immediately my heart started to pound. What was going on? He looked so serious. We had just been talking the night before about my prom dress and his tux and how they needed to color coordinate. How could we have gone from that lighthearted conversation to this heavy mood?

I looked around, beckoning for the other girl greeting that day to come take my place, and ushered Matt outside. We sat side by side on the curb, and he turned to me, taking my hands.

"I just made a decision that's going to affect us. Both of us," he said. "I really hope you'll be happy about it. But I need you to keep an open mind. Okay?"

I sat silent for a moment, racking my brain and going through our recent conversations in my mind, trying to figure out what on earth could have happened in the twenty-four hours since we had spoken that had cast this cloud over us and would potentially impact our relationship in what seemed like, from the expression on Matt's face, a negative way.

"What is it, Matt? You're scaring me," I said finally, squeezing his hand as a way to prompt him to continue.

He reached up and touched my cheek lightly, his face turning less serious as he realized how alarmed I was becoming.

"There's no need to be scared. It's really not bad," he said in a reassuring tone. "It's just . . . big."

"Okay . . . ," I replied, my voice trailing off. "Whatever it is, just tell me."

He took both my hands in his and looked down at his lap, like he was searching for the right words to say whatever monumental thing he was trying to tell me. Then he looked at me and smiled.

"I know I mentioned to you a couple of weeks ago that I met with a marine recruiter. Remember?"

I nodded slightly, recalling the brief conversation. At the time I had just assumed he had gotten roped into attending one of those standard recruiting meetings that the various branches of the military hold to recruit high school seniors. I never dreamed he was actually considering following up the meeting with action.

"Well, today I met with the staff sergeant again, the one I told you about that I really liked." He went on, "And, well, I joined the marines, Mandy. I just signed on the dotted line about an hour ago."

I let my breath out with a *whoosh* sound. "Oh my gosh! You scared me!" I playfully punched his arm in relief and stood. "I know a lot of guys who have joined the reserves. That's no big deal at all! It's just like one weekend out of the month and two weeks in the summer, right?"

He sat there, strangely silent.

Even as I rambled on in relief, I started to see a look of worry cross his face. He gazed at me lovingly and took my hand to pull me back down next to him.

"Mandy, I don't think you understand," he said. "I didn't sign up for the reserves. I signed up for active duty. I'll be gone for five years."

He paused, taking a deep breath before continuing.

"And I leave for boot camp in a month."

Chapter 3

Long-Distance Love

In the days that followed, I alternated between great pride that my boyfriend wanted to serve his country and great sadness that he was leaving behind a life with me to pursue his own path. I think it's probably the struggle that all military girlfriends and wives face. It's not that you're not happy, excited, and bursting with love for the person leaving; it's that you're struggling with the fact that you're the one being left behind. And right at the cusp of so many exciting things and new beginnings—prom, graduation, college—it was hard to accept that the most precious relationship of my life was coming to an end. Or at least it felt that way. Of course we had pledged to do the long-distance thing and make our relationship work, but the reality of the situation was, we were both eighteen. We were young. We were still becoming the people we were going to become. And our lives were taking us in two totally different directions.

Still, we had the excitement of prom to take our minds off of our impending separation, and as the night drew closer, I started to feel better and better about things. So we would deal with a little distance. We could handle it! This was my first love, my first real boyfriend, the guy I hoped to marry someday! Surely there was nothing we couldn't face down and come out on the other side, right? Sort of like the Bionic Boutonniere from homecoming? I felt confident our relationship could withstand a few hits and still come out unscathed.

We rented a big stretch limo for prom night, and Matt and I, along with Sherry and David and four or five other couples, rode in style to a fancy restaurant in Nashville before heading to the dance. Prom that year was at the country club in our small town, so we all felt extremely sophisticated to be at such a swanky venue, celebrating our official send-off into the real world and college and everything that being a grown-up entailed. But I quickly discovered that the real world was encroaching on our last night of magic and make-believe when the music started up and Matt refused to take the dance floor with me.

"What's wrong?" I asked, a bit impatiently. "We never sit on the sidelines at dances."

He winced as he settled into his chair, reaching down to massage a calf. "You know I've been training with Staff Sergeant Hal to get ready for boot camp," he explained. "We ran ten miles this morning, and my legs are killing me!"

I flopped down in the seat beside him, trying hard to be the understanding girlfriend.

"So you mean we can't dance . . . at *all*?" I asked.

"Sure we can. I just need to rest my legs for a few minutes, and then we'll be good to go."

A few minutes turned into an hour, until I finally gave up and took to the floor with Sherry and our other girlfriends, shooting glances over at Matt, silently willing him to stand up and grab hold of the moment in front of him instead of letting it pass us by. Though it was long before 9/11 and there were no major wars looming, there were still no guarantees when someone left to join the armed forces that they would be coming back. It's a sacrifice soldiers make, and in turn, a sacrifice soldiers' families make. I wanted us to live it up on the last night of celebration together, and make memories that would carry us through the next few months of separation while Matt was at boot camp and we wouldn't be able to even talk on the telephone. And all the while, he was sitting there just watching the precious moments dwindle away. It never occurred to me until later that maybe Matt was scared too. Maybe he didn't want to get lost in the moment because he knew if he did, the moment would end. Maybe he was sitting on the sidelines watching his peers dance the night away, thinking about the responsibility he had just taken onto his young shoulders. Maybe it felt frivolous and irresponsible to act like a kid when he had just signed away his childhood in favor of becoming a man much earlier than most of those guys shaking their hips on the dance floor would have to.

But in that moment, none of that occurred to me. In that moment, I was eighteen and saying good-bye to the boy I loved in two weeks, and I just wanted to dance with him one last time.

So after two hours of watching him sit on the sidelines of our senior prom, I had had enough. In true dramatic teenage-girl fashion, I huffed over to our table and grabbed my clutch. "What are you doing?" Matt asked, but I was too caught up in my own attitude to respond. I shot him a look, then turned on my heel and flounced off, with every intention of storming right out of the country club and, well, from there I wasn't sure, since the limo was long gone and Matt was supposed to drive me home.

Unfortunately, in the midst of my diva stomp, I failed to

remember that the entire front of the country club was a solid glass wall. Had I not been in such a tizzy, I would have found it odd that I could walk out of the ballroom where prom was and directly into the parking lot. But no, I was trying to prove a point, so I just kept right on huffing toward the parking lot until . . .

Bang!

I hit the glass wall so hard, I literally bounced backward and stood wavering back and forth on my feet—much like Tom flailing around in the air after Jerry has run him off a cliff—before tipping backward and falling flat on my back, legs shooting up straight in the air. And *of course* Matt had followed me out of the ballroom, so he was hot on my heels and saw the entire humiliating episode. Except, instead of being humiliated, I actually started to giggle. And then I started to guffaw. I looked up at Matt, who was standing over me with a horrified look on his face, and started to laugh even harder. Soon he was down on the ground in the middle of the country club floor with me, both of us rolling around in laughter at me in my fancy, sparkly dress, walking headfirst into a glass wall with the force of an angry bull. We laughed and laughed until we were gasping for breath and tears were rolling down our faces. And somewhere in the midst of that laughter, much like the laughter over his giant flower on our first date, the walls came down and the tension eased, and we knew that everything was going to be okay.

As our laughter started to die down, Matt reached over and pulled me to him fiercely, like he was trying to capture the moment and imprint it on his heart. And in that moment, as we held tightly to each other on the floor of the country club, I think we both accepted that the sweet, innocent, and carefree relationship we had known was over, and a new chapter was beginning.

———

Two weeks later Matt left for boot camp.

I knew it would take some time to get settled in and find time to write me. Finally, two weeks after he left, a letter!

I ripped it open in excited glee, hardly able to contain myself. And my heart jumped even more when I saw his words there, written in all caps so I grasped the significance of his message and the three little words he was saying to me for the very first time.

> I know it took me some time to say this, but being here and being away from you and finally seeing our relationship clearly, I couldn't wait another moment to tell you.
>
> Mandy Hale, I LOVE YOU!

I laughed and cried and cheered as I read his letter, which detailed his first two weeks of boot camp and everything he had been through. In just two weeks, his entire demeanor and attitude seemed to have changed. He had always been a good, solid, and kindhearted guy; but now he was loving, tender, and open in a way he had never been before. It was like boot camp had torn down the last remaining walls surrounding his heart, and he had finally and completely let me in!

Thus started a passionate exchange of letters, sometimes three and four a day. We started to number our letters because we sent so many, and we wanted to make sure we read them in order. Looking back on that time now, it always amazes me to think of the closeness that Matt and I achieved through only the written word. No e-mail, no Facebook, no texting, no phone calls—just good, old-fashioned, handwritten letters. I think that says a lot about how today's technology that's designed to bring us closer together might actually be a step or two behind the older form of communication. We poured our hearts and souls into those letters, holding nothing back. Never before, and honestly, never again after those three months of boot camp, did I feel closer to Matt.

Meanwhile, I was starting my own new beginning. I had just started my freshman fall semester at Middle Tennessee State University, and I was learning to navigate the waters of college life. I stumbled a little as I took those first few steps into adulthood, once again feeling as if I were starting at square one and struggling to fit in. Sherry had enrolled at a nearby community college, and though she was still close by, we no longer shared classes or a workplace or the same bond we had in high school, and that was tough.

Looking back at that era of my life, here is what I can see now that I couldn't have possibly seen then: God, in His infinite wisdom, was getting me to a place of complete and utter dependence upon Him. For so long I had looked to exterior things like my friendship with Sherry or my relationship with Matt for my identity and security and worth. And now here I was with no idea what I wanted to do with my life, and no boyfriend, or best friend to help me figure out my next step. Outside of my family, I felt completely and utterly alone.

So many people run from those seasons of loneliness out of fear. They never take the time to learn the lesson they're meant to learn from being alone. So you're lonely. Big deal! A little loneliness never hurt anyone. Learn to sit with it. Learn to appreciate loneliness for the gift that it truly is—a chance for God to finally get you alone so He can go to work on building a relationship with you. People need a little loneliness in life. Loneliness is where you find peace, reclaim your joy, and get to know the God who obviously loves you so much that He is going to great extremes to remove the distractions from your life so you can draw near to Him. When you look for your identity in anything other than Christ, eventually someone lets you down or you get fired or you break up or someone leaves, taking your identity with him or her, much the same way as my identity felt like it had taken a leave of absence during fall 1997. My God was going to great extremes to be alone with me, and at the time I couldn't even see it. Or appreciate it.

But a day was coming when I would.

Some days, the time Matt spent in boot camp seemed to fly by. I hadn't spoken to him outside of our letters or heard his voice in more than three months! And I had never physically heard him say those three little magic words, which was what I was most excited about.

Before I knew it, the day came when it was time to leave for Parris Island, South Carolina, with Matt's mom and sister to watch his Marine Corps graduation. And not only that, but we got to bring Matt home with us afterward for a few weeks of leave. I could barely sit still for the entire road trip to Parris Island.

The day of the graduation dawned humid and cloudy. Everywhere we looked, we saw recruits pounding the pavement in drills, runs, and other training exercises. Some were obviously brand new to boot camp. After we watched the graduation ceremony, we were directed to go outside and wait for all the battalions to march by in formation, after which the new marines would be allowed to find their family members in the crowd. I remember it being chaotic and frenzied as hundreds of young and newly minted soldiers started streaming into the crowd to reunite with their families, hugs and laughter and tears following in their wake. Matt's mom, Phyllis, and I were standing on our tiptoes searching frantically through the crowd for Matt. After what seemed like hours, I finally spotted a handsome, slimmed-down, and rather dashing young man galloping toward me in that familiar gait. Before I knew what was happening, he had swept me into a bear hug and was whispering in my ear, "I love you."

A photographer for the Marine Corps captured a photo of us there together in our first embrace, unbeknownst to us until a few months later when we received our USMC graduation-day yearbooks. It still brings a smile to my face to flip through the pages of that yearbook and land upon that moment of our youthful exuberance captured forever in time. We had no idea in that moment that soon growing pains, distance, and our ever-changing lives would sweep us apart, forever this time.

The truth is, Matt and I tried so hard to stay together. We managed to make it work for about a year after he joined the Marine Corps. He would come home for two or three days at a time, and every time I would be so thrilled and ecstatic and overjoyed about his arrival, only to have my heart break all over again when the time came, all too soon, for him to leave. It started to feel like a new breakup every time he left to go back to base—and he was stationed everywhere, from Pensacola, Florida, to Jacksonville, North Carolina, to somewhere in Vermont eventually. It was after one of those good-byes that I had my first panic attack. I had been watching the movie *In Love and War*, starring Sandra Bullock. It's a period piece about a soldier and a nurse who fall in love in wartime, and I can only guess that the parallels between the film and my relationship with Matt were just too much for me to handle. I can remember sitting on my bed, having just finished the movie, and the flowers on my bedspread suddenly started to spin. I grew very dizzy and started to feel as if every sensible thought I had ever had shot right out of my head. It was a frightening and unfamiliar sensation that I had never experienced before, and I called my dad in panic, begging him to come home and help me find my way back from this bottomless pit of anxiety. It felt like I was free-falling through space. Though I regained my composure fairly quickly, and the feeling dissipated almost as soon as it began, I started to feel as if something in me was broken that night. I even started meeting with a counselor once a week to work through my anxiety and fears and the growing sense of doom about my relationship with Matt, which helped some. Still, I knew that something had to change—and soon—if we were going to survive this five-year separation.

Matt tried hard to do everything he could to make the situation better. Once, while he was stationed somewhere in Vermont, he planned a trip to Tennessee on less than a day's notice to surprise me. He had a "seventy-two," as they call it in the corps, also known as a three-day leave, and he booked an insanely expensive flight home just a few hours in advance to see me. I had spoken to him the night before, and the Vermont number he was calling from flashed across the caller ID, so I had absolutely no reason to suspect he was going to be anywhere near Tennessee that weekend. We had gone five months without seeing each other, and we still had three more months to go. I think he detected the sadness in my voice as I pondered our future and the long stretches of time when we would be apart over the next four and a half years. So he flew all night and arrived at my door around eight the next morning. I was dead asleep when the doorbell rang. It was a Saturday, and I was a college student, so I never rose before eleven. I stumbled my way to the door in a haze of sleep, my hair standing in forty-seven different directions, only to be greeted by a giant vase full of at least two dozen roses. The bouquet was so big I couldn't see the person holding it.

"Oh my gosh!" I gasped, rubbing the sleep from my eyes. "Matt must have sent me flowers!"

"He did," piped up a voice from behind the ornate display of roses. "But he wanted to deliver them himself."

With a flourish, the mystery flower-delivery boy lowered the roses so I could see his face.

It was Matt! I was so stunned I stumbled backward until I hit the wall behind me, bursting into tears. Never before had anyone done something so unbelievably romantic for me. I grabbed the roses and darted over to the coffee table to set them down before tackling Matt with a giant bear hug, not caring that my hair was in complete disarray and I was wearing Minnie Mouse pajamas and my morning breath probably wasn't exactly, well, roses.

We spent a glorious weekend together, an unexpected wrinkle in time that neither of us had dared to anticipate for another three months. It was like time stood still.

Except that it didn't. Just two and a half days later it was time for Matt to leave again. And once again I was nursing a broken heart for a week after he left. No matter how hard he tried, I tried, we both tried, I just wasn't sure I was cut out for seeing the man I loved only two or three days out of every few months.

It might sound strange now, since Matt was my first real love and one of the most significant relationships of my life thus far, but I don't even remember the exact moment when we broke up. I remember it got bad; we started fighting, the distance between us stretched longer than ever, and whatever was holding us together just couldn't withstand the gap. I remember a series of stormy conversations and tears and angry words and apologies, but I don't remember the final good-bye. Isn't that odd? A part of me wonders if I don't remember because I don't want to remember, because I do recall feeling largely to blame for the breakup. I felt weak and flawed, like I just wasn't strong enough to be the military girlfriend he needed. But the reality was, I was human, nineteen years old, and just starting a whole new life with a million different paths and opportunities; and instead of seizing them, I was spending my life waiting on him. And I didn't like the person I was becoming. Matt had left the safety and the comfort and the familiarity of our hometown to go explore the world; and meanwhile, I felt stuck, trapped, like a rock at the bottom of the creek bed, just watching as the water, and life, flowed by me. Matt had gone out and found his new life, and now he was living it. It was time for me to go out and find mine.

So after two years and a lifetime of memories together, we went our separate ways. And following a short time of awkward silence between us, we managed to find our way back to each other as friends. Matt served his five years in the military, eventually being sent to Iraq and Afghanistan; and just as I was graduating college, he finally came home to begin college.

Then, five years ago, Matt was diagnosed with cancer.

He had a tumor on his spine and had to undergo a risky surgery to remove it, along with several rounds of chemotherapy. And though I was dating someone else at the time he was diagnosed, I rushed to Matt's side and sat with him through chemo, holding his hand and telling him funny stories. I brought him upbeat comedies to make him laugh, because I heard laughter is an important element to battling cancer, and books about the power of positive thinking. I prayed fervently with him and for him. In the years since we had broken up, we had both drawn closer to God. And after a few months of treatment and then rest and recuperation, Matt went into remission and was given a clean bill of health. Today he works as an air traffic controller somewhere in Georgia. We haven't spoken in several years, but I still love him like I would a member of my family. It's not a passionate, romantic love, but a steady, unfailing, unconditional love, like the love I would have for a brother.

Some relationships just don't work out, no matter how bad both parties might want them to. Sometimes time, distance, and circumstances get in the way. And sometimes we have a purpose for our lives that couldn't be fulfilled inside the bounds of that relationship. Looking back, I can see that every major shake-up in my life that ushered in a new era happened on the heels of a breakup, whether it was relational, situational, or professional. At age twenty it was the loss of my relationship with Matt that ultimately led to me finding my way back to God. Matt was a wonderful guy, but he wasn't *my* wonderful guy. And though I had a future all mapped out in my mind as Matt's wife, raising our kids in our hometown, and attending football games and recitals and living a safe, normal existence, God had a different plan for my life. It is only after surrendering what we think our lives are supposed to be that we can step into everything that our lives are meant to be. And the end of my relationship with Matt was my first step toward a life much bigger than I ever could have possibly imagined for myself.

Chapter 4

A New Copilot

Sometimes I am convinced that God allows us to fall into certain situations just because He gets a kick out of watching us get all tangled up in fiascos of our own making. He can tune in to just about any random day in my life and find something to tickle His funny bone, and spring 1998 must have been sweeps season, because I found myself in one unbelievable dating disaster after another.

After my breakup with Matt, I was back on the dating scene for the first time in two years, and it wasn't pretty. First there was the guy who was obsessed with bodybuilding, to the point where he had an actual life-size and extremely creepy cutout of Arnold Schwarzenegger in his dorm room. You can imagine my horror when I walked into Body Builder's room one evening to watch a movie and a glistening, sweaty, flexing-in-a-diaper Arnold was glowering at me from across the room. I screamed and darted back out the door, and not too long after, out of the relationship all together.

Then there was the guy who was so handsome, he bore a strong resemblance to James Dean. Yep, he very quickly won my heart when he approached me one night at a get-together I attended with friends and batted those baby blues in my direction. Unfortunately, "JD" lacked the coolness and smooth confidence of the real James Dean, and turned out to be the most insecure guy I had ever met. I discovered this one night as we were flipping through the channels and paused on a music video of a musician I thought was attractive. I made the mistake of telling JD not to turn the channel so I could see the rest of the video, and the way he looked at me, you would have thought I suggested he sprout wings and fly out of the room so I could be alone with the music video guy.

Around that time, two divine appointments happened in my life. The first came in the form of a coworker. I had started working for Mothers Against Drunk Driving in fall 1998 as a special projects assistant. MADD was looking to reach a younger audience with their message and hired me to help create a peer group of teens called Youth in Action to help combat the problem of underage drinking in high schools. One day at a national training in downtown Nashville, I met a young man who worked for MADD headquarters in Texas. His name was Scott, and he was so on fire for God that joy and peace oozed from him. As I jokingly shared some of my recent dating horror stories with him, lightheartedly complaining about modern dating, Scott turned to me with an earnest look on his face.

"You know there's a better way, right?" he asked.

"What? You mean online dating?" I joked. Online dating had just started to take off around that time, and I was highly skeptical of it. (Confession—I still kind of am.)

"No," Scott said. "I mean that God already has someone picked out for you, and you don't have to frantically search for him. When it's right, God will cross your paths."

His answer surprised me, to say the least. While I certainly believed in God and said my prayers (fairly regularly), I wasn't so sure He was overly concerned with the status of my love life. But as Scott continued to talk and share his story, my eyes began to be opened to the fact that God cares about every aspect of our lives, especially about the people we choose to spend our lives with.

The second divine appointment came from an unexpected place: my mother. She had started attending a new church a few months prior and absolutely loved it. It had reignited her faith in a way that she hadn't experienced in years. She called me almost every Sunday to invite me to church, and every Sunday I either turned off the ringer, rolled over and went back to sleep, or made up some excuse about why I couldn't go with her. A person can always find excuses not to change, but the thing about God is that He doesn't take rejection the same way humans do. When He sets His sights on you, He doesn't give up until He wins your affections. He is the ultimate Dream Guy. And so He kept prodding my mother to invite me to church, she kept inviting, and eventually I ran out of excuses.

I remember thinking I would go one Sunday, just to get my mom off my back. Off I went with my mom that day to church, where I spent much of the service looking around in awe. This wasn't just church, this was Church 2.0. The only churches I had attended as a child were old-school, traditional churches that weren't exactly known for coloring outside the lines. But this church was different. It was alive. It was electric. People were joyfully raising their hands to the music, tears were streaming down faces, and the music was lively and contemporary and unlike any church music I had ever heard. It felt more like I was at a rock concert than a worship service. It both unnerved me and intrigued me. The joy in the room was palpable. After the service, the pastor and his wife came right up to me and enveloped me in a huge hug.

"It's so nice to meet you!" the pastor said warmly. "Your mom has told us all about you. We were hoping we would get to meet you someday!"

Within minutes they were explaining their home groups and singles ministry and campus Bible studies to me. It was a little overwhelming, but I also felt something in my spirit responding. After my conversation with Scott at the MADD training, I had gone home and said a very specific prayer to God: "Dear Lord, if there is something to all this, and if there is a greater purpose for me and a mate already picked out for me, please send me a sign. Please help me find a church home and a church family. It's not something I've ever asked for before, but I feel like this is the direction You are calling me in. So please, just give me a nudge when I've found the place where I fit."

I had spent so much time in my life feeling like I didn't quite fit, and at age twenty, I finally found a place that was welcoming me with open arms. No conditions. No expectations. No standard of perfection I had to meet. I didn't have to audition. I didn't have to go through an interview process. I didn't have to be "picked." I was already chosen. It was one of the most peaceful, safe feelings I had ever experienced, to be brought into a fold of people who knew nothing about me but accepted me anyway. And as I began to look around, I saw people of all races, all backgrounds, and all walks of life. There were girls with pink hair and boys with Mohawks and athletes and brainiacs and older couples and children. No two people were the same. It was a wonderfully eclectic blend of imperfect humanity that had one thing in common: they loved God.

My one visit turned into two, which turned into three, which turned into me becoming a member of the church about six weeks after I started attending. More proof that one seemingly insignificant decision can alter the course of your entire life. God had created a perfect storm in the area where He knows I struggle the most—relationships—that resulted in me trading my dependence on them for dependence on Him. How amazing is it that He cares so much about our lives that He'll use something as silly as a series of bad dates to set His bigger plan in motion?

Something I was grappling with in my newfound walk with God was the issue of whether or not I needed or wanted to be baptized again. Although I had been baptized alongside my sister (in an actual creek, John-the-Baptist-style, no less) at age eleven, I didn't feel that it was a real turning point like the one I was currently experiencing. After that first baptism I had gone on to live life very much on my own terms rather than dying to myself and living for God. I had also lived a life of sin without true repentance. The Bible says in 2 Corinthians 5:17, "Therefore if anyone is in Christ, he is a new creation; old things have passed away; behold, all things have become new" (NKJV). But the problem was that after my first baptism, though I felt the stirrings of God in my heart, I didn't truly invite God into my heart. I didn't become a new creation. I went through the motions of what I thought I was supposed to do to be a Christian, but it was a matter of the head, not the heart. After thinking about it, praying about it, reading the Word about it, and consulting my pastors about it, I made the decision to be baptized. Only I didn't view it as being "rebaptized" or "baptized again," because I knew that while the first experience was a nice gesture, it didn't go any deeper than what could be seen on the surface. The water hit my skin but didn't penetrate my heart. This time around I was ready to truly wash away the old me and be reborn.

On December 12, 1999, I was immersed in water in the locker room of the MTSU basketball team's practice gym. How's that for a unique location? My baptism took place in a giant metal trough—or at least that's what it looked like to me—that athletes sat in to soak their injured limbs. I definitely win points for my bizarre baptismal sites. It just goes to show that God doesn't care how you come to Him or how you choose to serve Him, just that you *do* come to Him and *do* serve Him.

I came out of that water feeling so different, so alive, so changed. Gone was the Mandy who lived for herself, and in her place was the Mandy who was ready to live for God. Did this mean I was never going to sin or stumble or fall again? No! It meant I was going to get back up after my sins, stumbles, and falls and refuse to be defeated or defined by them, but rather use them for the glory of God. It meant that my mess was now my message—my tests were now my testimony. It meant I was born again, a new creation, and that as the popular shirts at the time said, Jesus was my homeboy.

I was so on fire for God that I was ready to jump into ministry opportunities at my church with both feet. Within a few months I was serving in the nursery, helping with campus Bible studies, participating in church plays, and teaching children's church. I was busy every night of the week. Gone were the lonely days of feeling as if I didn't fit in anywhere. I now fit in everywhere! I couldn't find enough places to plug into! I was so happy and joyful and filled with the love of God, it was spilling out of me. And miraculous things started to happen all around me. My dad joined the church with my mom and me, making it the first time he had regularly attended church since he was a teenager. I prayed fervently for a cousin's troubled marriage to be saved, and it was. I went to a specialist for my lifelong digestive issues and was told I had gallbladder disease, and the doctor was 99 percent sure I would need to have my gallbladder removed. I went immediately to my pastors, and they prayed over me for healing. When I went back to the doctor for follow-up tests a few days later, he shook his head in confusion.

"I'm not sure what happened here, Miss Hale, but your gallbladder is, well . . . it's well," the doctor said. "There are no signs of disease that we saw on the scans last week. It's baffling. I can honestly say I've never seen anything like this before."

Of course *I* knew what had happened. God happened! Hallelujah!

One Sunday we welcomed a prophetic minister to our church for a guest sermon. I was particularly excited about this, having witnessed other pastors with the gift of prophecy speak words over fellow church members. I sent a special prayer up to God that I would receive a word. I was still trying to figure out my future and what I was supposed to do with my life, and was feeling increasingly called into some area of ministry. I just couldn't figure out where. I didn't see myself as a full-blown pastor, or even a pastor's wife, so if God wanted to speak through one of His prophets and provide some direction and clarity about my life, I was all for it.

Sure enough, after the prophetic pastor, whom we'll call Pastor Dan, finished his sermon, he looked out to the audience and directly at me. I had prayed for a word, but never imagined I would be the first person in the congregation that day to receive one. Pastor Dan called me to the front and began to prophesy over me. If you're unsure about what it means to have the gift of prophecy, see 1 Corinthians 12:10 about the gifts of the Spirit:

> He gives one person the power to perform miracles, and another the ability to prophesy. He gives someone else the ability to discern whether a message is from the Spirit of God or from another spirit. Still another person is given the ability to speak in unknown languages, while another is given the ability to interpret what is being said. (NLT)

Though I can't remember Pastor Dan's prophecy verbatim, it went something like this:

> Mandy, there is something about you that is very precious to the Lord. I feel like He is saying, "Even in your mother's womb, I knew you." There have been seasons that you drifted away from God, but He always pulls you back. He's never been very far from you. I see you one day speaking into the lives of many young women. I see you on airplanes. [I shuddered a little bit at that one, since I'm sure you recall my love of airplanes from chapter 1.] I see you going . . . the sky is the limit!

Did you catch that? A full decade before I created The Single Woman, it was spoken over me that I would one day *speak into the lives of many young women*! How's that for God knowing who we are long before we figure it out?

Though I had a new life and a new beginning, some of the same old questions still kept coming up in my spirit: What is the best way to date and keep my morals and standards intact? Will God bring me someone miraculously, or am I supposed to go out and look for my mate? How will I know when I've met my potential mate? Is modern dating really the best way to go about meeting someone? Because of all my questions, I started doing what I usually do when I don't understand something: I researched. My digging led me to a book called *I Kissed Dating Goodbye* by a guy named Joshua Harris.* The book, in a nutshell, focuses on Harris's experiences as a young Christian who grew increasingly frustrated with the modern process of dating, so he made the decision to give it up in favor of the more traditional form of courtship. Courtship essentially entails hanging out in groups rather than one-on-one, getting to know other singles as friends and putting romance on hold, and waiting on God to speak to both of your hearts about whether or not you are meant to be together. It was a concept heavily endorsed by the church I was attending, so after giving it considerable thought, I decided to join the movement and "kiss dating goodbye" myself. We had a large singles' group at church to keep me busy and active. Who really needed to spend all their time obsessing over guys when there were so many other things I could be focusing on?

That decision started a five-year chapter in my life in which I didn't go out on a single date, didn't kiss a boy, didn't so much as hold hands with a member of the opposite sex. For a while it was fantastic. I felt free, like I was surrendering the outcome of my love life to God. Finally I could stop the endless cycle of bad dates and heartbreaks! I grew closer than ever to God; I had never

---

* Joshua Harris, *I Kissed Dating Goodbye* (Colorado Springs: Multnomah, 1997).

been more hungry for His Word and wisdom and guidance, and I finally felt as if I could exhale and release all the pressure and stress of finding a mate.

But about three years after I joined the church, I started to see some troubling trends.

Leadership had changed and a new pastor had taken over, and with the change came a feeling of oppression that I had never felt inside the four walls of our church. The attitude about dating and opposite-sex relationships felt particularly stifling. One day I was planning to carpool with a guy from our singles' group to a church-sponsored event in Nashville, and I was harshly reprimanded. "You must do everything you can to avoid the appearance of evil," I was told. I was baffled, and even hurt. How could carpooling to a church-sanctioned event in order to save much-needed money on gas ever be construed by anyone as "evil"? Because we happened to be of the opposite sex, riding in a car together would somehow cause our morals to fly out the window?

Another time a big group of us, a mixture of guys and girls, were sitting around watching movies together, and someone cracked a joke about "granny panties." The next thing I knew, leadership was bringing the girls in the group in to scold us about our improper topics of conversation, and how as ladies, it was our job not to make our brothers in Christ "stumble." (As anyone can attest to, there's absolutely nothing sexy about high-waisted granny panties, so if the thought of them made any of the guys stumble, there was an issue much deeper going on with them that had nothing whatsoever to do with us.)

The final straw for me was one Easter Sunday, when I was scheduled to be a greeter, welcoming people as they came in the door, which I did happily and enthusiastically while wearing a new black dress I loved and felt incredibly ladylike in. It was plain, short-sleeved, stopped around the knee, and was basically an A-line dress without too many bells and whistles, but very classy. I had twirled for my mom and dad that morning to show it off before I set off for church, and they approved. Yet, according to the leadership team, it was "too low cut" and proved I didn't have "good discernment in the area of clothing." I was told later the dress caused such a scandal that instead of just coming and talking to me about it directly, they called a leadership team meeting to discuss it. Once upon a time, we had held leadership meetings to discuss campus ministry and how to reach the unloved and how to further our missionary work, and now there were meetings being held in honor of my A-line Easter dress. (Which, for the record, was not the slightest bit scandalous or low cut. My mom would have never let me out of the house if it had been.)

Before long, I started to feel exhausted, and church started to feel like a chore. Suddenly all the endeavors and activities and volunteerism I was doing began to feel like a burden. And all around me I was watching couples walk around campus, holding hands, celebrating engagements, and whispering to their friends about the thrill of a first date. I began to feel more and more like I was giving up a vital part of life that I needed to experience to be a fully well-rounded person. I was experiencing the classic symptoms that any Christian struggles with when church becomes more about rules than about walking in the freedom Jesus bought and paid for with His own blood on the cross. For me, being a Christian wasn't about rules and regulations. It was about my relationship with God, which I cherished. A true, deep, and meaningful relationship with God provides one with guidance and conviction about how to live life that far transcends any legalistic rules.

Still, I stuck it out for another year and a half. This was the church in which I had truly become a Christian. This was a church that helped mold me and put me on my God-given path, and all those things meant something to me. What I was too naive to realize at the time was that the church itself is run by humans—humans just as fallible and capable of making wrong decisions and wrong turns and wrong calls as the rest of us. I don't think they had bad intentions; I just think they lost their vision. Their original fire, passion, joy, and freedom got lost in a sea of rules, regulations, and legalism. My volunteering on five committees, watching the kids in the nursery, and kissing dating good-bye wasn't going to get me into heaven. And it wasn't going to provide me with true happiness and meaning here on earth. My relationship with God *was*. And in trying to be pleasing, proper, and sanctified enough to maintain my relationship with the leadership staff, my relationship with God was suffering.

When I finally made the decision to walk away, it felt like a divorce. It was hard, painful, confusing, and heartbreaking. Ironically enough, I had kissed dating good-bye, and yet still wound up with a broken heart.

Let me be clear. It wasn't all the church's fault. It wasn't all the leadership team's fault. It wasn't all my fault. It wasn't Joshua Harris's fault. And it wasn't even a little bit God's fault. When a relationship of any kind ends, both parties are responsible. And maybe my need to please people had simply overshadowed my need to please God. There was no blame or anger or bitterness. It was just time to go. When you stop blooming where you've been planted, it's time to put down new roots.

I look back on my time there now with nothing but gratitude. I might never have gotten on track with God had I not gone to that church. I might never have had the seed planted in my heart that my destiny was to speak life and hope and healing into the lives of women across the world. And I most certainly wouldn't have become the woman I am today.

As for the kissing dating good-bye situation . . .

This is no criticism of Joshua Harris. He's a great writer and a great man of God, and I read his follow-up book, *Boy Meets Girl*, and loved it. But I do feel as though I missed out on very vital and formative dating years in the five-year gap when I kissed dating good-bye. The period from ages twenty to twenty-five is when most people really come into their own and figure out what they're looking for in love—and get their hearts broken enough times to learn a few lessons along the way. I have none of that knowledge or experience to fall back on. Do I regret making the decision I did? No, because everything happens for a reason, and I cherish that time I spent "dating" God. I know there was a purpose to choosing that path I might not understand fully for years to come. But would I recommend to someone else to abstain from dating? No. I would recommend that they abstain from dating in an unhealthy or immoral way. That they work on their relationship with God first, their relationship with themselves second, and only then focus on other relationships. You *can* date purely. To never put yourself in a situation that requires you to put your morals, self-love, dignity, and self-respect into practice is to assume that you aren't strong enough to put those things into practice, and that's insulting.

If you make the choice to abstain from dating in favor of courtship, that's great. I'm not discouraging that. I think it's a personal decision that everyone has to make for themselves. But do it for *you*. Do it for God. Don't do it because it's what you're expected to do or told to do, or because you're striving for someone else's approval. The only approval you need in this life is God's and your own. And you can never go wrong by following His lead on the dance floor of life, whether it means dancing solo or with a partner.

Chapter 5

A Few False Starts

Two years into college, I finally made the decision to declare my major as electronic media journalism. I'm not sure why it took me so long to reach that conclusion, since it perfectly combined my lifelong passion for movies, TV, and writing. I studied every aspect of the world of journalism, from creative writing to on-air talent to advertising to TV and radio production, and I absolutely loved every second of it. Finally, I had found my niche.

In spring 2002, I proudly walked across the stage to accept my diploma from Middle Tennessee State University with my parents frantically snapping pictures from the audience. I just knew I was going to go on to do great things, and the perfect TV job was going to drop from the heavens and into my lap.

Instead, I was about to fall through the looking glass into an insane kaleidoscope of careers that seemed better suited for the Mad Hatter than for a recent college graduate.

First, I saw an ad in the paper for a "Marketing Representative" at the local mall. This sounded right up my alley. An entry-level position, surrounded by clothes, flexing my newly minted marketing muscles; I could do this! I was surprised at how easily I got the position, and even more surprised when I arrived on my first day to discover that the mall was launching its Easter marketing campaign that weekend, and I was being dropped right into the middle of the chaos.

About ten minutes after I reported for duty, the mall's head PR person came galloping toward me, dragging a big, hairy bunny suit behind her.

"Mandy! Hi! We're so excited to have you on board!" she crowed.

"Um, hi," I replied, already feeling dread start to mount in my gut. "What can I do to help?"

"Well, you have perfect timing, because the high school student we hired to dress up like the Easter Bunny for our launch today dropped out just a few minutes ago," PR Girl chirped enthusiastically. "And we thought *you* could just 'hop' right in and replace him!" She giggled like her pun was the funniest thing in the world.

I looked down at my sweater set and dress pants, my effort to look professional on my first day, then looked over at the big lump of fur and massive bunny head lurking behind PR Girl.

"Well, okay," I said slowly, trying to rack my brain for reasons why I couldn't possibly don the giant suit. Wasn't I allergic to faux fur?! But it was my first day on the job after all, and I didn't want to walk away from my very first job out of college with my tail between my legs. Particularly a white, furry tail.

"Great!" PR Girl exclaimed, grabbing the huge, smiling bunny head and plunking it down on my head. "Now just pull this suit on over your clothes, and I'll point you in the right direction. You'll be launching the mall's Easter campaign by leading a processional of our kiddie models through the food court!"

I discovered in horror that my vision was extremely limited with the bunny head on, so I could scarcely see what was happening around me. How was I supposed to lead a processional anywhere when I couldn't see a foot in front of me? I had to gaze out of a small screen embedded in the bunny's teeth that had absolutely no peripheral vision. Before I knew what was happening, the music was starting up, and PR Girl was shoving me out onto the bright pink runway, where giggling, smiling, pastel-dressed clusters of children began to gather around me. One clutched my hand on each side and began to pull me down the runway.

Because I could only see straight in front of me, I'm pretty certain I sent children flying right and left all around me as I tried desperately to wave and look like a merry, friendly Easter Bunny instead of an irritated, humiliated twenty-something. Somehow I made it through the processional without doing any serious damage.

Real world: 1. Mandy: 0.

After a few months of working as the mall's "marketing rep," I quickly realized the only skill I was going to be learning on this career path was the bunny hop. It was time to look elsewhere.

Responding to an ad in the paper for a "Guest Services Ambassador" at Walmart felt like a solid next move—until I arrived for the interview and was promptly handed a red and green sparkly costume and shoes with pointy toes. They barely blew through a few questions before they pronounced me a perfect fit for the position of . . . elf.

Elf?

The job had been just a tad falsely advertised and wasn't even, in fact, a position at Walmart. It was a company that rented space *within* Walmart to operate a "workshop" where kids could come and purchase inexpensive Christmas presents for family members. The "elves" were responsible for helping the kids shop and wrapping the gifts. As much as I loved children, I had visions of the disastrous Easter Bunny episode on replay in my head. Not to mention that as a recent college grad, I was humiliated at the thought of being seen at the most public place in town—Walmart—dressed like something from the Island of Misfit Toys. But still, I needed the job to finance my own Christmas shopping, and I couldn't exactly be picky at this point. So I donned the costume, the workshop manager dubbed me Sparkles the Elf, and I wondered if God was trying to tell me that I had missed my calling in life as a Disney character.

Every day I slunk into work with my elf costume hidden away in my backpack, thinking that if I could just get into the workshop without being spotted, I could pull my elf hat down far enough over my eyes that no one passing by would recognize me.

That worked out great for a little while. Until the day I arrived at work to discover a film crew waiting for me.

A local talk show, *Talk of the Town*, was on the scene to do a feature story on the workshop, and my manager had decided that Sparkles the Elf would make the perfect interview subject. The show aired a couple of days later, and the phone calls didn't stop for a week afterward. My first fifteen minutes of fame out of college, and I was wearing green tights that jingled when I walked.

Real world: 2. Mandy: 0.

I kept applying and applying for TV jobs in Nashville, and to my frustration, I was getting absolutely no responses. It didn't help that my parents kept giving me lectures about how I needed to "get my head out of the clouds" and look for a "real job."

"You have bills to pay, Mandy," they said. "Working in television just isn't realistic. It's time to make some more practical career decisions."

I know my parents were worried about me and just wanted to see me find a career path that would be solid, steady, and successful. I know they were only trying to look out for me and protect me from disappointment. Still, their doubt, pragmatism, and logical arguments only fueled a fire in me to go after my dreams that much harder.

Finally, a month or so after my elf stint ended, I came across a listing in the paper for a leasing consultant at a local apartment complex. The money wasn't great, but it was enough, and surely working at an apartment complex couldn't involve any sort of character dress up, right?

I thrived at the job, getting along great with the apartment staff and forming fast friendships with both my manager and our residents. I helped brainstorm new marketing ideas, kept the apartment office decorated according to season, and designed cute promotional campaigns to target new residents. I still kept up the hustle, sending in resumes for jobs more suited to my major, but I finally felt as though I had found a solid, grown-up, postcollege job.

Then one day I walked into work to find my manager unwrapping a giant box.

"What's that?" I asked, peering over her shoulder.

She grinned slyly. "It's a new marketing tool that I thought you could help implement!" She opened the box with a flourish, and I looked inside to find a giant wizard head and costume staring up at me.

Oh no.

"What?!" I yelped. "What does a wizard costume have to do with our apartment complex?"

She reached underneath the costume and whipped out a bright yellow sign, which she brandished in front of me dramatically. The sign read, "Magical Move-In Specials!"

Three days later I was posted out front of the apartment complex, right on the edge of the road, peering through a small window in the wizard's mouth and waving the "Magical Move-In Specials" sign at cars as they whizzed by. Which wouldn't have been that bad, except humidity was setting in early that year, and the costume added about thirty degrees to the already almost eighty-degree temperature. I was dripping sweat and looked like a poor man's Gandalf the Grey. It was not a proud moment.

Real world: 3. Mandy: 0

After this latest career humiliation, I decided it was time for a vacation. One of my best friends Jennifer and I had developed an obsession with the WB show *Dawson's Creek* a couple of years prior. The idealistic beauty of the teenage soap had become even more beloved to me as I navigated the uncertain waters of postcollege life. The show was about a high-school-aged-turned-college-aged boy from fictional Capeside, Massachusetts, who wanted to be a filmmaker, and it served as my much-needed weekly dose of inspiration.

Jennifer and I got so caught up in the show that when we discovered it was filmed in Wilmington, North Carolina, a mere eleven-hour drive away from us, we knew instantly what was in our very near future: *Road trip!*

In spring 2003, we packed up my little red Ford and set out for Outer Banks, North Carolina, with my video camera in tow to document the entire experience. This was the last season of the show, and we knew it was now or never if we had any hope of catching a glimpse of the cast or the locations where the show was filmed.

I can remember whooping with joy as we crossed the big bridge over the Cape Fear River that led into Wilmington twelve hours after we left home. We were finally there, in Capeside, the fictional town we had fallen madly in love with! Immediately we started to recognize the scenery, pointing excitedly at landmarks we knew from the show.

Over the next two days, we gleefully toured the town, searching for landmarks, walking on the beach, touring Screen Gems Studios (where we actually got to step onto the set of *Dawson's Creek*, right into Dawson's living room!), and once even spotted the crew in town filming a scene with Katie Holmes and Oliver Hudson. We feverishly snapped photos and shot footage of every square inch of the town of Wilmington. We were even lucky enough to meet a man at a little ice-cream shop on the boardwalk who gave us very specific instructions on how to find several of the private residences that were used as the exteriors for the various characters' homes on the show. The first one we tracked down, Katie Holmes's character Joey Potter's house, also known as Potter's Bed & Breakfast, was not occupied, meaning we could pose for pics in front of the house, sit at the end of Joey's dock with our feet in the creek, and even peek in the windows. Somebody up there was watching out for us!

Later that day we followed the ice-cream shopkeeper's directions to two houses that were very much off the beaten path, which served as the exteriors for Dawson Leery's (James Van Der Beek) and Jen Lindley's (Michelle Williams) houses. These houses we were particular eager to see, since Dawson's house was the real centerpiece of the show. When our car reached the gravel path that allegedly led up to the houses, our plans were quickly derailed by two giant and rather unwelcoming Keep Out and No Trespassing signs.

"What do we do?" I whispered to Jennifer, as if the people in the houses could hear us. "It would be a shame to turn back now, right?"

"I don't know," Jennifer said. "We don't want to get arrested. I have a test on Monday!"

We looked at each other for a long moment, considering our options.

Finally, my voice shaking a bit, I said, "Let's just go for it!"

When we were two-thirds of the way up the gravel path, the houses suddenly came into focus. There, looming before us in all their majestic beauty, were Dawson's and Jen's houses! We started shrieking and bouncing up and down in our seats, oblivious to the fact that we were in a very pristine and quiet environment, the window was still rolled down, and these were clearly very private and very much lived-in residences.

Before we could go any farther, the door to one of the houses suddenly flew open, and a woman stepped out onto the front porch. We stopped in mid-shriek and looked at each other in panic. What to do? Not wasting a second, Jennifer slammed her foot down on the gas pedal as hard as she could and started peeling down the driveway. Backward. Did I mention it was a really long driveway? Gravel flew right and left, and squirrels on the path dove out of the way as Jennifer barreled on. Seconds later we shot back out onto the main road, both of us deathly quiet. It was only after we were safely a few miles away that we both started giggling.

"Well, I guess we won't be touring Jen's and Dawson's houses!" She laughed.

"I guess not!" I replied, wiping the tears from my eyes. "Unless we plan on touring the Wilmington jail immediately afterward!"

We consoled ourselves that night with a trip to Dunkin' Donuts. But even after almost getting caught trespassing and shooting away from the scene like Thelma and Louise, we still felt something calling us back to those houses. The next day was Sunday, and we were leaving. Since the pinnacle of our *Dawson's Creek* tour was seeing and snapping pictures of those two houses, we decided we would try again on our way out of town.

The next day we packed up our car and joined hands to say a prayer. "Dear God," we said, "we know that You're very busy and You probably have much more important things to be dealing with than our quest to see Dawson Leery's house. But still, we truly believe that You want us to come to You with anything. So here we are, two or more gathered together in agreement in Your name, and we are asking You to please help us find favor with someone at those houses. That is all we ask. In Jesus' name, amen."

Our faith and confidence buoyed, we headed out to try again.

We were just approaching the long gravel drive with the Keep Out signs when we noticed, coming toward us from the direction of the houses, a man on a bicycle flanked by two young girls also on bicycles. "Oh no! What do we do?" I hissed at Jennifer in panic.

"Just keep going," she urged. "Maybe he's the one who lives there! This might be our chance!"

I kept easing slowly up the driveway, until the man and the

two young girls were within a few feet of us. I rolled down my window and leaned out.

"Hello!" he called brightly to us.

"Hello!" I replied.

"What are you girls doing?" the man asked, drawing closer and peering in our window. The two little girls stayed behind him, whispering and giggling to each other.

I looked over at Jennifer.

"Well, we came to Wilmington to see the locations where *Dawson's Creek* is filmed," I began. "And we've been told that the homes used for exterior shots are down this path and were hoping to snap a few pictures."

The man's face softened.

"Well, these are the right houses, but I'm afraid they're private property," he said.

My spirits sagged. "Oh, okay. Well, we were just headed back to Tennessee and were hoping to catch a glimpse of the houses before we left town. But—"

"If you'd like to go down and turn around farther up the drive so you can see the houses up close, you're welcome to do that," the man said kindly. "But then I'm afraid you'll need to leave."

Jennifer piped up. "We understand," she said. "Thank you anyway."

The man and two girls started peddling slowly away, and feeling deflated, we did as we were instructed. We did manage to catch one more glimpse of the homes as we turned the car around and headed back up the path.

"Well, we gave it a shot," I reasoned.

Jennifer nodded in agreement. "Yes, and we . . ." She trailed off as we neared the end of the driveway. "Mandy, look."

I followed her gaze to the end of the path where the man and two young girls were waiting for us. What in the world was going on? He motioned for me to roll my window down again.

"Ladies, did you really come all the way from Tennessee just to see sights from *Dawson's Creek*?" he asked.

Hmm. This was an odd question.

"Yes, sir," I replied. "We're headed back right now."

He paused and looked us over one more time before reaching into his back pocket to pull out a business card.

"Well, the Lord works in mysterious ways." He chuckled. "I'm Mark Fincannon, the casting director for *Dawson's Creek*." He handed his business card to me through the window as Jennifer and I sat there with our jaws dropped far enough for a 757 to pass through them.

"And if you ladies could stick around for another day or two," he continued, "I can get you on as extras on the show."

––––––

A few phone calls and a little while later, we were ushered right into the casting offices on the Screen Gems lot to fill out some paperwork and get directions to the next day's filming location. The entire time we both kept pinching ourselves, expecting to wake up at any moment. Though I was due back at work the next day and Jennifer had a test, we both made some calls and shuffled some things around so we could stay and film the show. I could hardly believe it. My lifelong passion for film and television production was paying off in a big way!

At seven the next morning, we showed up to the extras holding location on Princess Street in downtown Wilmington.

We had absolutely no idea what to expect, and just assumed we would be part of a background or crowd scene. "We'll probably wind up on the cutting-room floor!" I giggled to Jennifer. But no, Mr. Fincannon had gone above and beyond to make our filming experience as memorable as possible, and we were stunned to be handed waitress costumes to change into upon our arrival on set.

"Ladies, there's a bathroom down the hall. You can change in there," a production assistant with a headset instructed us.

As soon as we entered the bathroom, we started jumping up and down like we were on pogo sticks, screaming silently so as not to alert anyone to our silly, fan-girl behavior. We held the waitress costumes up in the mirror, looking them over in awe. We were going to be waitresses at the fictional pub where the gang hung out on the show! How on earth did we get here?

What followed was one of the most amazing days of my life. We filmed for more than sixteen hours, getting to watch and be in several scenes with Katie Holmes and Oliver Hudson. Kerr Smith, who played Jack on the show, was also directing the episode. It was like we had stumbled directly into our wildest dreams. And though we only got paid minimum wage and just saw quick flashes of ourselves on-screen when the episode aired a month later, the experience was life-changing for me. We were immortalized on-screen on our all-time favorite TV show. How many people get to say that? I went to Wilmington to escape the reality of my disappointing postcollege career path, which seemed to be wandering further and further away from where I wanted to be. And six days later when I left, I had renewed faith in God and His divine order and plan for my life. And renewed faith in myself.

Now, I know what you might be thinking. Why would God

in all His infinite power and wisdom really care about such frivolous things as helping two girls get on a TV show? I think the reason is quite simple. He heard our prayer. He saw two naive, hopeful, young girls with huge amounts of faith asking Him to help make a small and simple dream come true. Nothing petitions the Lord on our behalf as much as unwavering faith and unfailing hope, and we had come to Him with both.

I also came to Him a little beaten up. The real world since college hadn't quite been what I was expecting, and I think maybe He recognized that I needed a little bit of a miracle. What happened in Wilmington gave me the push I needed to go back to Tennessee and secure my first real job in television. I can honestly say, more than a decade later, that Mr. Fincannon's kindness restored my belief in the industry and in my ability to succeed in it. Everything that unfolded afterward was another step toward my destiny. I like to jokingly tell people now that the Easter Bunny, the elf, and the wizard were all part of my "character work" in preparation for my big debut on *Dawson's Creek*.

One more reason for thinking God helped conspire to place us as extras on *Dawson's Creek*: like a proud papa, I think He sometimes does things for no other reason than to make His children smile.

The Lord works in mysterious ways, as Mr. Fincannon said.

When we left Wilmington the day after we wrapped shooting, the scoreboard was a little more even.

Real world: 3. Mandy: 1.

Chapter 6

Earning My Wings

A few days after we got back from Wilmington, I was running errands when I ran into my former college advisor, Dr. Thomas Berg, at the post office. I hadn't seen him since graduation, so it was a pleasant surprise. It also turned out to be another divine appointment.

"Hey, Dr. B! How are you?"

"Hey, Mandy! It's great to see you!" Dr. Berg shifted some boxes to one arm so he could give me a hug. "How goes the job search?"

"I'm still sending in resumes. Something's going to break sooner or later!"

Dr. Berg paused for a moment. "You know, I heard that Channel 4 is looking for associate producers. Or is it Channel 2?"

I looked at him excitedly. "Really? I hadn't heard that!"

He pulled out his BlackBerry. "Wait, let's see, yep, it's Channel 2. You should send in a resume. Use me as a reference."

"Perfect." I grinned. "Thanks, Dr. B. This is awesome!" I slid my letters into the mail slot and waved good-bye. "I'll let you know how it goes!"

Two weeks later I was sitting in front of the news director

at News 2, WKRN in Nashville. He was a large man, and rather intimidating.

"So, local news, huh? You sure about that?" he grunted.

"Oh, yes, sir!" I replied eagerly. "It's my dream to one day be a reporter."

"You don't say?" he asked, peering back down at my resume. "Well, let's have you do a writing test and see what we've got."

I must have had what it took, because about a week later I got the call that I was the newest associate producer at News 2.

I could barely contain my excitement. I felt so grown-up! So accomplished! So validated for not giving up on my dreams! I would be working "Nightside," which meant I would go in at one-thirty in the afternoon four days a week and work until after the ten newscast, meaning I usually got off around eleven at night. I would be helping to write stories for five daily evening newscasts (the 4:00, 4:30, 5:00, 6:00, and 10:00) as well as running scripts, answering phones, manning the teleprompter, and doing whatever else needed to be done that the producers didn't have time to do. I spent hours meticulously picking out my outfit for that first day on the job, and I just knew that like my longtime hero, Oprah, I was about to take the news world by storm. (Since she got her start in Nashville, I took that as a sign.)

I got to work extra early my first day on the job, expecting that there would be intensive training to be done before they would turn me loose. My "intensive training" consisted of someone sitting me down in front of a computer, facing me toward it, and saying, "Go." I have never felt more terrified or more like a fish out of water in my life. For the first hour I couldn't even figure out how to turn the computer on. No one gave me the log-in info, so I had to search frantically through an old, raggedy manual they had given me to see if I could find the right password. Meanwhile, everyone around me was typing fast and furiously. I felt beads of sweat start to drip down my back as I frantically jabbed at the computer, trying to pull up something, anything, so I could at least give the impression I was working. About two hours into my workday, I escaped to the bathroom to call my mother in tears from my cell phone.

"What is it?" she asked in alarm when she answered the phone and heard me sobbing. "What's wrong?"

"Mom, I can't do this," I sniffled. "I have no idea what I'm doing. No one is telling me what to do. I haven't received any training. I can't even get the computer to work. Can I just sneak out the back door and come home?"

My mom was silent for a moment. Then she said something I'll never forget.

"Yes, Mandy, you can come home." I sighed in relief. "But," she went on, "if you do, you'll regret it for the rest of your life."

"But, Mom—"

"You can do this. Listen to me. *You can do this.* Don't walk away from this. You wanted this so badly. Don't walk away and always wonder what might have been."

So I didn't. I stuck it out.

I quickly learned that there was a reason they didn't provide much in the way of training to the newbies. The news business is fast and furious, sink or swim, survival of the fittest. Things moved too quickly not to be. You pause, and you miss the story. You hesitate, and you get scooped. You leave, and someone else is lined up immediately to take your place. It's a brutal, dog-eat-dog business. But if you stick around, refuse to give up, and keep furiously paddling, eventually you'll stop sinking and start swimming. And I did.

Now, that's not to say I didn't have my share of newsroom fiascos.

The teleprompter was particularly evil. I'm not sure how it works now, but in those days, there was an ancient-looking computer screen with a little knob that you twisted to keep the story scrolling so the anchor could read it from the prompter and not have to stare down at his or her hard-copy script. The associate producers (AP) would sit at the prompter wearing headphones so we could listen to the director and the producer give directions from the control booth. If, along the way, a story got "killed," or taken out, the producer was supposed to remove it from the prompter; but sometimes a story died too late and didn't get taken out in time. When that happened, the AP was forced to switch to an even more ancient contraption that projected actual hard-copy scripts onto the screen for the anchor to see. We were responsible for cranking those through the machine manually. For the most part, I caught on to the ins and outs of the prompter pretty quickly. There were a couple of particular incidents, however, that still stick out in my mind as some of the most humiliating experiences of my early career.

One such incident occurred the day we were reporting on two stories back-to-back, one about a major drug bust and the next about a local state representative's latest campaign stop. Unfortunately, the two stories got swapped somehow in the prompter, so the anchor merrily launched into a story about the state rep while a graphic of a giant marijuana leaf loomed over his shoulder. By the time I realized what was happening, it was too late to do anything. So I watched in horror, sinking lower and lower in my chair as the news anchor grinned his way through the shiny, happy story while unknowingly linking the state representative to illicit drugs. I could hear the director screaming through my headphones, and for the second time in my short news career, I considered slinking out the back door and never looking back. But somehow, though I did suffer a seething tongue-lashing from the director, I managed to come out on the other side relatively unscathed. (My pride and the state representative's reputation, not so much.)

I had all sorts of wild adventures in that newsroom, from crawling under the news desk to deliver breaking news to the anchors via Post-it notes during bad weather, to fielding calls from crazies (one lady complained that our meteorologist yelled at her nightly through the TV), to handwriting an entire newscast worth of scripts the day every computer in the newsroom went on the fritz and didn't come back up until a half hour before our first newscast. Still another time I managed to singlehandedly shut down all the computers in the newsroom when I accidentally blew a fuse using my space heater. (It was freezing in that newsroom.) Thankfully the computers were only down for a few minutes, but my beloved space heater was confiscated as a result.

Still, through all the fiascos and shenanigans and meltdowns and teleprompter debacles, that newsroom was my training ground. It was where I learned to be a writer. If you could write compelling, bold, attention-grabbing copy while up against five different deadlines for five different newscasts on a daily basis, you could confidently call yourself a writer. And even though I managed to screw up royally a few times, I hustled, persisted, and didn't give up until I became the best AP I could be. That's what you do when you're tossed into a terrifying, unfamiliar, and intimidating situation. You scrape and claw and fight and challenge yourself until you rise to the occasion. Because no matter how bad you might mess up, or how foolish you might look, or how hard you might crash, there is absolutely nothing worse than the feeling of regret you will have if you don't try at all. My mom was right. Had I run out of the newsroom like a scared little girl that first day, I would have regretted it for the rest of my life.

About nine months after I started at News 2, I applied for a job at Country Music Television as a production assistant. It was a heavily sought-after position—basically my dream job—and I knew it was a long shot. But if my time at News 2 had taught me anything, it was to play the odds and bet on myself.

A few days later, much to my surprise and excitement, I got the job.

I didn't know it then, but because of my time and experience at Channel 2, I was about to walk into a new job that would change so much more than my career path. It would change my entire life.

———

I was happy and relieved to discover that my training would be much more involved and well-rounded than it was at my first television job. I would be working in the news department at CMT, so I shadowed one of the associate producers for about a week. She was very friendly and helpful, answering all my questions patiently, even though I'm sure I asked some pretty dumb ones. Within a couple of weeks, I was turned loose to start my official duties as production assistant. I transcribed tapes for hours, which basically meant I watched interviews conducted by producers and typed out everything that was said so the producer could go in and quickly pull sound bites for their news packages. I also logged tapes, ran errands, and conducted research—it was essentially grunt work, and I relished every second of it. I remember walking through the halls of CMT, looking around in amazement as I thought of how blessed and lucky I was to be there. And even though I was at the very bottom of the totem pole, the job came with some major perks. We would have up-and-coming musical groups brought in at lunchtime to play for us in the conference room. Once, a new and supercute artist set up a grill at lunchtime in the alley beside our building and grilled steaks for us. Every day it seemed there was something new and exciting to look forward to, to the point where it never felt like I was going to work. It felt like I was just showing up for another day of fun.

I was also starting to make new friends. One day I was typing away at my desk, transcribing a tape, when I looked up to see a skinny, adorable guy in glasses standing outside my cubicle.

"Mandy, this is our new producer, Jeremy," my boss piped up from the cubicle beside me. "He comes to us from E! News out in LA."

I stood up with a smile to shake Jeremy's hand and was instead enveloped in a huge hug.

"Hey, Mandy! It's so great to meet you!" Jeremy said excitedly.

"You too." I laughed. "I didn't know people from LA were so . . . huggy."

"Oh, well, my family is originally from Kentucky," Jeremy explained, gesturing to the University of Kentucky sweatshirt he was wearing. "So I have Southern roots."

Jeremy quickly became my partner in crime at CMT. The laughter never stopped. I'm happy to say that in the decade since, it still hasn't stopped. Jeremy is one of my very best friends to this day. His sister, Erin, would eventually move to Nashville from Arizona, and she would become one of my closest friends too. And her wedding a few years later would act as a major catalyst for the creation of *The Single Woman* blog—another example of how some of the smallest acts, like making a new friend, can lead to some of life's biggest moments.

About three months after I started working for CMT, I was called up to the fourth floor to the Really Big Guns' office. As in, my boss's boss. As in, Chet Flippo, world-famous journalist and former editor of *Rolling Stone*. I was a little terrified, wondering if I was in trouble or even getting fired. I couldn't understand why I would be summoned by Mr. Flippo upstairs unless it was a really big deal. I looked to my boss for reassurance as she escorted me up to the fourth floor, but she was tight-lipped. A sense of impending doom started to hover over me as we walked up the stairs, down the hallway, to Mr. Flippo's office door.

Knock, knock, knock.

"Come in!" I could hear him call from the other side.

We walked into his very grandiose office, and I glanced around nervously at the many awards lining his walls. I had never been in this office before, and I wanted to take it all in just in case it was the last time I saw it. His entire back wall was a picture window with a killer view of the riverfront. Pictures of Mr. Flippo with any and every country music star you could imagine lined his desk.

"Hello there, Mandy," Mr. Flippo greeted me.

"Hello?" I squeaked, more as a question than a response.

He laid down the file he had been looking through and peered across the desk at me intently. "We called you in here today to talk about something really important."

I closed my eyes for a second, frantically thinking about my last couple of weeks at work. Did I do something wrong? Did Jeremy and I create too much of a ruckus cutting up in the hallways? Was my dream job about to come to an unceremonious end?

"Okay," I said finally, holding my breath.

Mr. Flippo looked slightly amused. "I've heard that you've been doing some really good work for the news department. In fact," he went on, "I was told that you did a sample news package last week that was absolutely fantastic."

I exhaled in relief. This sounded like it could be really good! "Thank you so much, Mr. Flippo!" I replied with a big smile. "That means so much to hear, coming from you."

"We liked your news package so much, Mandy, we'd like you to consider stepping down from your production assistant position."

Wait, *what*?

"You see, we're looking to add a new associate producer to the team, and we'd like that person to be you."

Oh. They didn't want to fire me. They wanted to promote me!

"Oh wow!" I exclaimed. "Oh wow. That's so great! Wow. Of course! Of course I'll take the position!"

They went on to tell me that with the promotion, I would be getting a raise and increased responsibility. In fact, they were even entrusting me to cover an upcoming music video shoot! I could hardly believe it. My dream job had just gotten even dreamier. I said a silent prayer of gratitude as I made my way back to my cubicle. What a day! I was going to be writing news packages for national television! Me! Me, who just a year ago had been standing on the side of a highway dressed like Gandalf the Grey. I had come a long way, baby!

That's not to say my time at CMT was fiasco-free. It seems my "Mandy Moments," as I had come to call them, followed me across town from Channel 2 to my new job.

Once, the whole news team was at a party celebrating a number one hit for Dierks Bentley's single "What Was I Thinkin'." I thought Dierks was adorable, and I loved his music and could hardly believe I got to be included in such a momentous occasion. As any country music fan knows, Dierks has a cute Heinz 57 dog named Jake who has appeared in several of his music videos and has even walked the red carpet with him a few times. Well, just as Dierks was taking the stage to give his speech at the party, I helped myself to a giant Styrofoam cup of soda from the bar, filled to the brim with ice. It rivaled a Big Gulp from the 7-Eleven in size. I had hardly taken a sip of the soda when I tripped over a cord on the floor and nearly fell flat on my face, sending the massive soda flying into the air and all over me and several people in the near vicinity before it hit the ground with a nice, loud, wet splash. Not only did several people stop what they were doing and turn to see who was creating such a commotion, Jake the dog loped over and started excitedly lapping up the soda. And all of this just happened to go down right as Dierks was summoning Jake to join him onstage. (I have nothing if not impeccable timing.)

"Here, boy!" Dierks called, whistling. "Here, Jake!" He put his hand to his brow and peered out into the crowd. "Where is that dog?"

Much to my mortification, everyone in the room swiveled around to stare at Jake the dog eagerly licking up the spilled soda. My spilled soda. I wanted to melt into the floor as fast as the ice that was melting into Jake's mouth. I breathed a sigh of relief when someone finally managed to wrangle the dog away from the giant puddle of soda and onto the stage.

Another time I was rushing to get to work in time for our morning meeting when I got stuck behind a gigantic but super-slow-moving SUV in the parking garage. Since I had to climb eight or nine floors to get to the right entrance, getting trapped behind someone going at a snail's pace when in a rush was a nightmare. I sighed in frustration as I edged closer and closer to the SUV's bumper. Obviously, the driver had no idea where he was going. I didn't have time for this! I pressed my horn lightly, then a little harder as the SUV continued to creep up the levels like the chaffeur in *Driving Miss Daisy*. Finally, I got to the right level, my road rage levels at dangerous capacity. How dare this pokey SUV detain me from my morning meeting? I huffed all the way inside the building.

Later that day I was headed out the front door to lunch when I noticed that same SUV exiting the parking garage. It was so mammoth that it blocked the entire sidewalk, forcing me to stop and wait for him to pull out. I sighed. Twice in one day! "Who does this guy think he is, anyway?" I muttered to myself.

As he drove away, the driver turned back, and our eyes met. I was almost ready to make a very unfriendly (and not entirely Christian) gesture at him when I realized, *Wait a minute. He looks familiar. Is that . . .*

Kenny Chesney.

I had ridden Kenny Chesney's bumper all the way through the parking garage that morning and had honked repeatedly. I had gotten road rage at Kenny Chesney! Not exactly an enemy you want to make in the country music world. I tucked my head down and shuffled away down the sidewalk, hoping he wouldn't see me well enough to recognize the crazy-parking-garage-road-rage girl in any future red carpet encounters.

Of course you already know from chapter 1 the giant fool I made of myself on the red carpet at the CMT Music Awards, blowing past Loretta Lynn in my eagerness to get to Keith Urban, and the scene I caused on the airplane headed to Vegas, but those incidents wouldn't happen until a little ways down the road. In the meantime I got to cover the CMA Awards red carpet that year with another producer. I got to assist on a shoot with Dolly Parton. I got to tag along with our host, Katie Cook, as she interviewed Matthew McConaughey when he was on a promotional tour for a movie in Nashville (and yes, ladies, he is even more handsome in person). I was getting to do things far beyond my wildest dreams. God had promoted me to a place in my career I had once only dared to imagine I could be.

But you know what the problem was?

The further my career advanced, the further away from God I got. The more He blessed me, the more I forgot to thank Him for it. The more I looked to my new friends, my new job, and my new life for my identity, the less I looked to God for it. And that's a dangerous place to be. I wasn't out drinking or doing drugs or having multiple impure relationships, but my sin against God had never been more pronounced. I was ignoring Him. I became too busy for Him. I stopped giving Him credit for my amazing new life and started taking credit for it myself. And the fuller my life got, the emptier I got.

Things got worse when I made the decision to make the move from Murfreesboro, where I had lived my whole life, to Nashville. I had never lived farther than ten minutes from my family, even while I was in college. And now I was leaving them behind in favor of my new life. That wouldn't have been a bad thing had I been in a good place in my life, but at that moment, leaving my roots, my family, the people who loved me the most, was almost like the last stop on my tour of destruction. Even though Nashville was only a thirty- to forty-five-minute drive from Murfreesboro, it felt as if it were a million miles away. I didn't know myself anymore. I can remember feeling a cloud of darkness hanging over my head as I packed up my final box in my apartment and got ready to head to my new apartment in Nashville.

"What's wrong, Mandy?" my dad asked as my parents helped me make the final walk-through of my Murfreesboro apartment.

I stopped furiously poking the Swiffer sweeper into a corner and turned to face my mom and dad. They both had matching looks of concern on their faces.

"I don't know," I replied honestly, leaning against the wall before sinking to the floor. "I don't know. I just feel anxious. Sad. Like I'm not sure I'm doing the right thing. It's weird."

"Well, you can always cancel the move and stay here," my mom responded hopefully. I knew she didn't want me to go. I was her baby, and I was moving to the big city for the first time.

"No," I replied resolutely, standing to my feet and brushing the dust off my palms. "No. I'm just being a baby! It's just the stress of the move, I'm sure. I'm ready for this. I'm excited. It's time."

Sometimes in life you just have to learn your own lessons. I'm sure my parents sensed that all was not right with me. All hadn't been right in some time. I wasn't as close with them anymore, which was red flag number one. It's as if I didn't want them to ask about my relationship with God. I was afraid to really look them in the eyes and let them know that I had stopped praying and stopped reading my Bible and couldn't remember the last time I asked for God's guidance. I hadn't even consulted Him (or them) on my move to Nashville. I'm sure my parents saw what a colossal mistake I was making, uprooting myself at such a vulnerable time from everything I'd known in order to chase my own selfish desires and ego-driven dreams. And I know they saw right through me. They knew me better and still know me better than anyone in the world. They had seen the joy go out of my eyes. They had seen the abrupt change in my behavior. They had seen my eagerness to get to Nashville and out from under their watchful, knowing, loving eyes.

But they let me go anyway. Because sometimes, even when you see someone headed for a collision, all you can do is step out of the way and let it happen, hoping there will be something left to salvage after the wreckage is cleared.

So I went, despite my parents' reservations and despite my own hesitations. And I crashed and burned.

A few weeks after I moved to Nashville, the embarrassing airplane incident occurred. I crawled back into the office afterward with my tail between my legs, hoping and praying no one would ask about my panic attack on the plane. They did, and I deflected. Made jokes out of it. Tried to laugh it off. Inside, I was dying.

Even though my bosses acted as though they understood and promised they weren't angry or disappointed with me and my failure to complete the flight, I think after that incident they really started to lose faith in me. I know I had certainly lost faith in me. And I'm sure my performance at work suffered as a result. I know my attitude did.

A month or so later it was announced that new leadership had taken over at CMT, and there would be budget cuts and massive layoffs. The TV business in Nashville had really started to dry up. The economy was in the toilet. Jobs were being outsourced to cheaper production companies. No one felt safe, particularly me. Even though Jeremy and my other friends at work assured me that I was one of the best writers at CMT and there was no way they would even consider laying me off, I had a gnawing feeling in my gut. I felt as if everything had changed when I failed to make the flight to Vegas. I was getting weird vibes from my bosses, and I sensed something bad was coming.

Three months after I moved to Nashville, on a Friday

afternoon, I was called into the conference room at CMT and told they were eliminating my position, effective immediately. I was crushed. Physically, emotionally, mentally, spiritually—crushed. My bosses wouldn't look me in the eyes as hot tears started to roll down my cheeks.

What else was there to do but pack up my desk, turn in my badge, and walk out the front doors of CMT?

My TV career was over.

A few days after my abrupt and heartbreaking dismissal, I received an e-mail from Chet Flippo. It read:

> You're one of the good ones. You have what it takes to be a really good writer. Mainly: discipline, the ability to listen, the ability to observe, and the ability to tell the story without letting anything else get in the way. If you ever need a reference, remember me.

To receive such a vote of confidence from someone I looked up to as a career icon was a soothing balm to my heart during the challenging days that would follow. Chet was a humble genius, a silent hero who led by example, and he showed me such immense kindness and graciousness during my time at CMT. It was something I never forgot.

On June 19, 2013, Chet Flippo passed away, exactly eight years after the day he sent me that e-mail. I never had the pleasure of speaking to Chet again after my last day at CMT, but as he said to me in that e-mail I still have to this day: I will always remember you, Chet, as will the writing world. Thank you for believing in me at a moment when it felt like no one else did.

Chapter 7

A Crash Landing

$\mathcal{I}$ had invested my entire heart and soul into my job at CMT, so when it came to an abrupt end, I was completely and utterly lost.

All my friends were at CMT. My entire social circle was at CMT. My career was at CMT. I didn't even like going home on weekends; that's how much I loved it there. My complete identity had become wrapped up in CMT, and when it was gone, so was I.

I didn't understand this at the time, but here is what I know now, looking back. I was being called by God to do something very special with my life. He had blessed me and highly favored me in the area of my career. He had promoted me. He had placed my "hinds' feet on high places." He had blown open doors for me that most people knock on their entire lives. I was with Him in the valley, I was with Him on the climb, but I had gotten to the mountaintop and had forgotten all about who put me there. And now I was paying the price.

Does this mean we serve a cruel God who is out to punish us at the first wrong move we make? No, this means we serve a God who gives us free will. He allows us to choose our paths, even when they lead us into darkness. And He can't always magically swoop in and rescue us from the pits of hell when we make a conscious choice to travel there and without concern of how He feels about it. God had been my confidant, my copilot, my homeboy—until I got what I wanted. Then I got prideful, complacent, and completely, utterly satisfied. I was more concerned about earning the approval of country music stars than of the God who created the stars. If you make a conscious decision to follow Christ, it's not suddenly a magical cure that means the rest of your life is going to be perfect. It's actually quite often a hard and scary road paved with temptations and booby traps. The same job God had blessed me with became the very thing that lured me away from Him. And the road back to *me* wasn't going to be easy. Why? Because God didn't love me enough to come to my rescue? No, because He loved me too much not to allow me to learn the lesson I needed to learn so I would never again fall into the same sin.

The Bible says, "Do not be deceived, God is not mocked; for whatever a man sows, this he will also reap" (Gal. 6:7 NASB). For months I had been sowing pride, ego, conceit in my own abilities, and just plain rebellion, and I had a few months of reaping to do before I could expect to plant a new harvest.

One of my toxic seeds coming to fruition was the apartment in Nashville I had taken on, against God's will. The reason for me being in Nashville and needing the apartment was gone. I felt like a complete and utter failure. I had barely lived there three months, and now I was broke, jobless, and unable to make the rent. I was forced to break the lease, pack up, and move home with my parents.

I felt so embarrassed and defeated by the loss of my job, I turned off my phone and stopped talking to even my closest friends. No one knew what had happened to me. I was already isolated and away from the place of business that had been my second home for almost a year and a half and had abandoned the apartment in Nashville that was literally home. Isolating myself further from the friends who loved me and cared about me quickly sent me into full-blown depression. I never understood depression until I suffered from clinical depression. I think we tend to throw around the word *depression* too lightly, especially in America. If you've ever suffered from true depression, you know it's not about eating too much ice cream or listening to sad songs or not getting out of bed for a day. It's about not getting out of bed for a month. It's about feeling like the very life has been sucked out of you. It's about feeling like you'll never feel joy again. It's about losing the ability to laugh, or feel, or even care. I felt dead inside, and it terrified me.

I also felt like the rug had been ripped out from under me, and that led to massive anxiety. You might be thinking, *It was just a job. Get over it.* But for me, I had allowed the job to become my world. I was young and clueless and had just lost my dream job and the friends, the new city, and the life that had come along with it. It felt as if everything had been taken from me in five seconds flat. As a control freak by nature, the complete and total loss of control over my own life sent me spiraling.

Of course we're never really in control. God is. But when you've turned your back on God and placed your worth, your joy, your livelihood, your entire sense of self in something as fleeting as a job, when that job is taken away, it feels like you're left with nothing. That's why it's so dangerous to place our identities in anything other than Christ; people leave and die, jobs end, looks fade, and money is lost. Placing your entire life's purpose and meaning in any of those things is like placing your entire bet on red and having the roulette wheel land on black. Everything vanishes right before your eyes, and you're left empty-handed and just plain empty.

I was empty. I was jobless. I was penniless. I was directionless. I had swallowed my pride and moved back home with my parents. And I was avoiding my friends. I had hit rock bottom.

Over the next few weeks, I learned that rock bottom has many levels. Just when I thought things couldn't get any worse, they did. I started having massive anxiety attacks. The panic would hit and I would go into a tailspin, thinking I was having a heart attack or dying. That's one of the really awesome side effects of panic attacks; they make you feel as if your heart is literally about to explode in your chest. These were different from the panic attack I suffered when I was dealing with Matt's absence in college. These were more intense, more severe, more terrifying. Night after night, I made my dad rush me to the emergency room. I felt so hysterical and out of control. Hearing the doctor tell me time and time again that I was going to be okay somehow made me feel better, even as I racked up hospital bill after hospital bill.

I also lost my appetite as a side effect of the depression. I stopped eating, and within weeks, dropped from 120 pounds to a scary 106. On a frame of five feet seven inches, 106 is not a healthy weight. I was even skinnier than I had been in high school. Even size zeroes started to droop from my skinny waist, leaving my parents heartsick with worry.

It got to the point where I was afraid to leave the house for fear of having a massive panic attack. My world got smaller and smaller. I felt so hopeless, like this miserable existence was going to be my life and I would never be myself again, whoever that was. To make matters worse, I felt so ashamed about the way I had turned my back on God that I didn't feel worthy of His help now. I continued to avoid Him, not out of pride as I had before, but out of shame.

I was at the point where I was having full-blown panic attacks twenty-four hours a day and couldn't stop hysterically crying when I realized I had to take drastic action. I will say that no matter how bad things got for me, I never became suicidal. I'm one of the fortunate ones who had a strong support system that assured me there would be a day in the future when I would feel normal again, no matter how bad things got. I never wanted to end my life; I just wanted to end that era of my life and find a way to stop hurting and feeling terrified all the time. I drove to my family doctor's office one day and told him what was going on, spilling the full story as I wept, ending with: "I'm not leaving here until you find a way to help me." I couldn't go back home to another day of desperation, sadness, and fear. I needed help.

God is so faithful, even when we're not. He placed a team of doctors around me whom I credit with putting my life back together. My family doctor immediately got me in for an emergency session with a therapist he recommended, Dr. Thomas. I remember when I walked into Dr. Thomas's office that first day with my dad, I was in full-blown panic mode, crying hysterically, and my hands were shaking too hard to even fill out the paperwork. By the time I left an hour and a half later, I was weeping tears of joy.

"We're going to fix you, Mandy," Dr. Thomas had said, looking at me kindly.

"You mean I'm fixable?" I whispered, wiping a tear from my eye. I had fallen so far, I had come to believe I was beyond all hope. I thought I was going to be living in this anxious, miserable bubble for the rest of my life.

"You are 100 percent fixable. And we are going to fix you."

That was the first pebble of hope laid in the foundation of my new life. But I still had many more to go.

I now had my family and my doctors behind me, pushing me to get well, and I knew it was time for me to get on board as well. Along with the loss of my job and the depression, anxiety, and panic attacks had come no small amount of self-loathing. I began to realize I had been so busy beating myself up, I was actually keeping myself on rock bottom by never bothering to give myself a boost. The whole world can be behind you and believe in you, but if you can't believe in yourself, you're only going to stay stuck. So I began to take active steps in my own recovery.

I started where I always start: with research. I bought every book I could find on panic and fear and depression and anxiety, and I read every sentence, highlighting the parts that pertained the most to me. I created flash cards with positive affirmations and relaxation techniques that I carried with me every time I left the house. I began to take brisk walks around the block every morning to release tension and calm my nerves. It was during those walks that I began to have my first tentative conversations with God about everything that was going on. I journaled every night, as all the anxiety experts recommended, writing down my self-defeating and negative thoughts and replacing them with positive, powerful, self-affirming thoughts. I knew I had to purposefully change my thought patterns in order to stop the cycle of obsessive negative thoughts, so I worked diligently at staying focused on only the present moment right in front of me, not stressing over the past or obsessing over the future. I focused on the grass, the trees, and the birds as I walked. I focused on each word I was reading in every book as I read it instead of allowing myself to get lost in thought. I was absolutely relentless in my determination to get better.

My precious dad also found a way to help me gain back the weight I had lost. He knew I had a sweet tooth, and he had a sweet spot for Waffle House chocolate pie. Though you can typically only order by the slice, my dad would bring home full-size chocolate pies, and the two of us would stand over the pie pan at the kitchen counter, forks in hand, and dig in. My mom eventually gave up trying to make us use plates like proper people. The pies, coupled with the antidepressants the doctor had prescribed me, quickly brought my weight back up to 120.

Still, the dark days weren't completely over. Despite the intensive therapy and the medication and the self-help work I was doing on my own, I had good days and bad days. I remember one bad day when my dad had driven me to the bookstore to buy some new self-help books. I had a panic attack, out of the blue, right there in the parking lot. Since a father's job is to protect his children, my dad wanted so badly to make the fear go away for me. But he couldn't. He was powerless to help. So what he did was the only thing he knew to do: he turned it over to the heavenly Father. We sat in the car that day at Barnes and Noble, and my dad took my hands in his and prayed, "Dear God, we have asked You to take this panic away, and it's still here. So now we accept that maybe this is Mandy's cross to bear. And if that is the case, please give her the strength to endure it and the courage to learn the lesson from it."

Something about that sweet, simple, humble prayer from my earthly father to my heavenly one broke down the final wall between me and God, once and for all. I wept in my earthly father's arms that day, feeling the love of my heavenly Father permeating every inch of that car. I cried for a long time in the parking lot, finally allowing myself to grieve over the job and the career and the dreams and the life that I had lost. I also found the courage later that night to get down on my knees before God and ask for His forgiveness for everything I had done to disappoint Him over the past few months, and to thank Him for loving me enough to pluck me out of my life of sin and put me on a new and better path. I had lost everything but regained my soul.

Every day after that day in the car with my dad was a little bit better than the day before.

You see, Jesus didn't allow the cup to pass from me, as He prayed in His own hour of pain and torment in the Garden of Gethsemane. But He did give me the strength to carry it. And with the aid of doctors, therapy, love, family, and my own determination to get better, He eventually brought me out of the darkness and set me back on the right path: His path for my life. It was one of the hardest battles I have ever fought, and it wasn't won overnight. But it was won.

I'd like to be able to tell you that I was completely healed of anxiety and have never struggled with it again since that dark six months of my life, but that's not true. I fought the battle with depression and won, and it has never returned; but the anxiety is another issue. Though these days it doesn't often rear its ugly head, I am naturally a worrier and a control freak, and those two traits don't mix well together. I have learned to manage my anxiety, however, and turn it over to God when it arises and not let it control my life. In some ways, it has become my strength, because every time I have faced down a fear and won, I've become a little bit better, a little bit wiser, and a little bit stronger.

My point to all this is to let you know that it's okay if you are scared. It's okay if you have fear. It's okay if you suffer from panic attacks. It doesn't make you abnormal, flawed, or weird. And it doesn't have to control or ruin your life. Fear doesn't have to be merely your tormentor. You can allow it to become your counselor, and the lessons it teaches are powerful. It shows you how strong you are. It shows you what a fighter you are. And it shows you that there is nothing you can't overcome.

If you are struggling with anxiety or depression, don't let it win. There is help. There is life on the other side of it. I am proof of that. Find a doctor. Find a therapist. Tell a friend or a family member. Seek help. Read self-help books that teach you how to cope with anxiety and depression. Don't just try to struggle with it on your own. Don't surrender to it. Don't give up.

I am a girl who once struggled with anxiety so crippling that I couldn't leave the house. And a few months ago I stepped onto a stage and spoke in front of a crowd of ten thousand women, going on nothing but a wing and a prayer and the grace of God to pull me through. And He did.

If He can do it for me, He can do it for you.

Chapter 8

With a Broken Wing

In the months after my emotional breakdown, I slowly started to rejoin the land of the living, one step at a time. I was back on track with God, which was great. I also began to slowly reconnect with my friends.

My dad (God bless him) recognized that I needed to feel like I was regaining control over my life and that I couldn't do that while living under my parents' roof, so he loaned me the money to get my own apartment. Having my own place again helped boost my confidence even further. I had gone a couple of months without a panic attack, and now, securely settled into a new home, I finally felt ready to start looking for a job.

Of course I immediately went to the TV production listings, which at that point were few and far between. The TV business in Nashville was going through a dry spell, and jobs were scarce. Still, I was stubbornly determined to return to the career path I was passionate about and knew I could do well. I sent in resume after resume to local news channels, to production companies, and to CMT's competitor, GAC. I responded to any and every job posting having to do with television in Nashville, even some low-hanging jobs that I was vastly overqualified for. And you know what happened?

Absolutely nothing.

I got zero responses. Zilch. Nada. Nothing. Not even from companies in which I had connections and where someone put in a good word for me. It seemed I wasn't just hitting detours on my career path; I was being rerouted all together. And it took me a little while to realize what was going on.

God had shut the door on my television career with a resounding *thud*. It was over. It clearly wasn't the right path for me, and He was making that abundantly clear. It was time to move on to something else.

A few months before, I would have fought against the inevitable and banged on the door to my television career until my fists were bloody, but now I had been through the fire and recognized how to let something go that wasn't meant for me. If it wasn't in God's plan for my life, I didn't want it. So I surrendered my television dreams once and for all with this prayer:

God, I recognize that working in television is no longer in Your plan for my life—or at least not right now—so I am taking my hands off of it and giving it to You. Please show me the direction in which You would have me go. If You choose to resurrect my dreams of working in television someday for Your glory, so be it, but for now, I accept that season of my life is over, and I ask for Your guidance as I embark on a new career path, wherever that path may lead. In Jesus' name, amen.

As soon as I physically and emotionally released my own plans and asked God to have His way with my life, the floodgates began to open. I started getting responses from other jobs I had applied for outside of television, in public relations, marketing, and advertising. Since a great deal of the writing I did at CMT was for teasers and promotional spots designed to encourage people to tune in to various shows, I had developed a flair for public relations and marketing.

In November 2005, I interviewed for and was offered the position of vice president of communications at an international web-based company just making its move from London to the states. The company provided a platform and hosting that allowed people to create their own websites using simple templates, from celebratory websites like wedding or birth announcements to memorial websites in honor of someone who had passed. I was responsible for handling anything communications-related that came and went from the company, including press releases, customer e-mails, and everything in between. The great thing about the position was, since it was a web-based company, I would be allowed to work from home! I think God recognized that I was still very much in the healing process, and a nine-to-five rat race and long commute into an office every morning wasn't the best way to ease me back into the working world.

One of my first assignments at my new job was helping coordinate a major marketing event in Times Square on Valentine's Day 2006. Since the company was new and needed to gain much-needed brand recognition, we created the world's largest virtual valentine for the troops overseas in an effort to generate buzz. We were even attempting to set a Guinness World Record with the endeavor. I loved the concept because it wasn't just another empty, meaningless promotional gimmick; it was actually serving a greater purpose—honoring the troops. My time as a military girlfriend to Matt made it a cause very near and dear to my heart. My boss, Henry, and I worked our fingers to the bone in the weeks leading up to the launch to guarantee it was a resounding success.

All our hard work paid off in a big way. We wound up breaking the Guinness World Record for the world's largest virtual valentine created for our troops overseas, and I got to travel to New York City for the first time in my life with my parents to celebrate the milestone in Times Square on February 14 (we drove, as I still had regular flashbacks of my meltdown on the flight to Vegas and wasn't quite ready to try my luck at flying just yet). The network news stations heard about what we were doing and invited us to hit the early morning news circuit. I got to meet Diane Sawyer, Charles Gibson, and Robin Roberts at *Good Morning America*, and was even briefly interviewed by Al Roker on the *Today Show*! My love of television news came full circle that day in such a special way. Where once I had been the producer writing the news, now I was the one making the news.

I also fell in love with New York City on that trip. I loved the hustle and bustle and excitement everywhere you looked. I loved the energy, the exotic fashions, the endless choices, and the variety of opportunities. And I literally stood in the middle of Times Square and twirled around in circles, breathless as I took in all the colors, flashing lights, and massively tall billboards. It was like nothing I had ever seen. It was a whole new world—one that inspired, challenged, and energized me.

When I returned home to Tennessee, I took a good look at my life. My career was flourishing once again, my anxiety was in check, I was back on my feet, and yet I felt like something was missing. I was still working to repair friendships from CMT, and

I hadn't dated anyone in a really long time. I felt as though my personal life needed a major jump start, but I wasn't sure where to find it.

A couple of weeks later a friend quite serendipitously invited me to join her at a ballroom dance class. She had just gotten into ballroom dancing and had fallen in love with it. Quite coincidentally (or not, since coincidences never are), one of my New Year's resolutions had been to take ballroom dance lessons, so I quickly accepted her invitation. And I can't lie—since *Dirty Dancing* was my favorite movie growing up and I had seen it at least 2,347 times, visions of stepping into Baby Houseman's dance shoes and executing the perfect routine in the arms of a strong, mysterious Johnny Castle were also dancing in my head.

The first class consisted of learning the very basic steps to three popular dances—the waltz, the rumba, and the East Coast Swing—but by the end of the hour, I was hooked. I loved everything about it, particularly the simple charm and sweet nostalgia. After the difficult past few months of my life, getting transported back to a time of innocence like my childhood adoration of *Dirty Dancing* was simply magical.

I signed up for private lessons and was assigned a very patient and kindhearted dance instructor named Travis. Over the next few weeks, Travis took me through the basics of ballroom dance. It felt great to be a beginner at something again, to step out of my comfort zone, and to build the foundation of a new life's passion. I learned so much about life and myself just from the dancing. Who would have thought that the rumba would reconnect me with my vulnerability? That I would lose my inhibitions in the steps of the salsa? Or that I would find a beauty and grace within myself that I never knew existed in the waltz? But I did. All the months of grief, sadness, and turmoil were exorcised on that dance floor, and I held nothing back. And as I started to empty my heart and my emotional reserves of all the dark times I had been through, I started to make room for uninhibited, unfettered, and uncontrollable joy. That's the main thing dance represented to me: joy. It bubbled up in my spirit and flowed out of me, impacting every area of my life. I grew more social, making new friends at the dance studio and attending weekly dance parties that allowed students to practice their dance moves with one another. Soon my life began to resemble the East Coast Swing I loved so much: carefree, joyful, and wildly unexpected.

A couple of months into my dancing journey, Travis and I were invited to participate in a charity dance competition that would raise money for needy families. I was thrilled. On top of getting to help people and provide food for families in need, I would get to learn a complete dance routine to the song of my choice!

I knew instantly what it would be.

What better, more perfect song to dance to than "(I've Had) The Time of My Life"?

This dance felt like my victorious comeback, my chance to redeem the past few months of pain with a joyous routine to the soundtrack of my childhood. It was absolutely perfect. My life-long dreams of reenacting that legendary dance were about to become a reality!

But not without a great deal of hard work first.

Travis and I kicked our training into overdrive. Dancing requires you to step out of your comfort zone on a number of levels, particularly when you're prepping for a competition. You have to be willing to first and foremost risk making a complete

fool of yourself, both during training and during the live performance. And you have to be willing to dedicate the time and
discipline to training so that you *don't* make a complete fool of
yourself during the big night. You have to trust your dance partner immensely—trust him to train you, to catch you, to lead you,
and to push you to do your best. Since I knew what having the
rug pulled out from under me felt like, trust was something I
struggled with, and I carried that struggle onto the dance floor.
I overthought every single move and turn and instruction Travis
gave me, instead of just trusting the dance in the hands of the
professional. (See the obvious parallel here to trusting your life
in the hands of God?)

One day Travis and I were working on a turn that I just
couldn't seem to master. Actually, when I stopped overthinking
it and allowed my body to take over, I mastered it just fine. But for
some reason I was really stressing and sweating this turn. I was
firing off questions at poor Travis a mile a minute.

"*Mandy!* Stop!" he boomed. "Why are you overthinking
everything? Stop thinking, let me lead you, and just dance! You
got it right the first time!"

I stood frozen in my own muck of fear, hesitation, doubt, and
paralyzing indecision for a split second before we both burst into
uproarious laughter at the complete nonsensical mess I was making out of something as small and insignificant as one dance turn.
One turn, in an entire routine! Talk about missing the forest for
the trees. And you know what happened? When I exhaled, shut
off my mind, stopped asking questions, and just acted, allowing
my gut, my instincts, and my body to take over, I executed the
turn perfectly.

Isn't that such a perfect metaphor for life?

We can bring our lives to a screeching halt with overthinking. Lord knows I did that during my post-CMT meltdown. I almost drove myself mad with overthinking. When we overthink, we stop acting boldly and hide behind our endless streams of questions, objections, and insecurities. We drive away people and opportunities that are meant to be in our lives by overwhelming them with our expectations, stipulations, and worries. We shut off our hearts and allow our minds to work overtime, essentially turning ourselves into hamsters in wheels—endlessly grinding but going nowhere.

You just can't think your way into your destiny. More often than not, you have to feel your way there. Overthinking takes the very magic out of life because you're too busy planning the party to enjoy it. Trust me: the world will not screech to a halt if you step off the conveyor belt of overthinking. In fact, I'd venture to say it will spin a lot more peacefully on its axis.

Eventually we made it to D-day. I had a beautiful sparkly pink costume and silver dance slippers and felt like a princess. After months of training, Travis and I were ready to take the competition by storm!

Instead, we took dead last.

Since I pride myself on my dancing abilities, and since I knew Travis was a dance superstar, it was a bit of a blow to the ego. But you know what? If my post-CMT emotional wasteland had taught me nothing else, it taught me that sometimes a bad day for the ego is a great day for the spirit. I knew that Travis and I had done our very best. We had worked our butts off and challenged each other and pushed each other and poured our blood, sweat, and tears into that routine, and we still didn't make the cut. That's just the way it goes sometimes. Disappointments and failures are all a part of the process that makes you into the person you are meant to become. You can allow them to cause you to become bitter, angry, and hard, or you can accept them gratefully as the lessons that they are and use the experiences to be better the next time around. The choice you make will define whether the failure becomes a stepping-stone or a stumbling block.

For me, regardless of the trophy we lost, I had found so much more on the dance floor than I ever imagined possible. I found my way back out of my shell—the protective covering I had built around my heart after the disappointment at letting go of my television career. I found the ability to trust again—and not just someone else, but to trust myself. I reclaimed my belief in myself, my happiness, my fire, my spark. And I found the courage to accept my failure with the grace of a woman instead of the disdain of a child. I was learning on this journey we call life that failure is just a sentence in our stories. It doesn't have to overshadow the whole book.

Besides all that, dancing was just fun! It had opened me up to the magic and joy and possibilities of life again. For the first time in years, I felt brave enough and hopeful enough to believe that since I had rediscovered my ability to dream, maybe love wouldn't be far behind.

Chapter 9

Flying High

I can remember so clearly the first time I saw him. He danced by my table and into my life. *Poof!* There he was, as though he had always been there, just waiting for me to open my eyes and see him.

It was December 2006, and I had gone out with some friends from dance class to hear a band play and to practice our dance moves. We were sitting at our table, laughing, cutting up, and having a grand old time, when a very attractive guy with a fedora pulled down rather mysteriously over one eye walked by our table and shot us a grin. My heart instantly leapt, surprising me. It had been a very long time since I had any sort of butterflies over a guy.

Throughout the course of the next hour, as my friends and I danced, giggled, and sang along to the band, the mysterious guy kept shooting glances our way. He was with a large group of his own friends, obviously eclectic, colorful, and creative types. At one point he took to the dance floor alone to show off his solo moves, sliding across the floor with the agility and grace of Justin Timberlake. Who could this guy be? Nashville wasn't a huge town, and I knew I had never seen him before. Plus, the fedora and the dance moves made a very powerful yet enigmatic impression.

"What do you think his deal is?" I whispered to my friend Victoria.

"Who? Oh, you mean Mr. E?" she asked with a mischievous grin.

"Mr. E?" I asked in confusion.

"Mr. Fedora Guy. Mr. Mysterious. M-Y-S-T-E-R-Y, aka Mr. E. That's who you mean, right?"

I laughed, realizing what she meant. "Oh, that's perfect! Yes, Mr. E. Have you ever seen him before?"

She shook her head. "Nope. And I can't remember the last time I saw *you* so interested in a guy," she teased, both of us turning to watch him lounging languidly against the booth his friends were sitting at. "I think you should talk to him," she went on.

I blushed. "What? No! I can't. I don't go places and 'pick up guys.' That's not me! Besides," I said, shooting another look in Mr. E's direction, "look at him. He probably has a girlfriend."

"Only one way to find out!" Before I could object, Victoria strode over to his table and was greeting him and his friends enthusiastically. Then I saw her gesture over to our table. Oh no. I slid down in my seat a bit in embarrassment as he looked over my way with a smile. The next thing I knew, Victoria was pulling him over to our table.

"This is my friend Mandy I was telling you about," she said with a big smile, pointing to the empty seat beside me. "I think you two should get to know each other!" She leaned down and whispered covertly in my ear, "He's single!" Then she was gone, skipping off toward the dance floor, and Mr. E was sliding into the booth beside me. He was even cuter up close.

I smiled apologetically. "I'm sorry. My friend is a little over-eager for me to meet someone," I explained.

I sat there, fiddling with the straw in my soda cup for a long moment. This was the moment with guys where I usually froze up and transitioned into an awkward, rambling mess. Or worse, went completely mute. *Please, God, don't let me do that with this guy*, I silently prayed.

"So what's your story, Mandy?" Mr. E asked, tipping his fedora back a little on his head and shifting in his seat so we were face-to-face. His eyes were an interesting sea-foam color, not quite green yet not quite blue.

I took a deep breath and launched into the short version of my story. His eyes lit up as I mentioned my background in journalism.

"Wow, that's awesome! I'm a journalist!" he said brightly. "I actually just moved here from Wilmington, North Carolina, where I wrote for a—"

"Wait a minute," I interjected. "You moved here from where?"

"Wilmington, North Carolina. Have you heard of it? It's a great little town on the coast."

I laughed. "Heard of it? It's one of my favorite places in the world!"

He grinned. "No way! You've been there?"

"Yes, and I loved it. A friend and I visited because we were huge fans of the show *Dawson's Creek*, and we actually ended up getting to be extras on the show!"

He put his hand over his heart and looked at me intently. "Mandy, I was once an extra on *Dawson's Creek*," he said in amazement. He began to make a thumping motion with the hand that was over his heart. "This is incredible. Where have you been all my life?"

He went on to tell me he was from Boone, North Carolina, and had recently moved to Nashville to write for a small county newspaper just outside the city. He had a big family he was close to, he loved God, and he loved to dance. We even took a few turns on the dance floor that night, where he twirled me around and around until I was dizzy. Dizzy from the dancing or dizzy from the butterflies still fluttering away in my stomach, I wasn't sure. We sat in that booth and talked for hours that night, and I was already halfway in love with him by the time we got ready to say good night.

We made plans to see each other the following weekend. I asked him to attend a special formal dance with me at my studio, and he said yes without hesitation. He leaned in and gave me a quick peck on the cheek, releasing my hand so I could go join my friends.

"Hey!" I called out before he got too far away.

He paused, turning back to face me, people walking back and forth in the distance between us.

"Yes?" he asked.

"What would you have done if my friend hadn't 'picked you up' for me?" I finally asked.

He smiled, considering my question. Then he grinned brilliantly.

"I would have assumed you were already taken, or out of my league," he responded with a wink before touching the corner of his fedora in a farewell gesture and vanishing into the crowd.

Mr. E, indeed.

I went home that night and told my mom I had met the man I was going to marry. I told her how, much like Prince Charming, Mr. E had swept me out onto the dance floor and off of my feet. I told her about his family and about everything we had in common and about how excited I was to find a man who loved God. I told her he almost seemed too good to be true.

And I guess he was. He stood me up for our first date a week later. I couldn't believe it. How could I have been so wrong about him?

I sat in my car at the dance studio that night in my formal gown and cried tears of disappointment and embarrassment. He did at least call me to tell me he wasn't coming, which I guess was better than just not showing up, but still—it stung. My first foray back into the dating world in years, and it ended in disaster.

But I was all dressed up with someplace to go, so I dried my tears, deleted his number from my phone, and escorted myself to the ball.

After that, I tried to forget about Mr. E. It was clearly a giant red flag that he didn't show up for our first date, and I didn't want to sit around crying over a guy who obviously wasn't sitting around worrying about me. So I kept dancing, I hung out with my friends from the studio, and I even went out on a few dates. None were really worth writing home about, though.

As much as I tried to deny my wandering thoughts and tried not to let my mind drift to Mr. E, I still couldn't help but look around for him when I was out with friends. Particularly when we were somewhere with a dance floor. Regardless of his complete lack of first-date decorum, I still couldn't shake the nagging feeling that we had made a real connection.

It was five months later, right around the time that I stopped looking for Mr. E, when he reemerged. It was at a museum benefit in downtown Nashville. I was walking out of the ladies' room when I heard a voice behind me.

"Mandy?"

I turned, seeing him but not quite recognizing him.

"You're Mandy, right?" he went on, walking toward me.

"Yes," I replied, a little hesitantly. Did I know this guy?

"It's me. Mr. E." (Obviously he said his real name here, as he didn't know I referred to him as Mr. E. But he would no longer be a mystery if I revealed his identity.)

My face flushed as I finally made the connection. "Oh! H-hi," I stammered. "I didn't recognize you."

"I thought it was you." He smiled. "Or hoped, actually."

I gave him a Look. That's *Look* with a capital *L*.

"Really? Because you didn't seem too anxious to see me the night you stood me up," I said before I could stop myself.

"You're right," he replied sheepishly. "I was a jerk. I should have showed up that night."

"So why didn't you?" I asked. "I really thought we made a connection."

"We did," he interrupted. "Look." He pulled out his phone and scrolled through his contacts. "I got a new phone a couple of months ago, and I didn't transfer a lot of numbers over. But I transferred yours." He showed me the listing in his phone. "It was weird. Even though I knew you probably never wanted to talk to me again, I couldn't bring myself to take your number out of my phone."

I stared at him for a long moment, not really knowing what to believe. He held my gaze.

"I don't understand, though. Help me understand," I said. "If you thought we made a connection, and I thought we made a connection, why did you stand me up?"

"I don't know," he admitted, shaking his head. "I've asked myself the same thing. I guess I just got scared."

"C'mon," I scoffed. "Isn't that the oldest line in the book? Do guys even really get scared?"

"They do when they meet girls like you," he shot back, rendering me silent. Then suddenly he smiled.

"What?" I asked, trying to decide if I felt annoyed or charmed. Maybe a little bit of both.

"Let's dance!" He grabbed my hand and pulled me out on the dance floor where we ended up dancing the night away. It was impossible to stay mad at him. He was so filled with joy, mischief, and exuberance for life that he was almost childlike.

As we said good night a few hours later, I reached over and punched him lightly in the arm.

"So since you never erased my number from your phone, are you going to call me this time?" I asked with a grin.

He smiled.

"You can bet on it."

With that, he disappeared into the crowd, like he had the first time I met him.

A few moments later, as I was walking out of the museum with my girlfriends, my phone lit up. It was an unknown number.

"Hello?"

"Hi." It was him.

I smiled. "Hi."

"Told you I'd call you."

Thus began my summer of Mr. E.

We both loved to dance, so I think we hit every dance floor in Nashville that summer. Nashville has some of the best live music in the country, so we listened to a lot of it. He met my friends. I met his friends. I actually ended up becoming really good friends with his best friend, Crawford. Mr. E and I went to pool parties. He took me to see one of the *Pirates of the Caribbean* films, and I got more of a kick out of watching him than I did watching the movie. He sat in his seat, Indian-style, like a child, and laughed and cheered with abandon throughout the entire movie. He was so delightfully weird in the best possible way. The most appealing thing about him was that he lived almost entirely in the moment. He wasn't caught up in what had happened or what was going to happen. The *now* had his full and unwavering attention.

I soon learned that was also one of the most infuriating things about him. With Mr. E, if you were out of sight, you tended to be out of mind. He was so captivated by whatever and whoever was in front of him in the present moment, it was difficult to be the person who wasn't standing in front of him. We would have a great couple of weeks, then he would vanish for a month. We weren't boyfriend and girlfriend by any means, but it was still endlessly frustrating to feel as if we were finally getting close and then have him pull away. I swore every time he would do one of his vanishing acts that I was done, I was through, and I wasn't putting up with it anymore. Then he would reappear and be so fun, so charismatic, and so easy to be around that I would forget why I was ever upset with him in the first place.

He was incredibly adventurous and spontaneous. I would soon come to recognize the tone in his voice when he was about to drag me into an escapade that I would never have been brave enough to do on my own. "How adventurous are you feeling?" he would ask me with a grin, and then I knew something really crazy was coming, like "Let's climb up to the roof of my office building to look at the stars," or "Let's drive thirty minutes to the lake at two in the morning for night swimming."

Our first kiss happened on the other end of one of his "How adventurous are you feeling?" moments. It was the Fourth of July, and we had been to dinner with some of my friends and then watched the fireworks show over the Nashville riverfront. It was starting to get late, but all over the city, people were still shooting off their own firecrackers. We were walking hand in hand back to my car when he noticed, towering above us, a massive construction crane. There were some new high-rise condos going up, and the crane stretched at least twenty stories into the air.

"How adventurous are you feeling?" he said with a grin, looking from me to the crane and back again.

"Oh no," I said. "There is no way we are climbing that. Do you hear me? No way!"

A few minutes later, though, I was darting after him, giggling as we made our way through the dark construction site to find the foot of the crane. "We can't do this!" I whispered. "We're going to get in trouble!"

"C'mon," he said. "How many times in life do you think we're going to get a chance to do something like this? This is something we will never forget. You can probably see the entire city from up there!"

"Well, my guess would be zero more times, because we're probably going to plunge off of this crane to our deaths! It could be unstable, or broken, or someone might see us and call the cops!"

"Mandy, construction workers climb these every day," he reasoned. "It's not illegal."

Somehow his reasoning started to make sense, and a few minutes later I found myself removing my heels and following him up the ladder to the crane above. We climbed three or four stories before I convinced him that we were high enough. As we turned to face the city, I gasped.

Stretching before us, a sea of sparkly lights, was Nashville. All around the city, in different areas of town, people were shooting off firecrackers, and the lights from the fireworks combined with the lights of the city created a stunning effect.

"This is breathtaking," I breathed, hardly able to speak.

"So are you," he said, leaning over and kissing me for the first time.

He was right. It was a moment I never forgot.

Chapter 10

A Destination—or a Stop Along the Way?

𝓕or the rest of the summer and fall, very little changed between me and Mr. E. We always had a blast and continued to spend time together and see each other casually, but it didn't really feel like it was progressing. A lot of people might argue, "If the relationship wasn't moving forward, why did you stay in it?" And the reason was simple. I was only in my late twenties, and I wasn't looking to get married anytime soon anyway. Since I had missed out on so many dating experiences between the ages of twenty and twenty-five, why shouldn't I enjoy myself and have a good time now, since I felt absolutely no pressure to be married? Mr. E wasn't offering me a commitment, but I also wasn't asking for one, so what we had worked perfectly for me in that moment.

But even though my relationship with Mr. E wasn't moving forward, my life definitely was. By fall 2007, I had grown weary of working from home with only my cat to keep me company. I was becoming increasingly restless in my position with the web-based company and was eager for new opportunities. When

I came across a job listing for a public relations specialist position at a new nonprofit in Nashville, I decided I would fill out the online application and see what happened.

I was offered the job. Once again I would be commuting to Nashville from Murfreesboro and working in the big city for the first time since I worked at CMT. This was a big move for me, and I knew I was ready.

It was also time to start thinking about moving back to Nashville. Not on my own accord. Prayerfully this time. I talked to God about it and asked Him to open up the right doors at the right time and let me know when to walk through them.

On September 4, 2007, I started my new job. The company was a state-funded nonprofit working to make high-speed Internet available to everyone in Tennessee. Unbelievably, there were still people in rural areas of Tennessee who could only get access to dial-up (as in, Meg Ryan, Tom Hanks, *You've Got Mail*, you-can-hear-the-phone-dialing-and-ringing-as-it-connects dial-up). As the public relations specialist, I would be responsible for drafting communications pieces for the company, like newsletters, press releases, and media advisories. I fit in well with my coworkers, caught on to my job quickly, and knew I had made the right decision by following God's urging and my gut to embark on a new career path.

I was thrilled to learn that one of my job responsibilities would be coordinating one of the programs the company oversaw that provided free computers to underprivileged children and families. I got to be very hands-on with the program, actually traveling out into the community to meet the kids and families that the program was affecting. Their stories were amazing. It didn't take long for me to see how special the program was, and that got my wheels turning about how to better spotlight it.

Since I had laid down my TV ambitions two years prior, I hadn't worn my producer hat in a long time, but now I was suddenly itching to put it back on. The door on that part of my life had closed so suddenly and seemed so final that I hadn't even attempted to revisit it. But now, knowing we had a chance to touch even more families with this program if we could make more people aware of it, I began to hatch an idea to produce a short documentary, profiling one of the foster youths who received a computer from the program. I tapped Mr. E's best friend, Crawford, for the project since he was a director and ran his own freelance production company.

Crawford was a spirited, fun, insanely goofy guy who had never met a stranger and loved God with his whole being. He also happened to have a young son whom he adored and a wife who had just recently and very abruptly filed for divorce for reasons that weren't clear to Crawford. In spite of his heartbreak, he was always the brightest light in any room and was one of those rare people who never let his circumstances take away his joy. We had a blast as we started to plan the ins and outs of the documentary, and I knew I had made the right decision in bringing him in on the project.

One day we were sitting there going over our storyboards and talking about the best, most impactful way to tell the story when Crawford suddenly leapt to his feet. "Wait! That's it!" he exclaimed, raising one finger in the air, much like you would picture Albert Einstein doing upon his discovery of the theory of relativity. "I've got it!"

"You've got what?" I sat the chair up that he had tipped over in his excitement.

"You know who always gets the best version of every story?" Crawford asked, his eyes lit up like the Fourth of July. "Also known as the Best Interviewer in the World?!"

"Who?" I asked. Then it dawned on me. "Oh! You mean E?"

"Yes!" Crawford boomed. "You produce, I direct, and we bring E in to interview the subjects. It's perfect!"

I thought about it for a moment. It really was perfect. Even though Mr. E only wrote for a tiny, small-town newspaper, he was an amazing interviewer, and his articles were always brilliantly written.

Mr. E jumped onboard enthusiastically, and before I knew it, we were full steam ahead on the project. And a funny thing started to happen as Mr. E and I worked so closely together. We grew closer. Our relationship actually started to feel like, well, a relationship. I remember one day when we were all riding along to our next shoot, Crawford and Mr. E in the front seat and me in the back going over the notes for our next interview. Suddenly Mr. E reached his hand around from the front seat and clasped mine. We held hands the entire way, from front seat to back, until we got to our next stop. I glanced up at the rearview mirror at one point and saw him smiling back at me. He winked and squeezed my hand a little tighter. To anyone else this might seem like a fairly insignificant gesture, but to know Mr. E at all was to know better. Instead of his usual teasing or friendly slugging me in the arm or chasing me around to tickle me like we were eight, he just wanted to hold my hand. And when he reached back to hold my hand that day, he also grabbed my heart in a new way.

Finally the day came when the documentary was done and ready to be debuted at my company's very important quarterly meeting, where we would share with our stakeholders everything we had been working on for the past few months. I was a nervous wreck. I had really gone out on a limb at my new job to get approval to shoot the video. Plus, this was my first foray into producing since the Great CMT Debacle of '05. What if it was terrible? What if my boss hated it? What if we didn't convey the right message? *What if?*

I was drowning in a sea of what-ifs when I looked up and saw Mr. E coming toward me. He was there, at my very important meeting, to be my support system as the documentary debuted. Though I had mentioned the event to both him and Crawford in passing, I didn't actually expect them to show up. Guys can be terrible with details. How did Mr. E even remember the correct date and time of my little event when he could scarcely remember his own parents' birthdays?

Yet here I was, standing in the opulent hallway of the Frist Center for the Visual Arts and on the edge of what I hoped wasn't career suicide, and there he was, walking toward me in a suit and tie and with a fresh haircut and a big, encouraging smile on his face.

He had stepped up, and it meant the world to me. The documentary went off without a hitch. We even received a standing ovation.

How different things could go when you included God in the plan.

Over the next couple of weeks, Mr. E and I continued to spend more time together. We continued to grow closer, and for a moment, it seemed as if he was finally going to give in to whatever this thing was that we had between us and see what happened on the other side of taking a chance.

I was also quickly becoming besties with Crawford, which could have easily been awkward, since he was Mr. E's best friend, but it really wasn't. Crawford was going through so much turmoil at that moment in his life that it helped him to have a female friend to go to for understanding and clarity.

"I'll probably have to take on a roommate," Crawford explained to me one day as we sat at Starbucks, nursing his broken heart with a cookie and a Frappuccino. "I can't really afford to keep up the mortgage now that I'll be paying child support too."

"I'm so sorry, Crawford," I said sympathetically. "You don't deserve this. When I get back from Florida in a week or so, I'll come over and help you weed through applicants so you don't wind up living with a weirdo."

"Thanks." He shot me a halfhearted smile. "Where are you going in Florida again?"

"We're taking my nieces to Disney World for the first time. I can't wait!" I replied with a grin. My sister and her husband have two girls whom I positively adore: Emma, who was almost five at the time, and Olivia, who was one year old. To get to see their faces as they gazed upon Mickey and Minnie and the Magic Kingdom for the first time was worth the "vacation boot camp" my sister often put us through. She was a teacher, meaning she was the most organized person on the planet, and she had already issued itineraries to my mom and my dad and me, documenting our every move in Disney World. She had even scheduled in our bathroom breaks. And of course every day would begin, bright and early, at seven in the morning. My face turned from excited to glum as I thought about the week of structured "fun" I was about to endure.

"Maybe I should just stay here and help you interview roommates," I said, my shoulders slumping.

Crawford suddenly looked up from the table with realization, like he was about to have one of his Albert Einstein moments.

"You could," he said with a grin. "Or you could just *be* my roommate!"

"Wait, *what?*" I exclaimed in surprise. "Are you serious?"

"Think about it. It's perfect!" he replied with excitement. "You want to move back to Nashville. I need a roommate. We have a blast together. It would be awesome!"

I pondered the thought for a few moments.

"Hmm. Well, it's something to think about, I guess," I mused.

"Tell you what," Crawford said. "You pray about it while you're in Florida, and I'll be praying about it too, and when you get back, we'll see how we both feel. Sound good?"

"Sounds perfect!" I replied with a smile. We sealed the deal with a clink of our plastic Frappuccino cups.

Later that night a few of my close friends and Mr. E threw me a little send-off party at our friend Mike's house. Mike had a fabulous deck and backyard, and I remember being happy and carefree as we played music, danced, and enjoyed the beautiful spring evening. The next day I was leaving for a week in Florida, and Mr. E would be interviewing an infamous reality star we'll call Shayla Sanders, who had just moved to Nashville, for his column. We were all teasing Mr. E about it, since the starlet was known more for being a hot mess than for her hot-ness.

"Be careful when you're in the same room with her," I joked. "I hear she's a real Venus flytrap when it comes to men. Get anywhere in her vicinity, and she'll eat you alive!"

"I'm going to miss you while you're gone," he said, hugging me tight. "I'll call you every day." He pulled back and looked me deep in the eyes. "And I think we should have a talk when you get back. About us. Would that be okay?"

I smiled, my heart doing its usual flip-flop that it did when he was anywhere near.

"That sounds great," I replied, leaning in to give him a light kiss.

But that talk would never happen, for reasons I could never have imagined in that moment.

By the time I returned home from Disney World a week and a half later, Mr. E would be living with Shayla Sanders.

Mr. E's promise to call me every day in reality translated into one call, on the first day I was gone, and I missed it because my family and I were on the *Pirates of the Caribbean* ride. (You've gotta love the irony in that since that movie had been one of my first dates with Mr. E.) When I called him back later that night, I got no response. And then nine days went by without a single peep from him.

Still, I didn't really give it much thought since I was busy having so much fun with my family. We stayed at a hotel in the park that had two gigantic ceramic dogs from *101 Dalmations* in the courtyard, and my niece Olivia's reaction to them was priceless. Though she only knew a few words, every morning when we left the hotel to head over to the park, she would screech and squeal and wave her arms in the air in excitement.

"Doggie!" she crowed with the same exuberance every day as she had the very first time she saw them. "Doggie, doggie, doggie, doggie, doggie!"

We had a blast, despite my drill instructor's—oops—I mean, my *sister's* rigid itinerary. And despite the fact that she insisted on wearing a fanny pack all through the park, even though fanny packs were more extinct than the dinosaurs we saw in DinoLand at Animal Kingdom. We went on an African safari, visited the World Showcase at Epcot, had dinner in Cinderella's Magic

Castle, and watched the Main Street Electrical Parade and the fireworks display at the Magic Kingdom. It was reminiscent of the trip my parents had taken my sister and me on when we were just about my nieces' ages, and it was just as magical and wonderful seeing the park through their eyes as it was seeing it through my own eyes twenty-five years earlier.

I also had a chance to spend some alone time, praying about the idea of becoming Crawford's roommate. The more I prayed about it, the better I felt about it. Crawford was one of the most authentic Christians I had ever been around, and the idea of living in an environment of happiness, praise, and love for God just felt right. Plus, throw in the fact that his house was ten minutes from my office and the rent would be dirt cheap, and I was sold! I knew that when I got back to town, I was ready to tell him I wanted us to be roommates.

Another guy friend of mine with whom I had been friends for years, Steven, just happened to be visiting Orlando at the same time I was, and we had the chance to get together for lunch one day. Steven and I had hung out sporadically over the years and always had a good laugh when we got together. I had placed him firmly in the Friend Zone three years earlier, though, and couldn't imagine that he would ever find his way out. I just didn't have those kinds of feelings for him. Still, he was a supersweet guy, and I loved having someone to go to when I needed the male perspective on things. I filled him in on the latest with Mr. E over lunch and shared my excitement with him about the big talk Mr. E and I had planned when I returned home.

Of course, I should have known the fact that Mr. E had basically dropped off the face of the earth since I had been in Florida was foreshadowing of a deeper issue, but I was busy having fun with my family and didn't want to spend my entire vacation stressing and obsessing over a guy. It wasn't until my phone rang on the drive home that I got the first real hint that everything back home wasn't as I had left it.

It was one of my closest girlfriends Beth.

"Mandy," she said with a hint of foreboding. "We saw Mr. E out last night."

I was still so blissed out and relaxed from my vacation that I didn't catch on to the obvious undertone in her voice. "Okay?"

"He was with Shayla Sanders," Beth went on.

"Oh, right. Well, he's been working with her on a story, so I'm sure it was nothing," I replied, then paused. "Wait, are you saying it was something?"

Beth was quiet for a moment. "I don't want to ring the alarm prematurely, but, Mandy, it really looked like there could be something going on between them."

"Are you serious?" I gasped. "Between Mr. E and *Shayla Sanders*?!" I can honestly say the thought or concern had never entered my mind. I thought she had too many red flags surrounding her for Mr. E to even entertain the idea of her as anything other than an interview subject. She was basically a walking red flag.

"Well, have you heard from him since you've been in Florida?" Beth asked. "Maybe I'm just imagining things. I'm sure it's fine."

"Actually," I hesitated, "I've only heard from him once. Then when I called him back, he never returned my call." The first inklings of dread started to flare up in my gut.

"Oh," Beth replied. "Well, maybe it's still nothing. Just wait till you get back, and then you'll talk to him, and it will be fine."

"I hope so," I said with doubt, now feeling a nagging in my gut that I couldn't quite explain. "Thanks for telling me, Beth. I'll call you when I get home."

When I still hadn't heard from Mr. E by the time I got home, I tried reaching him again. Still no answer.

So I called Crawford, deciding there was no time like the present to tell him I wanted to be roommates.

Crawford answered the phone with a jubilant: "Mandy, I want us to be roommates!"

I giggled. "Me too! That's why I was calling you!"

"*Woo hoo!*" he bellowed, causing me to have to hold the phone out from my ear to keep my eardrum from bursting.

"Yeah, I've been thinking about it, and I don't think it will be weird at all. I adore you like a brother, and I know you feel the same way about me," I chirped excitedly. "And I know I had a moment of weirdness wondering if Mr. F. would be okay with it or if it would be awkward, but you know I've worked really hard to keep my friendship with you separate from him and not prod you for information about him. And besides, I really think things between me and E are about to take a more serious turn. So why would he care if I'm roommates with his best friend?"

Crawford got very quiet.

"What?" I asked. "Oh, did he not tell you about the talk we're supposed to have when I got back? He wants to talk about *us!*"

"Mandy," Crawford began slowly, "did he not call you while you were out of town?"

"Oh, yeah, he did, but I missed his call. Then when I tried calling him back I got no answer. But wait, why are you asking me that?"

"I mean, did he not call you and actually talk to you about anything going on *here*?" Crawford asked, a note of concern in his voice.

"No." My heart started to pound. "Why?"

Crawford sighed in frustration. "Mandy, you should call him and talk to him now. Right now."

"I've tried, and he won't answer my calls! Crawford, what's going on? You have to tell me."

"Mandy, I can't. This has to come from him."

"But he's avoiding me, obviously! And you're one of my best friends, so *please* just tell me what in the world is going on!" I was on the verge of tears.

Crawford heaved another deep sigh.

"Mandy, I don't even know how to say this to you," he began. "I can't believe I even have to say this to you." He took a deep breath. "Mandy, Mr. E moved in with Shayla Sanders a few days ago."

My heart skipped a beat. I started to grow faint. I could feel my lunch starting to rise in my throat.

"What?!"

And suddenly, even though everything was still fuzzy and wrong, the situation started to grow alarmingly clear.

Crawford went on to tell me, as lovingly as he possibly could, how Mr. E had interviewed Shayla for the story he was working on a week and a half prior, and how he came back raving about the "instant connection" they shared. It was an intensive piece that Mr. E was writing for his newspaper, and they were spending long hours of extreme intimacy together since the article was an exposé on Shayla's very colorful life. Within a few days, the two of them were together all the time. Then a couple of days ago Mr. E called Crawford to tell him that since he rented a one-room studio and Shayla had a large, sprawling home in one of the nicest neighborhoods in Nashville, it just made sense for him to give up his place and move in with her.

It "made sense"? Nothing about this made sense. I go out of town for a week and a half, and the entire *world* goes insane?

And how could Mr. E not have the decency to tell me himself instead of leaving it to his best friend to break the news to me? What kind of a person does that? How could he do something like this, when it felt like we were finally on the verge of becoming a real couple?

I was devastated. Absolutely crushed. Everything about our relationship, from day one, felt like it had been a lie. Particularly the new closeness and kinship we had developed over the days before I left for Florida.

The irony in the whole situation was now that Mr. E was with Shayla, he never darkened the door of Crawford's house anymore. So any lingering concerns about me becoming roommates with Crawford went right out the window because I wouldn't have to worry about bumping into Mr. E at Crawford's. Or anywhere, for that matter. He was completely, wholly, entirely consumed by this relationship. It was staggeringly difficult to make sense of. I knew Mr. E was a spontaneous person who tended to get swept up in the moment, but this was bizarre behavior, even for him. It was as if, overnight, he became someone I didn't know. But then again, maybe I had never truly known him.

My friend Steven came over the next day to help me start packing for my big move and found me in a mess of tears and wadded up tissues and melted ice cream. I relayed the whole story to him, and he sat there with his mouth hanging open in disbelief. He listened without judgment and let me rant, scream, throw things, and do everything I needed to do, then he put his arm around me and let me cry on his shoulder for hours without complaint. That's the great thing about guy friends—they have much broader shoulders to cry on. I was so grateful to Steven that night and in the days that followed, as he helped me navigate the often treacherous and unfriendly waters of complete and utter heartbreak.

I also cried out to God, asking Him why. Why was this happening? Why was Mr. E not the person I thought he was? Why did he choose Shayla over me? Why did he seemingly turn his back on God to follow his own selfish desires? Why, why, *why*? I have always had a very open, honest relationship with God, and sometimes that results in us having it out. I'll yell, I'll scream, I'll shake my fist, I'll tell God just how angry I am at Him, then I'll collapse on my face before Him in a heap of humility and surrender in unwavering love and tell Him that no matter what, I trust Him. Despite my confusion, pain, and feelings of betrayal about what Mr. E had done, I still knew in my heart that God was in control and was going to redeem this situation in some way. I still felt the calling in my life that I was meant to do something great, and if this was part of the plan to get me there, then so be it.

Two weeks after I returned home from Florida, I moved into Crawford's house, and we officially became roomies. I was more than ready for a fresh start. Steven, Crawford, and Beth were there to help me get settled in, and after a long day of moving, the four of us sleepily clinked our Starbucks cups together in celebration.

It was time for a new chapter.

Chapter 11

Highs and Lows

One day not long after my big move, I was at my parents' house packing up a few things I still had in storage there when I stumbled across the drawer of my New Kids on the Block stash. Like many girls of my generation, at the age of ten, I had fallen in love for the first time with not just one guy but five: Joey, Jordan, Jonathan, Donnie, and Danny—better known as the New Kids on the Block. As any thirty-something woman can attest, NKOTB were the Beatles of our era. Most women of my generation, when asked who their first love was, will sigh and say one of those five familiar names. Their exuberant innocence, rat tails, ripped jeans, and lovelorn lyrics melted the hearts of preteen and teenage girls across the world, much to the dismay of teenage boys across the world. As I poked through that drawer of memories almost twenty years later—the scrapbooks, posters, and a few fan letters my sister and I had written but never mailed—a very nostalgic feeling started to take over. The feeling stayed with me throughout the next few weeks, until one day I came upon an announcement as I was flipping through the channels looking for something to watch on TV.

"The New Kids on the Block Reunite!" the headline screamed, and though the teenybopper in me had long been replaced by a mature woman, my heart stopped and my face instantly flushed as my NKOTB radar surged back to life. I grabbed the nearest phone and punched in my sister's number at lightning speed.

"Oh my gosh, did you *hear*?" she screeched as soon as she picked up the phone.

"*Yes!* We have to go!"

Though the NKOTB stalkers in us had been lying dormant for twenty years, it was as though we had never skipped a beat. Instantly we were eleven and fourteen again, plotting our plan of attack for getting ourselves as close to the stage as we possibly could.

Seeing the New Kids as young girls, when we *thought* we were gorgeous and were convinced we were going to sweep them off their feet with one glance at our frizzy poodle perms, hot pink jelly shoes, and shoulder pads that rivaled those of an NFL linebacker, had been truly amazing. But to have the opportunity to see them again in our thirties, when we *knew* we were gorgeous and had driver's licenses, conditioned ends, and outfits with no shoulder pads, was beyond what I could really even put into words.

When we got to the show at the Bridgestone Arena in Nashville, decked out in all our grown-women glory, we automatically noticed that there was a blocked-off section right beside us that looked like a riser with a piano on it. We were ecstatic when the girls next to us arrived, seasoned veterans from attending the show in St. Louis, and explained that all five guys would be popping up on the riser during the show. Not only that, but they told us the exact moment during the show when it would happen.

When the guys came out to the platform in the middle of the show, we managed to work our way up to the blockade surrounding the riser and were the first to push our way through, which meant we were the closest to the guys. And when I say "managed to work our way up," I mean we blew past everyone and everything standing in our way—parting the Red Sea of fans with fixed determination that would make Charlton Heston proud—to secure a prime position against the railing. The girls behind us were pushing us up against the partition so hard that I made the bodyguard on the other side of the blockade promise to fish me out of the pile and carry me to safety should the crowd get unruly and storm the stage.

The momentary lack of oxygen was totally worth it, though, when the guys launched into three or four songs on the riser, only feet away from where we stood. I snapped pictures frantically while trying to flash my sweetest smiles and flirtiest eyes at Donnie. Since Donnie was the only single New Kid and I had developed my penchant for bad boys since the eighties, I had jumped ship from being a "Joey girl" to become a "Donnie girl". Unable to draw a deep breath because my ribcage was pressed up against the barricade, I feared my flirty glances came across more as pained grimaces. Apparently I did something right, though, because as the rest of the guys started to make their way back to the main stage, Donnie hopped down and began to work his way to my row. Then, as time stood still, he came toward me. Could it be? Was this really going to happen?

He swept me into an embrace, and the next thing I knew, Donnie Wahlberg's lips were on mine, my arms wrapped around him, my heart racing, my world stopping on its axis for what felt like half an hour (but was in reality only about three seconds, tops).

Then it was over, and I was left standing there, the eleven-year-old version of myself *freaking out* inside the body of my thirty-year-old self, my mouth hanging open in stunned silence, the culmination of every one of my wildest dreams as a child wrapped up in one moment. One of the biggest wishes of my idealistic, innocent, stubbornly faithful heart was granted, just like that, in one fell swoop.

When I was ten, my biggest dream was to kiss one of the New Kids on the Block. In fact, I used to kiss their posters every night before bed as practice. At age thirty, it actually happened. How many women can say they got to live out one of their childhood fantasies?

And after the crash and burn I had just been through, the pain, heartache, and disappointment of being passed up by Mr. E for another girl had left me feeling flawed and somehow just not good enough. Yet Donnie Wahlberg swept in, like a knight in shining armor, and made me feel beautiful, perfect, and special, just as I was.

I'm sure to some it might seem like nothing more than a silly, simple kiss, but for me it was a truly defining moment that reminded me that dreams *do* come true, and amazing things *can* happen, for no reason at all—and that I *was* worthy of the kind of kisses you only see in fairy tales. I walked out of that concert with a pep in my step and a confidence in my stride that hadn't been there in a very long time.

Soon it would be back to the real world, but for that night, feeling a bit like Cinderella, I went to sleep with a sweet smile on my face, memories of that night in my dreams, excitement for the future in my heart, and a kiss I had waited twenty years for on my lips.

Having a male roommate is sort of a twenty-four-hour-a-day, enter-at-your-own-risk type of situation. On any given day, you never know if you're going to open the fridge and find six-month-old milk growing a new species of antibiotics, head into the bathroom to find the toilet seat up and maybe his pants down, or be sitting innocently on the couch and have him fly across the room like a sumo wrestler and leap on top of you in all his giddy, puppy-like joy, thinking he's the most hilarious person on earth for pinning you to the couch and forcing you to sniff his socks. You have arguments over who scooped the kitty litter last and whose turn it is to take out the garbage and who used the last roll of toilet paper. Living with a boy is, in a word, chaos.

But . . .

It's also late-night trips to Walgreens to buy matching chocolate Ghirardelli candy bars when it feels like the whole world is against you. It's endless movie watching and spontaneous dance parties at midnight on your birthday and a big, broad shoulder to lean on when someone breaks your heart. It's a prayer partner who helps you carry the groceries, and also the weights of life. It's a best friend who loves you unconditionally, even when you have PMS, even when you're wearing rollers and zit cream, even when you are the most unlovable person on the face of the earth.

I loved living with Crawford. There was never a dull moment, and rarely a moment that we weren't laughing hysterically. We were both movie lovers and had ridiculously expansive DVD collections, so the first month or so that I lived there, we had nonstop movie marathons to the point where people started to send out search parties for us because we hadn't left the house in so long.

And since he was still going through his post-divorce heartache and I was going through my post-Mr. E heartache, we made the perfect pair. The perfect moody, often sniffling, sometimes crying, pajama-wearing, Ben & Jerry's–consuming pair.

A lot of nights when we couldn't sleep, Crawford and I would have prayer time together. It was so nice having a built-in prayer partner. We would pray for our families, our friends, our careers, our own heartbreaks, and our destinies. Though I loved my job, I still felt very much like there was something greater that I was meant to be doing with my life; I just didn't know what. And Crawford had a heart for missionary work and had taken several trips overseas to minister in different third-world countries over the years, and he very much hoped to do more in the future, as long as he had the finances to do so. We both knew God had a special plan for each of our lives, and prayed that we would be sensitive to His voice and know when to take action and when to simply be still and wait on Him.

Steven and I were also growing closer. Though I had only viewed him as a friend and nothing more for years, his kindness, understanding, and support during my whole Mr. E crash and burn had made me start to see him through new eyes. And my special kiss from Donnie Wahlberg had boosted my confidence about the idea of finding love again. Of course, I didn't realize at the time that my feelings for Steven were mostly misplaced feelings of insecurity and hurt from Mr. E's rejection. I even tried fasting from dating and relationships for forty days to try and work through my unresolved issues, but I still hadn't quite mastered the art of loving myself enough to wait on God's timing in the area of my love life instead of trying to manufacture love myself. I was rebounding in a big way, and instead of realizing

I needed a lot more than forty days to care for myself and give myself time to heal, I was masking the pain as so many people do by running headfirst into an ill-timed and ill-fated new romance. Steven and I started spending more and more time together, and when he finally confessed his true feelings for me a few months after I moved back to Nashville, I ignored the nagging doubts in my spirit and agreed to go on an actual date with him.

And while the spark between Steven and I was just starting to kindle, Mr. E's relationship with Shayla was coming to a fiery end.

Crawford and I hardly ever spoke of Mr. E anymore, even though I knew Crawford still talked to him on occasion. I respected my friendship with Crawford way too much to pump him for information about Mr. E, plus Mr. E had largely dropped off the face of the earth after he started dating Shayla, so there wasn't really anything to tell. And I was actually very okay with not knowing. I knew I couldn't fully let go of Mr. E if he was still lingering around, in person or merely in conversation. I was happily (or so I thought) moving on with my life with someone new, just like Mr. E was, and I had no desire to see him or hear about him.

So you can imagine my surprise the day I came home from work and Crawford broke the news to me that Mr. E would be coming to live with us.

"*What?*" I shrieked in disbelief. Had I heard him wrong?

"Well, not coming to *live* with us, per say," Crawford explained hesitantly, looking a little like he wondered if he should run for cover. "Just coming to stay with us for a bit."

"But why?" I asked. "Why in the world would he be coming to stay with us?"

"Well, he and Shayla got into a huge fight and broke up, and now she's kicked him out and he has nowhere to go."

"And this is our problem, why?"

Crawford looked sheepish. "Mandy, he really doesn't have anywhere else to go. He gave up his apartment a few months ago, and I'm his best friend. If you have a major problem with this, obviously I'll tell him no, but I'd really like to help him out and give him a place to crash. It will only be for a little while, I promise."

I sighed. "How long of a little while?"

"A few days—a week at the most," Crawford replied, looking at me hopefully. "So can he come? Are you okay with it?"

As furious as I might ever be with Mr. E, I didn't want to see him out on the streets, especially when he was probably already suffering a broken heart to boot. Plus, this was Crawford's house, and Mr. E was his best friend. I didn't really feel comfortable telling Crawford he couldn't provide a little solace and shelter to his best friend. I could certainly understand needing your best friend during a time of heartache. I wasn't going to be the one to stand in the way of that.

"Yes, he can come," I relented. "Although that's going to be an interesting conversation with Steven. How am I supposed to explain to my new guy that my old guy is coming to camp out on my sofa?"

Crawford and I looked at each other and started laughing.

"Wow, Mandy, you do find yourself in some bizarre situations," Crawford noted. "Like, truth-is-stranger-than-fiction situations. Have you ever thought about writing a book?"

———

Surprisingly, Steven was a lot cooler with the situation than I expected. Either that or he was lying through his teeth since we were newly dating, and he probably didn't want to come across as the overbearing psycho type. I breathed a sigh of relief when we hung up the phone, saying a silent prayer of gratitude. Thank goodness. This was a new relationship, and the last thing I wanted was to introduce any drama to it.

The next day drama walked into my living room in the form of Mr. E. Or at least, the remains of Mr. E. The scraggly, unwashed, uncombed, unkempt person who wandered into my house wearing a floor-length black trench coat in the dead of August sort of resembled Mr. E.

"Crawford!" I hissed as we huddled in the corner, watching Trench Coat Man shuffle across the room and collapse into a chair in front of Crawford's video game console. "*What is that?*"

Crawford looked a little nervous. "Mandy, I don't know what's going on. He looked like that when I picked him up. This is apparently his way of dealing with the breakup."

"By not bathing for what looks like"—I paused and sniffed the air—"and smells like a week?"

"You know how overly dramatic he is," Crawford said with a shrug. "He always grieves the end of relationships in colorful ways. I guess the trench coat and the whole, um, not bathing thing is just his way of dealing with his emotions."

Mr. E spent the next week in front of the video game console, dealing with his emotions. I went to bed, he was playing video games. I woke up, he was playing video games. I went to work, he was playing video games. I got home from work, and yep, you guessed it, he was playing video games. I'm not sure when he slept, or if he slept. And the trench coat remained firmly glued to his body, even as the temperature soared higher and higher outside.

This was not to negate Mr. E's feelings or to say that his broken heart wasn't valid. I'm sure he was working through his grief in his own way. Some of us eat ice cream and watch movies. He wore a trench coat and didn't bathe for ten days. I had battled depression myself and would never make light of anyone truly struggling with depression. But *this*, this felt like an act, a show, an overly theatrical stunt designed to get attention. And after everything I had already been through with Mr. E, my patience with his attention-seeking games was starting to wear thin.

On day ten, I marched into the den and tossed a bar of soap into his lap. He looked up at me with surprise.

"You have until five to get in the shower willingly, or so help me, I will drag you in there myself if I have to, kicking and screaming," I said evenly. "This is getting ridiculous. Crawford is kind enough to give you a place to stay. The least you could do is be respectful enough to take a shower."

He didn't respond, but simply went back to playing his video game.

When I got home that afternoon, the trench coat–covered lump was gone. His stuff that had been scattered around the living room had vanished. The empty box that had contained the bar of soap was the only thing left, sitting in the chair in front of the video game console.

"He left," Crawford said, walking up behind me.

"He left?" I asked in quiet surprise. "Where did he go?"

"He decided to go stay with his friend George for a few days, out at his house in the country. He thought it would be good for clearing his head, figuring out what to do next."

I picked up the empty soap box and sat down in the chair silently.

"And, Mandy," Crawford said, putting his hand on my shoulder gently.

"Yeah?"

"He said to tell you thanks."

A few weeks later Mr. E packed up and left for good. He moved back home to Boone, apparently to reevaluate, recharge, and get his life together. And just like that, I was free to move on with my life and with Steven, and see if this new relationship of mine might lead to the kind of happy ending that always seemed to elude me and Mr. E.

Except I wasn't really free. Not at all. I was still totally hung up on Mr. E and too prideful and stubborn to admit it to myself, so instead I continued to run from my feelings by hiding out in the safety of my relationship with Steven. Steven seemed to care for me so much, and he had been such a rock over the past few months, and a great friend for the past few years before that, it seemed at the time that I was making a healthy choice. Little did I know how soon that "healthy choice" would blow up in my face.

When Steven's birthday rolled around in October, I eagerly helped him plan his birthday fiesta. By that point we were boyfriend and girlfriend, and I was very much in the blissed-out, new-relationship state. By the end of the night, however, a skeleton that rivaled the size of Skeletor in *He-Man and the Masters of the Universe* would come bounding out of Steven's closet. (Since it was close to Halloween, I guess it was fitting.)

The party went well and things seemed perfectly fine and normal, until we got home. At some point between when we left the party and when we arrived back at my house, Steven experienced a case of the *Invasion of the Body Snatchers*. He went into a swift and completely unexplainable rage, ripping his shirt from his body, pouring a canister of motor oil over his head, and playing whack-a-mole with Crawford's birdfeeder, dashing it into a million tiny pieces. Miraculously, none of the neighbors or Crawford woke up to experience this one-man circus, and I was the only witness to the bizarre series of events. Though he didn't put his hands on me that night, his sudden fit of insanity should have tipped me off to the fact that something in him was broken, and I needed to get away before he tried to break me too. I was so stunned, I didn't know what to do. I simply couldn't understand how this man I had known for years could suddenly morph into this monster in the blink of an eye.

The next morning I ended the relationship. Steven objected and apologized and cried and begged me to give him a second chance, but I was unyielding. I was hurt, embarrassed, frightened, and beyond confused. And he hadn't just hurt me; he had hurt my roommate. Crawford had never been anything but kind to Steven, and now he was left picking up the pieces of his damaged belongings. I was mortified.

Over the next couple of weeks, Steven begged me to reconsider and give us another try. He had a million excuses about why he flipped out. His uncle had passed away a few months prior, and he blamed it on that. He blamed it on the stress in his life. He blamed it on something someone said to him at his party. He pointed his finger at everything and everyone except himself.

"Mandy, you know me," he pleaded. "You've known me for years! Have you ever seen me act like this before now?"

The truth was, no, I hadn't, which was part of the reason I was so stunned.

When he saw that his begging and pleading wasn't going to do the trick, he trotted a series of character witnesses (also known as his friends) past me to swear up and down that this was an isolated incident and they had *never* seen Steven lose his temper like this before. His friend John was particularly convincing.

"Mandy, he really cares about you," John reasoned. "He would never do anything to purposely hurt you if he was in his right mind. Something else had to be going on that night. Please think about giving him another chance."

In the end, I gave Steven another chance. Unfortunately at the time, I either didn't realize or didn't want to see that the crazy fit he threw wasn't just a giant red flag; it was like a blazing red fire, warning me to run for cover. Had I left then, I would have spared myself the next year of torment, lies, betrayal, and abuse. But then again, since the demise of that horrible relationship would ultimately lead to the creation of The Single Woman, how can I really regret a single second of it?

Chapter 12

Turbulence

After Steven's birthday rampage, things quieted down for a while. He was on his best behavior. I started to feel like maybe things were going to work out between us after all. It's amazing the lies we'll tell ourselves to maintain a relationship. My gut knew I needed to run, but my heart felt differently.

I was always one of those women who scoffed at the Lifetime movies that portrayed domestic violence situations, saying time and again, "I will never be one of *those* women. The minute a man lays a hand on me, I'm gone." I viewed *those* women as weak. I couldn't imagine anyone choosing to stay with someone who purposely hurt them, over and over again. The thing that I didn't understand at the time about domestic abuse is that it creeps up on you a little at a time. A push here. A grab there. It doesn't start with a bloody nose or a black eye. It starts so subtly, you don't even realize it's happening. And then the abuser, being the master manipulator, manages to convince you that it's somehow your fault. You nagged him too much. You picked a fight with him. You pushed him to hit you.

And then, ashamed, apologetic, and remorseful, the abuser

works overtime to make you forget what he did. He brings you flowers. He sends you sweet e-mails and texts. He cooks you dinner. He has no shortage of tricks up his sleeve to make you accept his profuse apologies. Before you know it, you're lulled into a peaceful oblivion, and all his powerful blows, hate-filled words, and broken promises are just a distant memory that seems more like a bad dream.

That was the process I went through with Steven following his birthday. I wanted so badly to believe in him, and I wanted so badly to make the relationship work, that I allowed myself to grow complacent. I allowed myself to turn off my inner voice and listen to Steven's seductive lies. I allowed myself to become one of *those* women I so pitied. I basically became the Queen of Bad Decisions. Which is not to say I deserved what Steven was dishing out, but I did actively choose to keep taking it. I do bear the burden of responsibility, not for his actions, but for my own. I'm not sure why I was clinging so tightly to the relationship. I think I knew in my gut that it was toxic, and that I didn't love him like I claimed to. But my relationship that I had believed so strongly in with Mr. E had gone up in smoke, and I hadn't managed to make any other relationship in the past five years work, so I think somewhere inside I believed that I was flawed, broken, and didn't deserve any better than Steven. Despite my inner hesitation, I forged blindly ahead with the relationship, determined to prove to myself and to the world that I could sustain love.

After a few months of dating, Steven came to me one day with a suggestion: "Why don't we move in together?"

My moral compass instantly recoiled at the suggestion. Despite the fact that Steven and I were already living in sin and having a sexual relationship, I couldn't imagine actually physically living with someone outside of marriage. Isn't it funny how we rate sin? How we think if we do *this* one but not *that* one, we're still doing okay?

I had made a vow to myself, many years before, that I would never live with a man before marriage. It just wasn't something that I wanted to do. I had very strong convictions about it and couldn't fathom breaking that vow to myself and to God. I know a lot of couples live together before marriage. I actually know several Christian couples active in the church—and who had been Christians and active in the church when they got together— who lived together before marriage. I'm not here to judge those people, as that's not my place. That's between them and God and their own personal convictions. But for me, living with someone I was in a romantic relationship with, but not married to, simply felt wrong.

"But you lived with Crawford," some people might object. I understand the comparison, but there's a major difference. Crawford was my strictly platonic best friend who just happened to be a male. Crawford and I had never so much as pecked each other on the cheek. We didn't share a bed. We didn't have any level of intimacy outside of friendship. He was basically my brother without the blood relation. To me, living with a male friend is no different from living with a female friend. My relationship with Crawford was innocent, pure, and completely God-centered.

My relationship with Steven, however, was the exact opposite. We were romantically and physically involved. I didn't feel right about living with him, plain and simple.

Still, I told him I'd think about it.

And just like that, sin creeps in.

Over the next few weeks, I started to convince myself that it wasn't that big of a deal. We were going to get married eventually anyway, I told myself. It's not like we'd just be arbitrarily living together. This relationship was going somewhere! This was just a prelude to marriage. And that was okay, right?

The more I considered it, the more I began to think about how fun it would be to live with Steven. I would have my partner, right there with me, all the time! And I would keep going to church and praying, which meant God would forgive me, right?

A few days later I said yes to Steven. The more I smiled and laughed on the outside, the more conflicted I felt on the inside. There's a scripture in Romans that encapsulates perfectly the internal struggle I was experiencing: "For I do not understand my own actions. For I do not do what I want, but I do the very thing I hate" (Rom. 7:15 ESV). I didn't really understand why I was doing what I was doing, and I silently hated my willingness to go against what I believed in so strongly for the sake of a relationship, yet I forged ahead anyway.

That spring I moved out of Crawford's house and into an apartment with Steven. Saying good-bye to Crawford was physically painful, since I knew he wanted to be happy for me but saw the compromises I was making in an effort to force this relationship to work. He knew I was going against everything I believed in. And he was the only one in my life who knew about Steven's birthday outburst because I was too embarrassed to tell any of my other friends. Obviously I couldn't hide it from Crawford, since his birdfeeder had taken the brunt of Steven's rage that night.

"I'll miss you," Crawford said sadly as he squeezed me into a tight hug on the front porch the day I left. "You know the door is always open for you here."

"I know," I whispered into his shoulder. "I love you."

"Love you too."

The apartment Steven and I would be sharing was in Murfreesboro, just a few miles away from my parents, but I didn't tell my parents Steven and I were moving in together. They had been to my new apartment, but assumed I would be living there by myself. I was afraid they wouldn't approve (which of course they wouldn't have), but mainly I was just ashamed. Ashamed to be going against my word to God and to myself, ashamed to be openly living in a way that would embarrass them, and ashamed to be doing something that would disappoint them (and God). Of course they figured out within a few weeks that Steven was there all the time, but once again stood out of the way and allowed me to make my own mistakes. I've never given my parents enough credit when it comes to knowing me better than I know myself. Here's the thing, though: if you have to lie about something to the people you love most in the world, and if you have to keep something a secret, it's not something you should be doing.

The first few weeks of living with Steven, picking out furniture, and designing our new place was fun, and the dark cloud over me started to lift. I felt like I had finally found a place where I fit. I was finally making a relationship work! Maybe I was just being silly worrying so much about the whole living together thing, I told myself. Everybody lives together before marriage these days, right? This didn't change who I was in the least. Maybe I needed to stop overthinking everything and learn to just go with it!

Then the walls of the carefully crafted lies I was telling myself started to crumble—just a bit at first.

It all started one night when Steven told me he wouldn't be home for dinner because he had a business meeting in Nashville. He was a real estate agent, and this sounded like a feasible story to me. I didn't think twice about it as I shot him a text back: "K. Have fun! See you when you get home."

I knew his meeting was at six in the evening, so I expected him home by nine, ten at the latest. But eleven rolled around, and he still wasn't home. Being my mother's daughter, I started to get a little worried, so I tried to call him. No answer. I sent him a text. No response. My pulse quickened. What if he had decided to have a few drinks at dinner and then drive home? I wasn't a drinker, but he was, so when we were together, I was always the designated driver. If he was with a bunch of guys, however, and everyone had drinks with dinner, he might have struck out for home without a designated driver. I knew his dinner meeting was at Merchants Restaurant downtown, so when I still hadn't heard a peep from him by midnight, I called the restaurant.

"I'm sorry to bother you, but I'm looking for my boyfriend, and I can't reach him on his cell. Can you tell me if he's anywhere in your restaurant, or maybe at the bar?"

"Ma'am, there's no one left in the restaurant or in the bar. We closed an hour ago."

Hmm.

I hung up the phone, wondering what to do next. Just then my phone lit up with a text.

"Still hung up at Merchants. Leaving in a half hour."

Obviously I knew he was lying, but for what reason? Where was he?

Suddenly something hit me, and I knew where he was. To this day I can't tell you how I knew, as I had absolutely no reason for suspecting this and no evidence to prove it. Call it female intuition or divine inspiration, but I knew in my gut where he was.

I tapped out a text: "Hope you're having fun at the strip club."

Five minutes later my phone rang. It was him, raging at me through the phone.

"How do you know where I am? Are you having me followed now?" he screamed.

"No, Steven. I am not having you followed. I actually didn't know where you were until this moment. I just took a shot. Thanks for confirming it, though."

I hung up the phone.

He blew up my cell for what I can only assume was his entire drive home. By the time he finally got there, there was a pillow and blanket waiting for him on the couch, and I was in the bedroom with the door locked. He pounded and pounded, but I ignored him. Finally he wore himself out and stopped, but I got very little sleep that night. It was already 2:00 a.m, and I had to be up at 6:00 a.m. to get ready for work. I felt like such a fool. How could I have ever trusted Steven again after his inexcusable behavior on his birthday? And not only that—I had moved in with him! Now I felt trapped.

Of course the next morning I woke up to a decadent breakfast and a million apologies.

"Mandy, I'm so sorry. I feel so horrible about everything that happened last night," Steven said in a pleading tone as I tried to force down some eggs. "The prospective clients wanted to go to this gentlemen's club, and I didn't know how to say no without losing their business! Can't you understand that?"

Honestly, I didn't understand. I didn't understand at all. But I had made a commitment to live with this person and to make this relationship work, and I was stubbornly determined to see it through.

So I stayed.

That's just one of the many problems with making the choice to live with someone you're not married to. There's a false sense of obligation that doesn't exist when you're simply dating someone and not living with them. Even though the apartment was in my name, and I could tell Steven to pack his bags and get out at any time, the decision to move in together felt binding, almost like the responsibility of marriage without any of the perks. Had I really been honest with myself, I would have realized that Steven wasn't truly committed to me and our relationship, or he never would have even considered stepping one foot into a place that defiled women and completely obliterated the bonds of our relationship. And things were only going to get worse.

I soon figured out that Steven was a pathological liar. He would lie about things that made no sense to lie about. He would lie when the truth was better. Some of the lies I caught him in were absolutely ridiculous, like pretending to be sick so he could stay home and have his buddies over to watch a ball game instead of coming to a work function with me. Of course I got home later that night and figured out from the beer cans and pizza boxes cluttering the garbage can that he wasn't really sick. So why lie instead of just telling me that he'd rather hang out with his friends than go to dinner with me and my coworkers? Big lies, little lies, they were all the same to Steven.

It was a month or so after we moved in together that he got physical with me for the first time.

Arguing a lot was normal for us, and screaming matches frequently broke out, but on this particular night, Steven was even angrier than usual. He was stalking around the room, ranting and raving and shaking his fists. When I went to speak up, he thundered over to me and kicked my feet out from under me as

I stood on the hard tile kitchen floor. I crashed to the ground, my ankle pinned beneath me at an unnatural angle. At first he ignored my screams of pain, telling me I was faking my tears. It was only when he saw me attempt to stand to my feet and my legs crumpled beneath me that a look of guilt started to register on his face.

I called in sick to work the next day, pretending to have the flu. And I limped for three days after. But only in private. In public, I steeled myself to walk as normally as possible to keep anyone from asking questions about what had happened. I protected him, while he was doing nothing to protect me.

Slowly the violence started to escalate. Steven would grab my arms and shake me, leaving dark purple bruises all up and down my arms. Bruises that my coworker Jane would notice.

"Mandy," she said with concern the first time she saw them, "what's going on?"

I looked down at my arms. Darn it! I had absentmindedly worn a sleeveless top to work that day. Looking back on it now, maybe it actually wasn't absentminded at all. Maybe it was a cry for help.

I immediately went into defense mode.

"Oh, nothing! It's fine. Steven and I got into an argument, and he grabbed me a little too hard, but honestly, it was my fault. He was exhausted, and I was nagging him to take out the garbage. I can be so overbearing sometimes!" I laughed like it was the funniest thing in the world, barely even recognizing the sound of my own voice. My entire life had become one big lie.

Soon the grabbing and the shaking escalated to the next level. While on a weekend trip to the mountains to try and work on our rapidly deteriorating relationship, Steven head-butted me in the parking garage of our hotel, causing me to fall to the ground and literally see stars. I laid there, a searing pain shooting through my head, unable to move.

"Mandy, I'm so sorry. I don't know what's wrong with me." Steven knelt next to me and gently picked me up from the pavement. "Please forgive me. I just love you so much, sometimes my emotions get the best of me."

Here's a hint, ladies: there's no such thing as "loving someone so much" you're forced to hit them. True love doesn't hurt, and it doesn't hit.

A few weeks after the disastrous trip, we were having one of our usual arguments outside because he would dart out of the house the minute I tried to communicate with him about anything. It was impossible to have a normal, adult discussion with Steven because he would instantly accuse me of nagging him and either start screaming and hitting or simply run away, like a child. I was getting so desperate to make things work, I chased him out the door to continue the conversation. That's when he turned on me, slamming me down so hard against the hood of my car, I thought I was going to black out. I slid off the hood and to the ground and just lay there in a heap. Instead of staying to see if I was okay, Steven jumped in his car and peeled out of the driveway. I limped back inside and lay down gingerly on the couch, wondering what in the world I was doing and why I was choosing to remain in such a toxic situation.

I knew where a lot of my hesitance to sever the relationship stemmed from: Steven and our dysfunction had become my whole world. Because of my embarrassment about the violent, unhealthy nature of our relationship, I had started dodging my friends' phone calls and avoiding anyone in my life who knew me well enough to take one look at me and know something was desperately wrong. This included my friends, my coworkers, my parents, and my church. I had done what so many victims of domestic abuse do—I had closed myself off from any other lines of communication outside of my abuser. I didn't want to look in the faces of the people who loved me and see how far I had fallen mirrored in their eyes. I had frozen out my support system, the very people who cared about me the most in the world, and all the while I was clinging for dear life to a sinking ship.

One night he told me an old female friend that he had known for years was coming into town later that week, and he wanted us to have dinner with her. This sounded reasonable to me, so I quickly agreed. Obviously he was including me in the plans, so he must not have anything to hide, right?

Wrong.

The night of the planned dinner, Steven never came home from work to pick me up. I never heard a peep from him. He disappeared into the night, presumably with this woman. It was completely and utterly baffling. I called him, texted him, left voice mails, and got no response. That is, until six the next morning, when he finally reappeared. Not in person. In my text message inbox. "Sorry, got caught up at work and then went on to dinner with Anna without you because I figured you were already asleep." That was it. No explanation about why he never came home or where he had spent the night. Or why he had spent the night. It was clear to me what was going on, and the implication of his infidelity devastated me. Were the lies and the rage and the drinking and the hitting not enough? Did he have to humiliate me further by cheating on me?

Eventually we had it out, and he claimed he, Anna, and his friend John had gone to dinner and then stayed the night at John's house because they all had too much to drink. This still didn't explain why he had cut me out of the dinner or why he didn't just call to tell me any of this, especially knowing how much I would worry. Steven swore up, down, and sideways that he did not cheat on me, but I wasn't hearing it.

"Mandy, you have to believe me. She's just a friend!" he pleaded. "I would never cheat on you!"

This time, though, I was unmoved by his empty apologies. I told him to get out and not come back. I had put up with a lot, but blatant infidelity was not something I was willing to turn the other cheek to.

That was the beginning of one of the most unbelievable and bizarre incidents to ever occur to me. It's so bizarre, in fact, I'm almost embarrassed to write about it. It sounds more like something that would happen on the *Jerry Springer Show* than something that would happen to me. But in the spirit of transparency, just so you can fully appreciate the sheer depth of Steven's lies and dishonesty, here's what happened next.

Steven started begging me to let him take a lie detector test to prove he hadn't cheated on me. The first time he brought it up, in an e-mail, since I was unwilling to speak to him, I laughed until I cried. Then I just cried. Was this guy serious? How many more levels of complete and utter lunacy was he going to ask me to descend to?

But he wasn't giving up. E-mail after e-mail poured in, with statistics about the accuracy of lie detector tests along with his list of reasons of why I should go along while he submitted to one. I continued to dismiss him. This was insane. I would not allow myself to stoop to such shenanigans for someone who wouldn't know the truth if it smacked him right across the face.

After two weeks of hounding e-mails, though, I was ready

to reconsider. He clearly wasn't going to give up this fight, and if nothing else, this would surely provide some much-needed comic relief. So I called him.

"If you are determined to do this," I asserted, "you find someone to administer the test, you pay for it, and I will go along and watch this train wreck happen since you are obviously not going to leave me alone until I do."

He paused. "Really?" he asked in a tone that I thought bordered on panic-stricken. I honestly don't think he expected me to give in and agree to his little plan, so when I did, he realized he was going to have to pony up and actually follow through with it.

"Yes, really," I said. "Call me with the details, and tell me where and when to be there."

A few days later I was in the seedy-looking office of a private detective somewhere in a part of Nashville that I hope to never return to. And sitting across from me was Steven, sleeve rolled up, eyes as big as silver dollars, ready to strap himself to a machine to prove, once and for all, that he might be a liar, but he wasn't a cheater.

Except (and I know you're going to be truly shocked by this news) he only managed to dig an even deeper hole for himself. After the test was over, the administrator called us both in to go over the results.

"See these lines here?" the administrator asked, pointing at a series of wavy lines zigzagging across the paper. "These show a high level of deception."

I shot Steven a look across the table.

"Really?" I asked. "And on what question?"

The administrator looked over at Steven with a withering look. "The question that inquired about whether or not Steven has been physically involved with another woman since starting his relationship with you."

Oh, the irony.

Steven started to angrily protest as I stood up and shook the administrator's hand.

"Thank you, sir, for telling me all I need to know. Good day." I gathered my purse and my coat and turned to leave. "Oh and, Steven? Good-bye."

Thus began weeks of barraging e-mails from Steven about the *in*accuracy of polygraph tests. I'm embarrassed to say that I actually started reading some of the articles he sent through and eventually convinced myself that there had to be some glitch that caused the test to say Steven was lying when he wasn't. I'm even more embarrassed to admit that I took Steven back—again. Yes, despite his glaring lies and raging temper and cheating ways, I allowed him to move back into our apartment and back into my life. It seemed there was nothing Steven could do to hurt me badly enough to make me walk away once and for all.

But God was about to intervene.

———

Although my prayer time and relationship with God had clearly suffered since I moved in with Steven, I still spent time with God regularly and talked to Him about things going on in my life. I don't think my problem was that I stopped talking to God; I think it's that I stopped listening to Him. In late summer 2009, God started to lay something very heavily on my heart—a realization that I wanted to ignore but knew I couldn't hide from as easily as I was hiding from my closest friends and family.

"If you don't get out of this relationship with Steven, you are going to end up hurt badly, or worse," I felt like God was saying.

Still, despite everything I had been through with Steven, I felt powerless to leave. I was scared, uncertain, and so beaten down by the constant arguing, violence, and lies that I felt trapped in a prison of my own making. I wasn't yet ready to heed God's urging, so instead I began to cry out to Him like never before. At night, when Steven was in the living room watching TV or tapping away on his laptop, I would sneak away to the bathroom, lock the door, and fall onto my knees on the hard tile, begging God to give me the strength to walk away, once and for all.

"God, I know I have turned my back on You, disappointed You, and disobeyed You, and I humbly ask for Your forgiveness," I would pray. "And I know I don't deserve Your mercy, but I am asking for it anyway. Please help me find the strength to walk away from this toxic situation. Please give me the courage and boldness I need to disentangle myself from this dark relationship and find my way back to the light. When I am weak, I pray that You would be my strength. And I am so very weak right now. Where You lead, I will follow. Just show me where to go. Show me what to do. And give me the courage to be obedient."

Night after night, I prayed this prayer. And night after night, as God supernaturally conspired to bring the perfect circumstances together to ensure my exit from the relationship, I slowly started to feel myself growing a little stronger.

Two events happened simultaneously to bring this prayer to fruition. First, Jeremy's sister, Erin, with whom I had become dear friends several years prior, had moved back to Arizona and was getting married. She had asked me to be a bridesmaid in her wedding, and I was honored to say yes and thrilled to get to travel to Arizona to see her. Originally Steven was supposed to go with me, and we had discussed the idea of flying out West together. As the date drew closer, however, he decided he couldn't take that much time off work, and my dad volunteered to be my travel partner instead.

My dad and I decided that since my history with airplanes was less than stellar, we would both take a week off work and drive out to Arizona on a father-daughter road trip. It would be a much-needed break for me and would give me time and space to clear my head, heal, spend time with my dad, and see some beautiful sights along the way.

A few nights before we were set to leave, though, something drastic happened.

After another heated argument over me catching Steven in yet another lie, I got out of bed to get a drink of water. His cell phone happened to be lying on the kitchen counter. Desperate to know the truth and to find out once and for all whether or not he had cheated on me (I had never gotten over the failed polygraph), I picked up his phone and started going through it. Mind you, *I do not recommend or condone this type of behavior at all.* He was the first and only guy I have ever deployed these tactics with, and I will never do it again. But after being repeatedly lied to and kicked around and insulted for months on end, knowing in my heart that he had cheated on me was the final indignity. I just needed proof. Proof that would finally make me strong enough to walk away.

At that moment, Steven came into the kitchen and saw me holding his phone. In a fit of white-hot anger, he picked me up and threw me onto the floor as hard as he could, pinning me to the floor and wrapping his hands around my neck, choking me. I was kicking and flailing with as much strength as I could muster to get him off of me, but he was short, stocky, and strong, and my 125-pound frame and tiny fists did little damage. Finally I started screaming at the top of my lungs, which caused him to grab my face and cover both my mouth and my nose with his hand, positioning himself in such a way that I couldn't breathe. I was getting no oxygen. In a panic, as the blood began to drain from my face, I found enough gumption to bite down on his finger as hard as I could, which caused him to yelp like a wounded puppy and back away from me. Gasping for breath, I ran to the phone and dialed the first number I could think of. 9-1-1.

That night Steven was arrested. The premonition God had laid on my heart weeks earlier played on repeat in my mind. "If you don't get out of this relationship with Steven, you are going to end up hurt badly, or worse." I realized I could have easily been killed, and the thought of it made me shudder.

By the time Steven was released from jail, I was well on my way to Arizona with my dad. I left him a note on our kitchen counter: "I don't want to speak to you while I'm gone. We will talk when I get back."

Over the next three days, I took in the sights, sounds, and smells of the wide-open road, feeling a sense of freedom I hadn't felt in years. My dad and I drove through the flat, dusty plains of Texas and the beautiful mesas of New Mexico, finally reaching the rolling deserts of Arizona. I could feel God's presence all around as I took in His beautiful handiwork. Traveling those roads with my dad, sometimes singing, sometimes listening to audiobooks, and sometimes sitting in companionable silence as we rolled along, was like chicken soup for my soul.

It was equally wonderful to arrive in Arizona and dash right over to Erin's house to see her, Jeremy, and their entire family.

Everyone was so friendly and welcoming, and though we had left behind gray and chilly October skies in Tennessee, the sun in Arizona was as warm and comforting as its people.

Over the next two days, we feted Erin's wedding, and I had the great privilege of witnessing many beautiful walking, breathing portrayals of love in action—of healthy relationships—of marriages that were strong, successful, and thriving. It's almost as though God wanted to show me examples of the kind of love I should be striving for, instead of the kind I was currently settling for. Erin's relationship with her new husband, Keith, was particularly moving. You could see the joy in both of their faces when they simply caught each other's eyes from across the room. His whole being would light up at the mere sight of her. It filled my heart with hope. It helped me see what was possible. It was what I so desperately needed in that moment to finally make me realize how much I had been settling for rocks when God wanted to bring me diamonds.

The festivities culminated in a lively reception, which took place outside under the stars at Erin's mom's house. White lights hung all around, a cool breeze tickled my skin, and I could scarcely recall the last time I was so happy. I danced until I nearly wore holes in the bottoms of my shoes, and then I kicked them off and danced some more. Jeremy joined in on "The Devil Went Down to Georgia," swinging me wildly around the dance floor. I was dizzy with laughter and full of love for my friends, and I never wanted the night to end.

I had stopped dancing long enough to grab a sip of water and was standing off to the side of the dance floor, watching the joy and the wonderful chaos all around me, when Erin's new father-in-law, Shep, came over with a smile. He was a kind and fun-loving man with an infectious laugh, and in the two days I had been around, I had already witnessed how he loved to tease people and bring smiles to their faces. Maybe he caught a fleeting glimpse of sadness cross my face in that moment, I don't know, but he leaned against the pole beside me and crossed his arms over his chest.

"So, what's your story, Mandy?" he boomed in his kindly way. "Are you married?"

"No, sir," I responded with a rueful smile. "Not yet. I have a boyfriend, though."

"But he's not here." It was more a statement than a question.

I shook my head. "No, sir. He couldn't make it." I looked down at my water. "He's not a very nice guy, though."

Shep stood quietly for a minute, scratching his chin.

"Well, then you know what I say?" he said finally, giving me a wink. "I say you head on back to Tennessee and kick his butt to the curb." He chuckled, patted me on the back, and walked away.

I stood there for a moment considering this advice, then grinned broadly and rejoined my friends on the dance floor. It was time for Erin to toss the bouquet!

As luck or fate or providence would have it, I caught Erin's bouquet that night. And I think everyone at the reception felt the magic the moment my fingers closed around it. It was like God was sending me a sign from heaven to restore my hope, my faith, and my belief in happy endings. Erin turned to look and see who caught it, and we both burst into laughter, tears of joy running down both our faces. I have a wonderful picture of the two of us hugging the moment after I caught the bouquet, my face lit up with laughter and happiness. It's one of the most precious portraits of friendship I have.

It's also the portrait of the moment I found myself again. Somewhere on that dance floor in Arizona, thousands of miles from home, surrounded by people I loved, and celebrating one of the most significant moments of my friend's life, the broken pieces of my soul were put back together and sealed with friendship, laughter, and love. God knew exactly what it would take to get me back to *me*: a trip to Arizona. And He orchestrated it as only He can.

The next day my dad and I left Arizona. And as we rolled down the highway later that night, I gazed out the window and up at the pitch-black, velvety sky. The lack of street lamps or city lights made the stars look as bright as diamonds. As I watched, praying silently to God, one star broke away from the rest and shot across the sky in a brilliant silvery streak, confirming what I already knew in my heart to be true. My fervent prayers, spoken in secret to God from my bathroom floor night after night, month after month, had been answered. I knew I was finally strong enough to walk away.

When I got home to my apartment the next evening, I walked right in and ended the relationship with Steven, once and for all. "I don't know much about love," I told him, "but I know I deserve better than this." He looked stunned, shell-shocked even. I honestly think he believed he could do anything to me and I would stick around.

Since our apartment was in my name, I told Steven to pack up his stuff and be gone by the time I got home from work the next day. Even though I'm pretty sure he thought I was going to change my mind, like I had the other five thousand times before, by the time I returned home from work the next evening, all his belongings were gone. My apartment was completely stripped of his presence. Since we had combined our furnishings to decorate the apartment, the missing pieces here and there created an odd effect, almost like looking at a gap-toothed child. Everything appeared essentially the same on the surface, but if you looked a little closer, you would find a nail where a painting once hung, a TV stand with no TV, an end table with no lamp. I still had the foundation of an apartment, but not the trimmings, bells, and whistles that make a house a home. It was rather representative of what was going on inside my soul. Steven had taken a part of me here and a piece of me there, leaving me feeling a bit vacant and strangely unfinished; yet the foundation of who I was couldn't be shaken. Philippians 1:6 says, "He who began a good work in you will carry it on to completion." And though at that moment I had absolutely no idea how God was going to carry out His good work in me, as I walked through the rooms of my half-stripped apartment later that night, the one thing I knew for certain was that the end of my relationship with Steven was the beginning of everything else.

Chapter 13

Grounded in God

It was October 13, 2009, when I ended my relationship with Steven and took my first uncertain but brave steps back into the world as a single girl for the first time in a year and a half. And if you count all the chaos and confusion with Mr. E before that, this was really the first time I had felt truly single, free, and unattached in more than three years. It was scary, a little overwhelming, and completely wonderful.

Over the next couple of months, I found the courage to dream new dreams and have new adventures and restore old relationships. I saw a counselor. I found healing. I adopted a wonderful seven-year-old white, fluffy, and cantankerous Persian by the name of Jeeves from a rescue shelter. But most of all I worked on restoring my relationship with God, and with myself. I owed both of us a big apology for putting up with so much abuse for so long. When you're in the midst of an abusive relationship and being constantly demeaned and degraded, it's hard to remember how you got there or imagine a time when you would be able to break free. But your reaction about the ending of something will go a long way in telling you your true feelings about it. Did I have a few moments of sadness, and even doubt, about walking away from my relationship with Steven? Absolutely. But was it enough to make me return to the scene of the crime? Absolutely not! Endings, even endings that need to happen, always come with a certain amount of sadness. But trust me on this one: it's better to face a few fleeting moments of sadness any day than to spend a lifetime of misery clinging to the wrong person.

Feeling so empowered in my new single life and learning something new about myself every day, I wanted to find other people who were experiencing similar *aha* moments, so I turned to my usual method of research when it comes to learning everything I can about something I'm going through. I flipped on the TV, but the only examples I saw of single life there were endless shows warning women about the "dangers" of being single past a certain age. ("Your eggs are drying up!" "You're past your prime childbearing years!" "You're more likely to get struck by lightning than to find love over the age of thirty!") Then there were the "reality" dating shows depicting women pawing and fighting and scratching each other's eyes out to get to a guy who wasn't even that great. *Whose reality is this?* I wondered. It certainly wasn't mine. I wandered the aisles of bookstores and found endless books with candy-colored covers offering to help women "find a man" and "keep a man," and my personal favorite, "make any man fall in love with you!" But I found absolutely nothing offering to help women simply become better women. Was this what the single journey was truly about in the eyes of Hollywood, literature, and pop culture? Either wringing your hands over the tragedy of your singleness or wringing your hands in desperation as you tried anything and everything to end your singleness, even if it meant settling for a relationship or a life far inferior to what you deserve?

Something had to be done. There had to be a better way to be single.

I had been working for the nonprofit organization for more than two years by that point and was starting to feel a little uninspired. Since it was a technology company, and the subject of technology wasn't something I was particularly fired up about, I felt that my imagination wasn't being stimulated and my creativity was lying dormant. I wanted to find a way to tap into my lifelong passion for writing and get the creative juices flowing again. But what to write about?

Then it dawned on me. Since I couldn't find the sassy, confident, independent, inspired single role model I was looking for, maybe I could become it. After all, they always say that you should "write what you know," right? If I knew anything, I knew single life. I had spent five very formative single years in my twenties learning how to stand alone. And over the past few years, I had experienced great love, great heartache, and enough crazy exes to make my writing entertaining. I felt uniquely qualified to write about being single, and to write about it with the passion, honesty, and flair that I felt was largely missing from most of the current dialogue about single life.

The idea sort of thrilled me a little. I started praying that God would show me the right platform from which to share my thoughts with the world. I even made it a New Year's resolution to find an outlet for my writing. And just a few days into 2010, I stumbled across a listing on Examiner.com for a "Nashville Single Women Examiner." If you're not familiar with the *Examiner*, it's basically an online newspaper that allows people from all over the world to write articles based on their expertise. There's an *Examiner* for any and every subject you can think of: reality

TV, scrapbooking, gardening, nightlife, underwater basket weaving—you get the picture. I responded eagerly to the ad, sending in samples of my writing, and was ecstatic to get a response back a few days later, offering me the position as the Nashville Single Women Examiner. The position would only pay me a few pennies every time someone clicked on my articles, so I definitely wasn't doing it for the money. And I had to figure out a way to balance my new writing position with my full-time job, but having something I felt passionate about again was worth any inconvenience I might have experienced. I would dart home from work every day to write and submit a new column, and even though I had no idea if two people or two thousand people were reading my work, it felt great to be contributing what I felt was much-needed positive commentary to the subject of single life.

I wrote about confidence; I wrote about dating; I wrote about red flags, friendships, and breakups; I debunked popular myths about single life. I wrote about anything and everything I thought other single women could benefit from, and I wrote about things that I struggled with because I knew if I struggled with them, chances were someone else out there did too. I applied all the wisdom I had picked up along my own journey to my articles, not talking down to women from the platform of an expert or guru, but talking to them as an honest, real, and transparent single woman.

In February, about a month after I started writing my column, I decided I should try and find some creative ways to promote it. I was fairly new to Twitter and only had a personal page with a couple hundred followers. Early 2010 was still very much what I consider to be the early days of Twitter, when people and companies and brands were just starting to figure out how the platform could benefit them. I decided to start a page specifically for the purpose of promoting my column, separate from my personal page. I thought I might be able to pick up a few hundred followers to plug my column to and share my own unique brand of wisdom with. But what to call it?

I pondered this question as I typed in a few different screen names. "The Single Girl"? No, that sounded too young. Wait! I've got it! "The Single Lady"! Beyonce's song "Single Ladies" was fiercely popular at the time, and I thought the spirited, feisty tone of the song would resonate perfectly with the message I wanted to send. I typed in the name excitedly, but was disappointed to discover it was already taken. Hmm. Well, my column was called the "Nashville Single Women Examiner," so why not try "The Single Woman"? Surprisingly, the name was available! On February 1, 2010, The Single Woman was officially born.

Of course, I had absolutely no idea at the time what I had stumbled upon. And I really didn't have much of an idea of what I wanted to do with the Twitter page. I especially didn't have any clue about what lay ahead for me and how that simple, less-than-five-minute act of setting up a Twitter account would soon come to change my life. So as I pondered what I should choose as my very first tweet to shoot out into the Twitterverse, I decided a fun, spirited quote by Katherine Hepburn that I had always loved was the perfect sentiment: "If you obey all the rules, you miss all the fun."*

Nowadays there's all sorts of fancy software you can purchase to grow your Twitter following, and I've even heard talk of "buying followers," but in 2010, if that type of software existed, I didn't know about it. Not that I would have used it anyway. I

---

* *Quotations Book*, accessed August 19, 2013, http://quotationsbook.com /quote/34884/.

built my platform organically, from the ground up, starting with a whopping zero followers, and watched in amazement as it grew to 550,000 people across the world (as of the moment I write this).

But how? you might be wondering. Well, with a little bit of luck and a whole lot of God. The first rule I knew to be true from my personal Twitter page was that you had to follow to be followed. So I decided to tap into an audience of women who I knew I had at least one thing in common with: fans of the New Kids on the Block. My reasoning was fairly simple. I knew these women would be around my age, I assumed a fair percentage of them would still be single like me and would appreciate my message, and I knew them to be fiercely loyal. Once they loved you, they loved you for life, as I had witnessed through their undying devotion to NKOTB more than twenty-five years after the band had first appeared on the scene. So I went through and started following any and every woman who followed any of the five members of NKOTB. And pretty quickly, I realized my suspicions were accurate. The ladies loved my message, started telling everyone they knew about me, retweeted everything I had to say, and ultimately helped build my Twitter following far beyond what I ever could have hoped for or imagined. Many of these ladies I still follow to this day, and I am both moved and inspired by their bond with one another and their loyalty to me.

The second proponent of my message who played a huge role in creating early buzz for The Single Woman was a guy by the name of Mastin Kipp, also known as the creator of *The Daily Love*. *The Daily Love* at that time was a daily motivational blog coupled with a hugely popular Twitter page and a couple hundred thousand followers. (Now *The Daily Love* is so much bigger than that. Just Google it.) Mastin and I had become friends through my personal Twitter page a few months prior, and I considered him a mentor and one of the big inspirations behind the creation of my own inspirational blog and Twitter page. Mastin saw what I was doing with The Single Woman and did me the huge favor of lending his support and stamp of approval, regularly promoting my page to his followers and even recommending it to one of his many celebrity followers, Kim Kardashian. Kim became my first celebrity follower, and I was soon followed by many more. Before I knew it, my Twitter audience had grown from one hundred followers to one thousand followers to ten thousand and counting. In those early days I would watch the numbers continue to rise with wide eyes, hardly believing the way the message was spreading like wildfire. At the time, I was still naive enough to think I was building a Twitter page. I had no idea I was building a movement, a future, a destiny, and all the while becoming a voice of hope, healing, and inspiration for women across the world.

None of these appointments were anything less than divine. A few weeks after I started The Single Woman, I was leaving work when my license plate caught my attention. I stopped in my tracks, doing a double take. Then I started laughing and pulled out my phone to snap a picture. Completely by coincidence, because I had bought these tags long before I started The Single Woman, the last three letters of my license plate were TSW! It was such a great God moment for me, standing there in the parking garage, gazing at my license plate in amazement as I realized that God had known who I was long before I ever figured it out. Nothing about The Single Woman was orchestrated by me. From day one it was God at the wheel, and it has stayed that way, which is why it has been a success. And I love how He brought my twenty-five-year-old affections for New Kids on the Block around full circle, making their fans a cornerstone of the foundation of The Single Woman's success. Something seemingly insignificant, like my love of a boy band, became yet another tool God used to help launch me into my destiny. I often call myself the queen of full-circle moments, but He is truly the author of them.

Now you might be wondering why He would care so much about a Twitter page. And my answer is this: I didn't know it yet, but He was bringing about the prophecy I received a decade before—"You will one day speak into the lives of many young women." He was just using unorthodox methods to do so. He cared about a Twitter page because it was a Twitter page that gave life, hope, and courage to single women across the world. He cared about a Twitter page because I laid hands over it and prayed healing over the women it represented at least once a week, asking Him to allow me to be His vessel to speak to them. He cared about a Twitter page because it was never just a Twitter page. It was the first step in me discovering my destiny, and in hundreds of thousands of women across the globe discovering theirs, right along with me. He cared about a Twitter page because even in that first moment I created it, He knew it would one day lead to the writing of this book, and He knew that you would be one of the people to read this book. He foresaw a day when you would hold this book in your hands and read these words, and in the midst of traveling my journey with me, you might find a bit of bravery and boldness and encouragement for your own journey. He cared about a Twitter page simply because *He loves you that much.*

In the early days I stuck mainly to posting inspirational quotes from other people and pulling quotes from the columns I was writing for the *Examiner.* I was still trying to set the tone for The Single Woman and hadn't really settled on the direction

I wanted to go. Obviously I wanted it to be inspirational, but initially I also wove in facts and statistics about single life. It's funny to look back at my early tweet logs and watch the evolution of my message. I was incredibly inspired by the fictional character Sarah Jessica Parker played on *Sex and the City*, Carrie Bradshaw; and despite the show's racy image, I always managed to find a nugget of truth and wisdom in every episode. I loved Parker's portrayal of a single woman—in the early episodes of *SATC*, the show felt more authentic than the later days of all the Gucci and Prada and Manolo Blahniks—and how she didn't have it all together. She didn't have the perfect hair or the perfect nose or the perfect clothes, but she still felt she deserved the world. I wanted to convey that same spirit with my message, subtracting the raciness and adding godliness. Basically I saw myself as the edited-for-TV version of Carrie Bradshaw, with a little Joyce Meyer tossed in for good measure. As my message grew and evolved, I stopped relying so much on wisdom from other people and started finding my own voice, one that I hoped combined humor with straight talk and simple truth.

Pretty quickly after the creation of The Single Woman, I knew that it was going to be something pretty special. The response I was getting was nothing short of amazing. I received some invitations that were amazingly wonderful and beyond my wildest expectations, and some that were amazingly weird. I got invited to audition for *The Bachelor*. I had meetings with Bravo and Warner Brothers, both to discuss potential reality show ideas. I was contacted by several production companies, all vying to option my story for a reality show. I was invited to audition for a hosting gig on a dating show. Someone wanted to name a chocolate after me. At one point I was even offered a show and handed a contract, but I walked away. Nothing felt like the right fit. The me from a few years ago would have jumped at any of these opportunities. But the me I had become had handed the reins of The Single Woman over to God, and I was determined to let Him lead me where He wanted me to go. I knew that if it was from Him and of Him I would feel it in my spirit. I would know when He wanted me to act, and so far I felt strongly that He was telling me to wait. I knew in my gut that inspiring single women was my calling in life, but until you are called up to the majors, you still have to work your rear off in the minors, and that's what I was doing. I started to joke with people that I felt a little like Superwoman, working my PR job all day, then disappearing into the phone booth, whirling around, and becoming my alter ego, The Single Woman, at night. I was essentially juggling the dream and the job, and I would continue to do so for almost three years. That's what you do when you know you're called to do something, but you can't make that "something" pay the bills yet. You hustle. You sacrifice sleep. You do whatever it takes to keep your dream alive. I knew that in due time, God would reveal His master plan, but while I was waiting, I would do everything I could to be ready for it.

One of my favorite meetings that I took in the early days of The Single Woman was at CMT. As in, my old stomping grounds. One of their producers had caught wind of my column and heard that I lived in Nashville, so she contacted me and asked me to come in and have a chat. By that point, CMT, like most networks, had become heavily reality-TV-show driven, and they were looking to add more programming directed at singles. It was a market they hadn't really tapped into before, and one that they knew they needed to capture to achieve the kind of ratings they wanted.

I was so nervous as I got ready for the meeting. I wore a dress I called my (Carrie Bradshaw) dress, cream with black stripes and a belted waist. It was very ladylike and had an almost Parisian feel to it, so when I put it on, I instantly felt prettier and more confident.

Five years after I slunk out of CMT with my tail between my legs after being given the boot, I walked confidently through the front doors and was whisked right up to the fourth floor, which as I'm sure you recall is where all the Really Big Guns' offices are located. I was given nothing but VIP treatment that day, and as I walked through those familiar halls, it hit me how powerfully my life had come full circle. Losing my job at CMT had ultimately led to my emotional breakdown, which changed my entire life. It had given me a strength and a wisdom and a willingness to risk failure that I hadn't possessed before. Meaning I had the courage to walk into that meeting at CMT and lay it all on the line without fear of whether or not they accepted or rejected me. Why? Because the power was no longer in their hands. It was in God's.

In the end, nothing came of that meeting. Well, nothing in terms of a show or a deal or a contract. But it wasn't a waste of time at all, because it sent my faith in God and His plan and my God-given destiny shooting right through the roof. The things I had gone through since leaving CMT had given me the strength to walk back into that building with my head held high and my self-worth unwavering. Trust me on this one: allow God to settle your accounts, friends. Allow Him to right the wrongs in your life. His vindication and redemption are far superior to any petty revenge you could ever seek.

I was also forced to face my anxiety head-on at several speaking engagements that I was invited to participate in, giving me the first hints that public speaking would be a part of my ultimate destiny. And though I would walk out onto whatever stage I was speaking from shaking, sweating, and feeling like I was going to pass out, God always got me through it. A moment or two after I took the stage, I would feel a complete peace wash over me, and I would carry on with my speech confidently. It was such a feeling of achievement to kick anxiety's butt. Though I didn't always win my battles with anxiety in other situations, like flying, I was still determined to show up to the fight and not back down. And here's the thing I was learning: what you are most afraid of is probably holding the key to your destiny. Why? Ephesians 6:12 says, "For we wrestle not against flesh and blood, but against principalities, against powers, against the rulers of the darkness of this world, against spiritual wickedness in high places" (KJV). Light is the enemy of darkness, and when you are doing anything at all that matters in this world, the enemy is going to attempt to attack you at your weakest places to stop you from becoming the person you are meant to be and to keep you from changing the lives you are meant to change. The good news? The Bible goes on to say a few verses later, "In all circumstances take up the shield of faith, with which you can extinguish all the flaming darts of the evil one" (v. 16 ESV). There is no fiery dart, no weapon formed against you, no evil plot from the bowels of hell that can stop you from realizing your destiny when you are under the umbrella of God's protection. Period. End of story.

Every day during the first year of The Single Woman, I was realizing a new dream, reaching a new level of trust in God, and setting new goals, always aiming a little higher and a little bigger than I did the day before. I created a vision board, listing all the things I hoped to achieve over the next few months, and hung it in a place where I would see it every morning when I woke up and every night before I fell asleep. There is something very powerful about putting your dreams into writing. I began to realize that, good or bad, you could speak your life into existence. Proverbs 18:21 says, "The tongue has the power of life and death." I would be joking around with a friend saying how I hoped to have my own reality show someday, and a few days later I would get an e-mail from a network or a production company wanting to discuss a pitch for a reality show. I would dream aloud about how I wanted a certain celebrity to follow me on Twitter, and a week or so later they would start following me. It wasn't magic. It was the power of choosing to speak words of life, hope, and achievement over my life rather than negativity, pessimism, or defeat. A few of the goals I listed on that first vision board that seemed at the time like pie-in-the-sky dreams were:

1. I will meet Oprah.
2. I will sign a book deal.
3. I will leave my day job and will be a full-time writer.

Within two years, all those dreams would become realities.

Chapter 14

New Attitude, New Adventures

It was late spring 2010, I was thriving at work and loving my single life, and the future of The Single Woman had never looked brighter. Little did I know that my life was about to come full circle in another wonderfully unexpected way. One of the little girls I babysat in my youth was coming to intern with my company for the summer.

The oldest of her sisters, Alli was now a twenty-year-old senior at the University of Tennessee in Knoxville. I hadn't laid eyes on her in about eight years, but we had recently reconnected on Facebook. When she learned that I was working in PR, she inquired about whether my company might be hiring interns for the summer. Her degree was in communications, so it seemed like a perfect fit. My boss conducted a quick phone interview and, much to my delight, gave Alli the stamp of approval! I could hardly wait to get to spend some time with her and get to know her as an adult. I wondered what she would be like now and how my memories of her as a child would compare with her grown-up version.

After my first few weeks of working with Alli that spring, I no longer saw her as merely "the little girl I used to babysit." She began to feel like my little sister.

I like to think that all the summers she spent with me as her babysitter were foreshadowing the summer that Alli and I were about to embark upon together, although I don't think anything could have prepared either of us for the unbelievable adventures we would find ourselves in.

The first hint that we were in for a wild ride came the night of the CMT Music Awards (again proving that my past and present were inextricably linked). A connection I had made on Twitter offered me tickets to the event that night, and I invited Alli to go as my guest, but I didn't find out for sure I was getting the tickets until about four hours before the show.

The show was spectacular, and afterward, we had already decided in advance, we were going to do a little detective work to try and sniff out where some of the top secret after-parties were so we could try and ogle some of our favorite celebs. This was a big year for the CMT Awards, and stars like Ryan Seacrest, John Mayer, and even the cast of *Jersey Shore*—what they had to do with country music, we had no idea—were in town for the show.

"Think, think, think. Where would be the most likely location for a top secret after-party to be held?" I asked, tapping my thumbs against the steering wheel.

"Hmm, the Hutton?" Alli piped up.

"Good call!" I exclaimed, pointing my car in the direction of the fancy West End hotel. "Let's go scope it out!"

We were disappointed to see no signs of Hollywood shenanigans at the Hutton, nor at any of the other four or five obvious hot spots we cruised past over the next hour. By this point it was getting late, and since we both had to work the next morning, we decided to give up the ghost and hit the interstate back to Murfreesboro.

"*Wait!*" Alli screeched just as I pulled onto the entrance ramp to I-40.

"What is it?" I cried, pulling to the far right lane in case we needed to turn around.

"Someone just tweeted about an after-party at 'WK.' What's WK?" Alli asked, looking puzzled.

"WK, WK . . . ," I said aloud. Then we both looked at each other.

"Whiskey Kitchen!"

I got off at the next exit and whipped the car around to head back downtown. I'm not sure what we were thinking or what our plan was for getting into this party. It's not like we had invitations or were on any lists. But we were resolute. We would find a way in!

"I say we just wander in like we know exactly what we're doing," said Alli. "Anytime you walk in somewhere with confidence, people tend to just let you slide on by."

Okay, so we did have a plan.

We pulled into the packed parking lot across the street from the Whiskey Kitchen. It was an up-and-coming restaurant and lounge located in one of Nashville's trendiest new areas of town, nicknamed the Gulch, so it made sense that a big-time celebrity would be having a party there. As we crept through the parking lot, looking right and left to see who we could see, we noticed a long, black Lincoln town car parked diagonally in the parking lot, taking up several spaces. A driver was propped up against the car door, looking bored. He nodded at us as we darted past, trying not to be too obvious about our gawking. Looking back, I'm sure we were about as subtle as a herd of gazelles.

As we got closer to the door, we changed our stance, pushing our shoulders back and attempting to suavely stroll right past the doorman, who was standing behind a podium, checking people off a list.

"Ladies," the man called out as we were about halfway past him. "Excuse me. Ladies! May I have your names please?"

Alli looked at him with wide eyes.

"Oh, we're not on the list," she explained innocently. "We thought we could just walk in, like any other night. Is there something going on here tonight?"

The man looked at us skeptically, like he didn't buy our story. Not one word of it.

"Well, yes, there is," he replied. "This is a VIP event, and if you're not on the list, I'm afraid I can't let you in."

Embarrassed now, we slunk away in a cloud of humiliation, hoping we could scurry back to our car without receiving any pity-filled glances from the people in line behind us who heard the whole exchange. We were just approaching the parking lot when the driver of the Lincoln town car called out to us.

"Leaving so soon?" he asked.

"Oh, well, it's a private event, and we're not on the list, so we're just going to call it a night," I called back. He held out a hand to stop us, then beckoned us over.

"So you girls really wanna get into that party?" he asked with a smile.

"Well," Alli replied, "we did think it would be kinda cool. We don't even know whose party it is, though."

"It's Kid Rock's," the driver explained. "And it just so happens that I'm his driver. If you girls could wait just a minute, I could go talk to him and get you in. If you really wanna get in."

Alli and I looked at each other in disbelief. What dumb luck must we have to just happen upon Kid Rock's driver? Kid Rock, whose party was going on inside and whose list we had just been rejected from?

"Well, sure," I blurted, trying to temper my excitement. "I mean, if it's not too much trouble."

"Hang tight just a minute," the man said. He dashed across the street. We saw him walk around to the outdoor patio of the restaurant, where some revelers were hanging out, and lean down to whisper in the ear of who we could only guess was Kid Rock himself.

A few seconds later the driver waved us over, gesturing for us to go around the doorman and come directly to the back patio. And just like that, we sailed right into Kid Rock's CMT after-party, thanking his driver profusely before darting straight to the ladies' room to scream and jump up and down in circles like total fan girls.

"We got into Kid Rock's after-party!" Alli squealed. "We actually did it!"

In a state of disbelief and shocked glee, we wandered around the party that night, hardly believing what we were seeing. We spotted Uncle Kracker standing by the bar. We took our picture with Mike "the Situation" from *Jersey Shore*. We even heard whispers that Ryan Seacrest was hidden away in some top secret VIP area, but, the rare unicorn of Hollywood royalty that he is, we never actually saw him.

As crazy as it might sound, I firmly believe we spoke our CMT after-party adventure into existence that night. We simply believed that we would find a way in, refused to admit defeat, and *poof!* The door opened for us. Sometimes all it takes in life is a little stubborn determination.

It was the kind of spontaneous adventure I love, the kind that sneaks up and surprises you and winds up becoming a day you look back on with laughter for many years to come. And although Alli is almost a decade younger than I am, she was quickly becoming one of my closest friends. When she came back into my life, I was at a point where I desperately needed a little fun in my life. I was working feverishly to get The Single Woman off the ground. I was working just as feverishly at my full-time job. I was healing from my relationship with Steven and learning to love my single life, but I still had a thing or two to learn about the importance of just plain fun. Of silliness. Of going on wild adventures with your girlfriends and sneaking into rock stars' parties and being spontaneous. That's what my friendship with Alli, and what the summer of 2010, was coming to mean to me—incorporating the fun back into my life and working hard but also allowing myself the grace to relax, breathe, and laugh. I took the position of influence that God had given me through the platform of The Single Woman so seriously that sometimes I forgot to just be Mandy. Learning to reconcile my two worlds was made a little easier by the fun-loving, exuberant girl I literally had known since she was in her mother's womb. We shared a rare and special bond.

I also confided my Mr. E story to Alli, filling her in on the whole saga, and finding the courage to admit to her and to myself that I still had unresolved feelings for him. I hadn't heard from him in over a year by that point, and I had no idea how he was doing or where his life had taken him. After finally disentangling myself from Steven, I was able to see clearly how I had rushed into that relationship as a way to avoid dealing with my feelings for Mr. E. Strangely, I felt like the closer I got to God and the more I prayed about His will for my life, the more I thought about Mr. E. Of course, summer always made me think of Mr. E. Warm weather, sunshine, carefree days, and breezy nights seemed to evoke nostalgia about the summer we had spent together two years earlier. But he was gone now, and I was moving on with my life, so what did it really matter anyway?

Perhaps, though, all those unresolved feelings suddenly coming to the surface weren't just a fluke after all, but foreshadowing. A few days later I heard from Mr. E for the first time in a year and a half. It was in the form of a Facebook friend request, but it still rocked my world.

At some point or another, every girl has to respond to the inevitable earth-shattering Facebook friend request. The ex that appears out of nowhere. The high school sweetheart who's suddenly single again and wants to know what you're up to these days. The old friend you had a major falling out with and never thought you'd hear from again, suddenly ready to let bygones be bygones. Yes, Facebook is much like the ghost of Christmas past, always waiting to come dragging its chains into your present with faces you thought you had left safely in your yesterdays. And most of the time you can overlook the person's infractions, whatever they might have been, and hand them an all-access pass to your online existence, if for no other reason than to show them how *fabulous* your life turned out. But when it comes to someone who once owned your heart, it's never that simple. Actually, I guess you could say with Mr. E, it was more like rent-to-own, since he never seemed to generate enough interest to own it outright; but nonetheless, allowing him access to my life, even just my online life, was allowing him access to my heart. A heart that had long ago closed the door on the idea of him, convinced that he would never be the man I needed him to be.

Though I briefly considered denying his request for friendship, something told me there was something deeper and more complicated at work here—that this was simply a prologue to a much bigger chapter in my life. I had been praying for a resolution to my Mr. E saga. Could I really walk away from what might be a blatant answer to that prayer?

Besides, I didn't want to run from this. I didn't want to hide. *I'm not the same girl he left behind a year and a half ago*, I thought, mentally stepping into my Single Woman stilettos.

"How adventurous are you feeling?" I heard the echo of Mr. E's voice in my mind.

I clicked Confirm.

Chapter 15

A Stop Along the Way— or a Destination?

Though Mr. E and I were now Facebook friends, I wasn't brave enough to actually venture onto his page yet. That would actually make his brief reappearance in my life real. Plus, with all my new-found girl power, I felt like *he* should be the one to reach out to *me*.

I did keep one eye constantly on my own Facebook page over the next few days, I must confess, waiting for the inevitable moment when he would send me a message, a comment, or at least a poke, but day after day, nothing. While the surprise request in my inbox had put Mr. E back on my radar, he was definitely still off the map. After a week or two of complete radio silence, I finally gave up and went back to my regularly scheduled programming, refusing to allow myself to sit around and wait on him to make contact any longer. I was in a great place in my life, possibly the best ever, and I knew that when time, circumstance, and God were ready for our paths to cross again—somewhere other than cyberspace—they would. Besides, Alli and I were having an epic summer, and I wasn't going to allow Mr. E to disrupt that. I had way too much in my life to look forward to, to keep looking back.

"Any word yet?" Alli asked me at work the next day as she breezed into my office for our morning chat.

"Nope!" I said cheerily, firm in my resolve to stop monitoring Facebook like it was the Dow. "Not a peep. But it's okay. I've called off the Facebook stakeout. I've decided to let it go, and whatever will be, will be!" Alli looked impressed, and I have to say, I was feeling pretty impressed with myself. This was a huge moment in the life of Mandy, and I was as cool as a cucumber. As zen as the Dalai Lama. As laid-back as . . .

"Wait a minute! Did you see *this*?" I screeched to Alli as I opened up a Facebook invitation to my friend Brad's pool party, which was now just two short weeks away. Brad has this incredible house in one of the wealthier areas of the city and is famous for the legendary pool parties he throws each summer that leave you feeling like you've just been dropped off in the middle of an episode of *MTV Cribs*. Seriously. You stand there waiting for P. Diddy to float by with a fruity beverage in his hand.

"What is it?" Alli asked, dashing over to my computer to see what had unnerved me so much. "Oh!" she said, seeing the picture that was there, clear as day, under the attending guests.

Mr. E.

He was also a friend of Brad's. And he had RSVP'd to the pool party. The pool party that was happening in two weeks. The pool party that I was now RSVP'ing to, which meant we would be in the same vicinity, under the same roof, in the same *room*, for the first time in a year and a half. And this was all going down in just two short weeks.

Alli and I looked at each other, our eyes wide.

"Wow," she whispered. "We have a lot of planning to do!"

Planning? This was going to take serious strategizing.

It happens to every single girl sooner or later, and usually at the most unassuming times. You know the drill: you're sashaying along through life, happy as can be, not a care in the world, when all of a sudden, you turn a corner and come face-to-face with Your Past. Also known as: the Ex. Not just *an* ex, but *the* Ex. The one who can melt you into a puddle of mush with one glance in your direction. The one who most likely broke your heart— maybe even unintentionally. And the one who still possesses the power to single-handedly rock your world more than the entire cast of *People*'s Sexiest Man Alive issue showing up on your front doorstep would.

I knew that after our year-and-a-half-long hiatus, the very combination of Mr. E and me in one room would quite possibly send the earth rotating the wrong way on its axis. I mean, this was (almost) as big as the New Kids on the Block reuniting. The way I looked at it, I had three paths I could take when this climactic life moment occurred:

A) Run in the opposite direction with my tail between my legs.
B) Stand frozen, without moving an inch, and maybe wear a camouflage bikini to try and blend in with Brad's shrubbery.
C) Take a deep breath, face the moment head-on with a smile, and be my most rockstar self. Not the Mandy that he walked away from, but the Mandy that he won't remember *why* he walked away from once he sees the fabulous transformation I had made since he exited stage left.

I knew what I had to do.

I wasn't the same Mandy Mr. E had left behind. I wasn't the

weak, scared, insecure girl that went flying into Steven's arms the minute Mr. E broke my heart. The last time I saw Mr. E, I was a single woman. Now I was *The* Single Woman. With my own words of advice echoing in my ears, the support of my beautiful readers and followers began to transform my wishbone into a backbone.

Over the next two weeks, Alli and I planned out my pool party wardrobe meticulously. I wanted to put my best foot forward after all. And even more important than focusing on the outside, I also went to work on the inside, preparing myself for whatever might happen when I came face-to-face with the guy who had shattered my heart even more than he had stolen it. Mr. E had been missing in action for a year and a half. As in, I practically needed to go buy a carton of milk with a gigantic "Have You Seen Me?" emblazoned on the side to remember what he looked like. And this was Mr. E we were talking about. Missing for him meant he might have run off with the circus, joined the witness protection program, or become a folk singer in an Amish community. I knew how I had changed, but how had he changed? Had he grown? Had he matured? Had he thought about me at all over the past year and a half?

Finally, after two weeks of more precision, planning, and prayer than the Yalta Conference, D-day arrived. I was ready.

Alli, our friend Amber, and I got to Brad's before Mr. E arrived, as planned. I wanted to have time to get settled in and establish a comfort zone at the party before taking a dive right into the deep end of my gigantic whirlpool of emotions. Ironically, Mr. E was coming to the party with Crawford, my ex-roomie and our co-best friend.

The girls and I mingled, ate lunch, and checked out the scene, Amber and Alli stopping to perform routine checks on me every five minutes as though I were a car with an oil leak. "How are you doing?" they would ask, or "Are you nervous?"

I heard him before I saw him. The joyful voice that was once music to my ears, which I hadn't heard in so long, and the sound of party guests who hadn't seen him in a while greeting him excitedly.

"Hey, man! How are you doing?"

"Dude! Where have you *been*?"

"Mr. E!"

I heard Crawford and his goofy laugh. I heard my heart thumping in my ears. And I knew if I didn't get out of there, the next sound I heard would be the sound of me hitting the floor when I fainted dead away. Without looking in his direction, I motioned for the girls to follow me, and I darted downstairs to the dance floor area, my face flushed, my breath coming in short spurts, wondering if it was possible to develop asthma at age thirty-one.

"Mandy! Are you okay?" Alli asked as she and Amber hoofed it down the stairs after me.

"I'm not ready yet. I'm not ready," I replied. "I don't think I can do this."

I raced outside, past the pool, past the crowd—ignoring the splashing and laughter and music and other jovial sounds—to the steps at the side of the house. I just needed some distance, some clarity, some space. I leaned up against the fence for support and tried to catch my breath. Why was I letting him affect me like this? After everything I'd been through, overcome, and faced down, I was going to run scared at the sight of my past? No! I couldn't do that. There was no reason to be afraid of the past; it didn't last! I did!

I was just turning to go back into the house, feeling silly for being so overly dramatic, when I heard a voice behind me.

"Mandy?"

It was Mr. E.

He looked . . . different. Happier. More peaceful and content. He had always been one of those people with a glow about him, only now it seemed to come not from his handsome exterior but from somewhere deeper within.

I smiled, my nerves suddenly gone. "Hi."

He smiled back, then crossed the distance between us in a few short steps and swept me into a giant bear hug. We stood there for a long moment, the time, distance, and space between us suddenly melting in the power of unspoken forgiveness, and I knew that everything was going to be okay. Even if Mr. E never became anything else to me, he was a dear friend whom I cared deeply about, and it warmed my heart to see him looking so happy and well. I pulled back suddenly to look at him and realized that like mine, his eyes were brimming with tears. We both laughed, the tears spilling over, and then he pulled me back into a hug, kissing the top of my head affectionately.

Then the silence was broken, and we were both talking a mile a minute, eager to catch each other up on everything the last year and a half had contained. We found a large shade tree to relax under and talk away from the craziness of the party. Mr. E told me he had been living at home in Boone, near his family, and had never been happier. He had recently gone through a bad breakup, like me; but also like me, he knew it was for the best and was moving on with his life. He had found a church that he loved and said he was closer to God than ever before in his life.

"I can see it in your eyes," I told him. "I knew something was different."

He had also discovered a new career path—politics!—and was working as the campaign manager for a candidate in whom he believed very strongly, a family friend who had decided to run for an open state representative slot. Mr. E said he really felt like he had found his calling.

"Mandy, I'm so good at it!" he exclaimed. "It's bizarre. I have no background or qualifications in politics, yet I feel like it's what I was born to do."

Most of all, Mr. E said, he wanted me to know how sorry he was for everything that had happened a couple of years ago with Shayla Sanders and for hurting me like he did.

"Mandy, I was an idiot," he said. "I look back at it now, and it's like I was up to bat at the most important game of my life, and I swung at the wrong pitch. I want you to know, though, I *need* you to know, that my feelings for you were genuine. I was really falling for you. I just did what I always do and ran instead of giving us a chance. I'm so sorry for everything I did to hurt you." He took my hands in his as he said this, and I looked into his eyes and could see he was being genuine. As flighty and flaky and elusive as Mr. E could be, he wasn't a malicious person, and he never intended or set out to purposely hurt me. I knew that. Now, that didn't mean he didn't hurt me anyway, when, like a child, he dropped me like a toy he was tired of playing with and moved on to the next person. But that was almost two years ago. We were both thirty-one now. We had both moved on with our lives, had our hearts kicked around, and had grown up separately from each other. Perhaps sometimes in life, no matter how much you want to, you can't grow into the person you are meant to be while you're standing in the shade *or* the sunlight of someone else. Maybe, as much as it hurts, you have to grow apart to truly grow together.

"But what's been going on with you?" Mr. E asked. "I want to know everything!"

So I launched into my own tale, telling him all about my relationship with Steven, how I prayed my way out of it, repaired my relationship with God, got back on my feet, and started The Single Woman. Mr. E's eyes lit up as I filled him in on everything. He asked a million questions, and I could tell he was impressed with the new direction my life had taken.

"I've found my calling in life," I told him with a smile. "And I've never felt so peaceful or so sure about anything. I'm blown away by everything God is doing. I can't take credit for any of it."

"I want to pray for you!" Mr. E said enthusiastically. "Let's pray for covering and guidance as you move forward with The Single Woman. What you're doing is so important, I want to ask God to close the wrong doors and open the right ones."

And so Mr. E and I clasped hands, bowed our heads, and began to pray together. He said an impassioned prayer for me and for everything I was walking into with my newfound calling with The Single Woman, and then I prayed the same covering for him and his newfound calling in politics. We both asked for forgiveness for things we had done to hurt one another in the past, and we thanked God for finding a way to bring us back together. "We give You the glory, God, for this friendship and for whatever it might lead to," Mr. E prayed. It was the first time we had ever prayed together, and it was a beautiful moment. The prayer went on and on, and by the time it was finished, both of us were crying.

Two hours after we first sat under the shade tree, we rose to our feet to go rejoin the party. I knew Alli and Amber must be dying to know what had happened with Mr. E, and they were probably about ready to send out a search party.

Of course they instantly dragged me into a secluded corner the minute Mr. E and I returned to the house.

"What happened?" they asked, their eyes wide. "You guys were gone for so long!"

"It was really wonderful," I said with a smile. "We talked and caught up, and we even said a prayer together. He's so different," I went on. "It seems like he's been through a lot, and it has really changed him for the better. Oh! And he finally apologized for the whole Shayla Sanders nightmare. He told me he knew he 'swung at the wrong pitch.' And that he was starting to really fall for me before he swung at that wrong pitch."

"Wow!" Alli exclaimed. "That had to be nice to hear."

"It really was!" I replied, taking a sip of water. "But you know what the best part was? We didn't orchestrate this meeting. It just happened naturally. Both of us just happened to show up to the same pool party. Nothing about this has been forced. And nothing between us felt forced. It just feels so different this time. Like we're friends who are leaving the door open for more, and it's okay whichever way it goes."

And it was true. I did feel peaceful. Suddenly all the angst and planning and worry I had put into preparing to see Mr. E felt unnecessary. God had orchestrated this meeting between us. Why did I doubt for a second that He would have my back? Hearing Mr. E's apology and finally feeling the weight of the hurt I had been carrying around for the past two years lift left me feeling like a new person. I had prayed for a resolution with Mr. E, and I had found one. And whatever happened between us next was entirely up to God.

The girls and I went out to relax by the pool and read some magazines, and the rest of the afternoon went by like a dream. I would see Mr. E in passing, or hang out with him briefly in the pool, but I didn't spend the day obsessing over him like the old Mandy would have done.

As the day turned into night, we changed into sundresses and went inside to join the dance party that had broken out in Brad's workout room. The furniture had been pushed back, the music had been cranked up, and at least fifty people were shimmying around the makeshift dance floor. It was wonderful chaos. Mr. E and Crawford soon joined us, and it wasn't long before Mr. E and I were revisiting our old dance moves from two summers before. "I think we've still got it!" I laughed as he spun me wildly around the floor.

Mr. E was returning to Boone the next morning after the pool party, but as we said our good-byes that night, he held on to me extra tight and whispered in my ear, "I'll call you." And unlike his promise to call me on the very first night we met, I knew he really would this time. I knew in my heart that no matter what happened between us and where our lives took us, Mr. E would always be someone very special to me. And instead of fighting it, I was at peace about it, perhaps for the first time since I met him all those years before. I went home that night with a big smile on my face, feeling incredibly blessed to be in the moment that I was in, living the life that I led, surrounded by people I adored, and on the cusp of what might just finally be love.

Chapter 16

Walking on Air

*M*r. E did call. He called and he e-mailed and he texted and he Facebooked. We were communicating regularly, sharing openly, and building the foundation of something that finally felt real and honest. I gave him PR tips as he got further into his political campaign, and he gave me writing tips as I continued to build The Single Woman. We prayed together regularly about our individual destinies, and as we did, something interesting started to happen. It started to feel as though our two separate paths, which had been diverged for so long, were finally starting to run more parallel with each other. I was determined not to read too much into it and not to rush things, but the closer I drew to God, the closer I felt to Mr. E. That felt really nice. Comforting, even.

As the campaign Mr. E was managing drew to a frenzied finale, he asked me if I might be up for traveling to Boone for election night. "I'd love to have you there with me, whichever way it goes," he said sincerely. Since election night happened to fall a day or two before the Fourth of July, he invited me to stay on for the weekend and spend the holiday with him and his family. "I'd love for you to meet my mom and dad. I know they're going to love you." He told me I could just stay in his parents' guest room, so I wouldn't even have to find a hotel. To say that this was a huge development in our relationship is the understatement of the century.

I knew Mr. E was close with his family, and I had heard from Crawford that they were wonderful, kind, God-fearing people. But Mr. E always kept his worlds so compartmentalized that that aspect of his life had always seemed incredibly guarded, even secretive. I had started to view his family more as a mythical, magical entity rather than a reality, sort of like Mr. Snuffleupagus on *Sesame Street*. I knew they existed, but only Mr. E could see them. The opportunity to actually meet the people who had hatched Mr. E in all his delightfully eccentric weirdness was intriguing, to say the least.

I pondered the invitation for a day or two. I prayed about it, weighed the pros and cons, and talked to my girlfriends about it before finally deciding that much like everything else that summer, I had to embrace the unexpected and seize the day. I was flattered that Mr. E wanted me there for his big moment on election night, and I couldn't wait to see the town, the people, and the family that helped mold him. So much of what Mr. E and I had always had was based in the present moment, in the here and now; and while that was good, it also left a lot of gaps that had never been filled in. Where did he come from? What kind of childhood had he had? What was his family like? I felt like seeing a glimpse of Mr. E's past might help me understand him better in the present.

So a couple of days later I packed up my car and headed east, toward North Carolina. Boone was about six hours from Nashville, and I looked forward to the time alone in the car to pray, think, and prepare to meet Mr. E's parents for the first time.

Boone was a beautiful little town nestled in the Blue Ridge Mountains, and I fell in love with the quaint, historic downtown area as I navigated my way to the local high school where Mr. E had directed me to join him later that afternoon. The election party was being held at the school, and I knew things would be extremely busy and chaotic for E as the results from the different voting precincts started to roll in. Both of his parents would be at the party, however, so I would have ample time to spend getting to know them.

I parked my car in front of the school, checking my reflection in the mirror one last time before heading inside. I had purchased a conservative but stylish pink dress with black embellishments for the occasion, pairing it with black wedge sandals. I wanted to look cute and classy without going too over the top.

"*Woo, wee*—look at *you*!" I heard a voice exclaim as soon as I walked in the door. It was Mr. E, of course. He pulled me into a hug, then twirled me around to get the full effect. "Am I ever proud to walk into the party with you on my arm!"

I blushed. "Thank you," I said, dropping into a mock curtsy. "I am here and ready to be your arm candy, you big, important campaign manager, you!"

He escorted me out of the classroom and down to the gym, where he held open the door for me, then turned to offer me his arm.

"Shall we, my lady?"

"Yes, we shall," I responded, not able to suppress a huge, goofy grin from spreading across my face. He had a way of turning even the most ordinary moments into grand occasions. Life to him was a grand adventure, and it was enchanting to be a part of that adventure.

As we made our way into the gym, I got swept up in the excitement all around us. Some people were talking animatedly into cell phones. Others were eagerly watching the election coverage that was projected onto a large screen in the middle of the room. Still others were passing out buttons, party hats, and noisemakers for when the results would come in. There was a feeling of optimism and hope and urgency in the room, and the energy was infectious.

I noticed a striking couple making their way toward us, a woman who was petite, attractive, and blonde, and a man who was tall, strapping, and tan. "Those are my parents," Mr. E said with a smile. My mouth dropped. Wow. I could certainly see where he got his good looks from! And I soon discovered their stunning exteriors, if possible, paled in comparison to the beauty of their hearts.

"Well, hello there!" Mr. E's dad boomed as they drew closer. "You must be Mandy. We could not be more delighted to meet you!"

Mr. E's mom swept me into a hug. "Mandy," she said softly against my cheek. "We have heard the most wonderful things about you. Thank you for traveling all the way here to be here for our son."

Any nerves I had about "meeting the parents" immediately dissipated in the presence of these warm, caring people. "Thank you so much for inviting me!" I replied, overwhelmed by their sincerity and kindness. "It's an honor to meet you both. This feels like it's going to be a very exciting night!"

Just then someone swept Mr. E away to handle a campaign emergency, and when E's dad decided to join him in putting out whatever fire had flared up, I was left alone to chat with his mom. We settled into chairs at one of the many round tables scattered throughout the gym.

"I know how deeply you must care about our son," she said. "And I also know how incredibly frustrating he can be. He's been that way his whole life—never settled, always restless, always running."

She had hit the nail on the head, on all points. "Yes, ma'am," I responded. "I do care about him, very much."

"There's something you need to know about the men in this family, though," she went on. "They all tend to struggle with the idea of commitment—even E's dad. He asked me to marry him, then changed his mind and canceled the wedding four different times before we finally made it down the aisle."

My eyes widened. "Four times?!" I exclaimed. "How on earth did you handle that?"

She reached over and patted my hand. "God, honey. God is how I handled it. He had told me who I was going to marry, and I never wavered in His promise, no matter how ridiculous E's dad acted." She chuckled. "He would call to cancel the wedding, I'd say, 'Okay. Call me when you change your mind again.' Then he'd call to say he wanted to marry me, and he couldn't imagine his life without me in it, and I'd say, 'Okay. I knew all along how this was going to play out.' I just stood on God's word. And eventually, E's dad stopped running from what he knew God was telling him, and the rest is history."

I shook my head. "Wow. Your faith . . . Wow. I'm in awe of you right now!" We both laughed. "I wish I could have one speck of the faith you must have had to keep taking him back, even after he canceled on you so many times. I probably would have given up after the first time or two and told him to get lost!"

"I thought about it," she admitted. "Believe me, I thought about it. But thirty-five years and four kids later, I wouldn't trade any of it for the world."

We sat in companionable silence for a moment. Then she spoke up again.

"Mandy, Mr. E received a prophecy over his life when he was very young that he was going to one day be a world changer, and his dad and I aren't letting go of that promise without a fight. We're not giving up on him. No matter how far he strays from the path or how far from home he wanders, we've never lost hope that God would bring that prophecy to fruition." She looked over at me with a smile. "Don't you give up on him either."

"No, ma'am, I won't," I promised.

We were distracted a moment later when someone cried out, "The final precinct is in!" Someone else grabbed the remote and cranked up the volume on the TV. This was it. The vote was too close to call, and it was down to one final precinct to decide the outcome of the election.

When the numbers were tallied on the screen, revealing the final vote, a disappointed silence fell over the room. Next to me, E's mom sighed deeply. E's candidate had lost.

I stood and looked around the room for him, my eyes darting right and left. Where was he? I needed to see him, to be there for him in that moment, to smile and let him know that it would be okay.

Suddenly I spotted him on the other side of the room. He was standing there, alone and rather forlorn, a short distance away from the crowd. As I watched him, he reached up to push his hair back with one hand, then turned to scan the crowd just as I had been doing only moments before. His eyes finally landed on me, and I knew he had found his target. We stood there, crowds of people milling around between us, the chatter in the room picking up as people began to hug, console one another, and congratulate the candidate on a solid campaign. His eyes had such a look of disappointment, my heart broke for him. Then, with a sad smile, he lifted his shoulders in a slight shrug, as if to say, "Well, what are you gonna do? You win some, you lose some." It was in that moment, watching him rally from a gut-wrenching loss from across the room of a gymnasium in Boone, North Carolina, that I realized I was in love with Mr. E. Hopelessly, helplessly, madly in love with him. I guess perhaps I had known it since the first time I spotted him across the room in that silly fedora four years earlier, but it took seeing this vulnerable, open, unguarded side of him to really bring my feelings into focus. And to give me the courage to be just as vulnerable, open, and unguarded with him. It was time to let down the walls.

The next morning Mr. E, his parents, and I went to church together. It was wonderful to stand next to him in that church pew and for the first time get to watch him worship God. He had such a look of intensity, passion, and awe on his face as he raised his hands to heaven and sang, I think it made me fall in love with him a little bit more.

The next day was the Fourth, and we were hanging out at Mr. E's parents' pool that morning when his cell phone rang. It was Crawford! Quite coincidentally, Crawford was returning home from another part of North Carolina with his friend Joy and thought since they were close by, they would just stop off in Boone and spend the Fourth of July with us. This was turning into one heck of a holiday! Crawford and Joy arrived later that day, and the four of us joined E's parents, his brother, his sister-in-law, and his two nieces downtown for the parade and fireworks show.

It was an absolutely magical night.

We strolled through the streets of beautiful downtown Boone, hand in hand, surrounded by Mr. E's tribe of wonderful friends and family, and I didn't think my heart had ever been so full. We played games, drank lemonade, and ate cotton candy, and later, as Mr. E and I sat side by side on a park bench, I looked over at him and nudged his shoulder with mine.

"Hey, remember our first kiss?" I asked him.

He looked up at me with a brilliant smile. "How could I ever forget? It was two years ago on this very night, several stories up in the skies of Nashville." He took my hand. "That's a memory I will always hold right here," he said, bringing our clasped hands up to his heart. He leaned over then, a serious expression on his face, drawing closer and closer, until . . .

Boom! Just then the fireworks started with a bang. He stopped, looked at me with a rueful smile, then stood and pulled me to my feet so we could rejoin the group. As we stood there with everyone watching the firecrackers light up the sky above us, my head leaning against his shoulder in contentment, an idea came to me.

"Hey," I whispered in his ear, over the sound of the fireworks. "Come back with me tomorrow when I leave."

He looked over at me with surprise.

"Really?"

I nodded enthusiastically. "Yes! It would be so much fun! You can meet my parents and my sister and my nieces. I can give you the grand tour of Murfreesboro, Tennessee, and heck, I'll even take you to see the World's Largest Cedar Bucket."

He laughed. "Well, I could only stay for a few days. I'm supposed to go to the beach with my family next week. Would that be okay?"

"Of course!" I said. "Joy is coming back to Nashville with Crawford, and she has to drive right through Boone on her way home in a few days anyway. You can ride to Tennessee with me and hitch a ride back home with her. It will be perfect!"

He looked at me with a grin. "Okay! Let's do it!"

That night we all piled in at Mr. E's parents' house for what felt like a giant slumber party, E and Crawford sleeping on the pull-out couch in the living room and Joy and me bunking in the guest room. The next morning we awoke to find Mr. E cooking a grand breakfast for the entire gang; he was even decked out in an apron and a chef's hat for the occasion. He looked so silly, I had to giggle.

Before Mr. E, Crawford, Joy, and I set out for Nashville, Mr. E's parents wanted to have a group prayer. Joy was going through a painful divorce, Crawford was just beginning the first phases of what was sure to be a long custody battle, E had just lost the campaign he had worked so hard on, and I was still balancing my full-time job with my responsibilities to The Single Woman. All of us were at very defining crossroads in our lives, and E's dad wanted to cover us in prayer.

We all gathered in the living room and prayed fervently as a group for almost two hours that morning. Mr. E's dad was a powerful intercessory pray-er, and it didn't take long until tears were running down all of our faces. He prayed so passionately for The Single Woman platform that day, claiming that lives would be changed and souls would be won for the kingdom through my message, that God would open new doors and lead me to the right opportunities, and that my Twitter following would experience a growth spurt unlike anything I had experienced over the past six months. As we loaded up our luggage and said our final good-byes a little later, I turned to Mr. E's parents. They both held out their arms, and I embraced them simultaneously.

"Thank you both, so much, for everything," I said, feeling a little choked up. "You've both been so wonderful. I have absolutely loved spending this time with you and getting to know you."

"We feel the same," Mr. E's mom said, giving me a kiss on the cheek. "Now don't be a stranger. Come back and see us real soon."

The four of us hit the open road, Crawford and Joy leading the way in her SUV, me and Mr. E trailing behind in my little sedan. I breathed a sigh of contentment as we rolled down the open road. What a spectacularly amazing weekend it had been. I almost hated to get back to the real world so soon.

We were about an hour into our trip when I happened to glance up and see signs for Lake Lure, North Carolina. That sounded familiar. Why did I feel like I had heard of that town before?

Then it hit me.

I grabbed my BlackBerry and quickly tapped the name of the town into Google search. When the results popped up a second later, I bounced in my seat and started clapping with excitement.

"Oh my gosh! Oh my *gosh!*" I cried, barely able to contain my elation.

Mr. E looked over at me with a confused smile. "What is it?"

"Those signs back there said 'Lake Lure, North Carolina.' Do you know the significance of Lake Lure, North Carolina?" I asked, grinning from ear to ear.

Mr. E shook his head. "Nope. What?"

"Parts of *Dirty Dancing* were filmed there!" I screeched. "We have to go!"

"Really?" Mr. E asked. "Oh, wow, that would be cool! Do you know how far off the exit Lake Lure is?"

I did another quick search. "The town of Lake Lure is only about six miles off the exit!"

Mr. E and I exchanged glances. "Let's do it!" we agreed in unison, doing a fist bump.

I called Crawford to tell him that we were stopping off in Lake Lure to scope out the locations where *Dirty Dancing* was filmed and that he and Joy could go on if they wanted, and we would catch up. A few minutes later Mr. E and I were winding our way down a narrow two-lane road toward Lake Lure.

"Isn't this how most horror movies begin?" he cracked. "If both of our cell phones lose service, we're outta here!"

The Blue Ridge Mountains rose up all around us. The view was absolutely breathtaking. Finally we came upon the quaint, little town of Lake Lure. To the left of us stretched an expansive blue lake lined with adorable little lake houses. We could see boats floating out on the water, people kicked back on docks with fishing reels skimming the lake, and cyclists peddling through town in twos and threes. It was simply beautiful. But how on earth to figure out exactly where *Dirty Dancing* was filmed? I instantly recognized the lake from the movie, but the research I was able to do on my phone before losing my signal also said something about Lake Lure being home to the rock steps that Baby practices her dance moves on. It was one of the most iconic scenes in the film. I needed to see those steps.

"Okay, the Internet said something about a 'Boys Camp Road,'" I told E as I fiddled with my phone, trying to find a signal.

"There it is!" I cried, seeing the sign in front of us. Mr. E turned onto the road, and I looked around eagerly for familiar sights, but all we could see was what looked like a clubhouse for an apartment community to our right. There were no apartments, just the clubhouse. We decided to pay a visit to the clubhouse and see if we could find anyone to point us in the right direction.

"Future site of Firefly Cove at Lake Lure!" a sign boasted as we made our way into the building.

"Hello?" I called as we walked in to what looked like a beautiful but vacant sitting room. There didn't seem to be a soul in sight. "Is anyone here?"

Suddenly we heard the sounds of shuffling feet running toward us, followed by the excited giggles of what sounded like two young children. Two boys burst into the room like wriggling puppies, a man following right on their heels.

"Oh, hi," the man greeted us. "I'm sorry, my boys and I were swimming out back and didn't hear you pull up. How can I help you?"

I somewhat sheepishly explained to him that we were just passing through and saw the sign for Lake Lure, and my lifelong love of the movie *Dirty Dancing* inspired us to pay the town a quick visit to see if any of the old filming locations were still standing. The man smiled, obviously having heard this same story a time or two.

"Sure, I can tell you exactly where to go," he said. "I'm actually one of the developers for the new community of homes going up in this area, Firefly Cove. Firefly Cove is being built on the grounds where the movie was filmed, an old children's camp called Camp Chimney Rock. Most of the cabins and other buildings that you might recognize from the film have been torn down, but the steps leading up into what was the dance hall in the movie are still standing."

I looked over at Mr. E with an excited grin. Jackpot!

The man beckoned for his boys to wait for him on the couch,

then walked Mr. E and me out onto the front porch. "Just continue down this path a little less than a mile." He gestured to the road in front of the clubhouse. "And you'll come to a clearing on the left. That's where the steps are. Now, keep in mind, the bridge in front of the steps is gone, which throws some people off. And the steps have been damaged some over the years, so they don't look exactly how they looked in the movie. But people still get excited to see them, so I'm sure if you're an avid fan of the film, you'll recognize them automatically."

We thanked him, Mr. E shaking his hand, then turned to go. "I hope you enjoy the sights!" the man called after us.

We got back in the car and continued down the path. It felt like we were meant to be here, meant to be on this journey together. I had always wanted to see the locations where *Dirty Dancing* was filmed; I just never dreamed Mr. E would be the one beside me when I did. It was almost more than my childlike, movie-obsessed, Hollywood-ending-loving heart could take.

"Wait, there!" Mr. E cried, pointing off the left. "There are the steps!"

I looked up the hill in the direction he was pointing, and suddenly I saw them. Those were the steps. A little worn down maybe, and a little aged by the hands of time, but those were the steps. I started squealing in delight as Mr. E pulled off to the side of the road so we could get a closer look.

I darted out of the car ahead of him, stopping at the foot of the steps to gaze up at them in awe. These were the very steps that Jennifer Grey had sashayed up twenty-five years earlier. The very spot where film captured one of the most iconic scenes in my favorite movie of all time. Mr. E loped up behind me, snapping photos as I climbed the steps, turned to look playfully over my shoulder, and began emulating Baby's dance moves all the way up the staircase. What a magical moment!

We climbed the final few steps together, pausing at the top, where Mr. E took my hand and asked me, "Remember that day you got to kiss a handsome gentleman on the *Dirty Dancing* steps?" Then with a dramatic flourish, he kissed me on the steps where my childlike heart had already been a thousand times before in my mind. I never dared to imagine that my "Johnny" would turn out to be the boy I had loved for as long as I could remember.

———

The next few days with Mr. E went by in a whirlwind. I had managed to take a couple of days off work, but the third day Alli and I would have to travel to Memphis for a work trip. Mr. E excitedly volunteered to go with us. He was always up for a spontaneous road trip.

I was thrilled to get to introduce Mr. E to my parents, and he and my dad quickly bonded. Even though Mr. E was more than a little eccentric, my parents had never seen me this excited over a guy before, so they welcomed him with open arms and open minds. "He is a good guy until proven otherwise," my attorney father surmised.

The trip to Memphis, though something I had been dreading a bit, turned into another fun adventure with Mr. E along for the ride. He had a friend who lived in Memphis whom he wanted to spend an hour or so with while we were there. After our work event, Alli and I dropped him off to hang with his friend Pete while we strolled along the riverfront in downtown Memphis and chatted. It was a beautiful, perfect summer day—not a single cloud in the sky. Alli and I found a little ice-cream shop on Beale Street and relaxed at a shaded table out front with ice-cream cones while we waited for Mr. E.

"It seems like you two are getting a lot closer," she said as we sat there enjoying our ice cream and an unexpected breeze.

"Yeah," I agreed. "We really are. He seems to finally be allowing himself to care about me without running from it. And because of that, I'm allowing my guard to come down with him. It's a little terrifying," I confessed. "I guess I know somewhere in the back of my mind that he could run, hurt me, or disappear again, but it's like it just doesn't matter anymore. At some point in life, you just have to be willing to take the risk."

Alli agreed. She was working on preparing for her own risk when college wrapped up for her in a few months, opting to pursue her lifelong dream of acting instead of rushing right into a full-time, nine-to-five job after graduation.

"I'm so proud of you," I told her fondly. "I'm so proud of *us*! Look at the summer we've had. We've worked hard, played hard, loved hard, and risked hard. This has truly been the summer of no regrets." I held out my pinky to her and she smiled, hooking her pinky in mine. We shook on it.

"Summer of no regrets," she agreed.

On Mr. E's last night, I told him I wanted to take him somewhere special.

Murfreesboro is home to a little colonial village called Cannonsburgh, which is supposed to represent the way the town looked in the 1800s. A few years earlier, my mom and I had visited the village on a fluke one day when looking for some-where to sit outside and have lunch. We both fell in love with it, me in particular. The village has a mock mill, schoolhouse, gen-eral store, doctor's office, and more, plus a beautiful little chapel where people hold weddings and a gazebo in the middle of the town that houses receptions. We loved to take my nieces there on warm summer days and have picnic lunches, and my nieces have grown to adore the village as much as we do. One of their favor-ite things to do is crank up the music on one of our cell phones and have a spontaneous dance party right there in the middle of the gazebo. One night when we were there at dusk, I discovered a switch that turns on strands of white twinkly lights lining the gazebo, and I knew right then and there that someday I wanted to bring the man I loved, whoever he might be, to that gazebo and dance under those lights.

Mr. E and I stopped to grab sandwiches on the way so we could have a picnic dinner. It was pitch-black when we pulled up, as Cannonsburgh was already closed for the night, but I grabbed Mr. E's hand and we dashed across the wooden bridge to the vil-lage anyway.

Mr. E and I sat under the stars at a picnic table and had a quiet dinner; both of us, I think, were thinking of the next day when he would return home to Boone. We had been together almost nonstop for over a week at that point, and the idea of not knowing the next time I would see him made my heart hurt a little. But the past week had been so magical, I didn't want to ruin it by focusing on it coming to an end. After we finished eating, I jumped to my feet.

"I have a surprise for you!" I said excitedly. I dashed over to the gazebo, and, with a flourish, hit the light switch. Suddenly the gazebo lit up brilliantly in the night, creating the effect of hundreds of twinkly stars shining above us.

A look of affection crossed Mr. E's face. He knew me well enough to know what a movie moment like this meant to me. He crossed over to where I was standing in the gazebo and brushed a few strands of hair away from my face. Then he held out his hand.

"May I have this dance?"

And that's how, underneath the twinkly lights of the gazebo in the center of the small-town colonial village I loved, a moment I had pictured in my mind for years came to pass, in a way that was so much more special than I had ever dared to hope it would be. Mr. E and I slow danced under those lights, with nothing to keep the beat except the sound of our own hearts.

It was and remains one of the most romantic moments of my life.

Then he dipped me grandly, holding me there in place so I could stare up at the twinkling lights above us.

"I want you to remember this moment forever," he said quietly, not unlike that night long ago atop a construction crane in downtown Nashville.

And also just like that night, I knew that I would.

———

Early the next morning Joy came to get Mr. E so they could set off for North Carolina.

Mr. E and I stood outside Joy's car, face-to-face, not saying a word. I was holding back my tears. I didn't want to cry until he'd gone. I didn't want any sadness to mar the beautiful week we had just spent.

Suddenly he pulled me into a fierce hug, holding on to me so tightly I could hardly breathe for a long moment. Then just as suddenly, he kissed me on top of my head, got in the car, and a moment later he was gone.

I watched with my heart in my throat as Joy's car disappeared into the early-morning light, carrying away my love. Then I wiped away a tear, mentally handed the situation to God, and went about my day.

I never could have imagined in that moment that our goodbye outside Joy's car would be the last time I would lay eyes on Mr. E for more than a year.

Chapter 17

Finding My Own Way

Over the next couple of weeks, Mr. E's dad's prayer began to yield powerful results. The Single Woman Twitter page took off in leaps and bounds, surpassing one hundred thousand followers in just under six months. As I watched the numbers grow exponentially every day, I was struck by the trust God was placing in me to speak into the lives of these precious women. E-mails started to pour in from all over the world. I noticed I seemed to have a particularly large following in the Philippines and in South Africa, which simply astonished me. My toes had never so much as touched the soil of those countries, yet my words were being heard and their impact was being felt there. I continued to lay hands on my computer screen at least once a week, crying out to God on behalf of the souls of each one of my Twitter followers and blog readers. "More of You, less of me, Lord," I would pray. "I am humbled to be Your vessel, and I pray that You would help me get out of the way so You can work through me. Give me the right words to say to speak hope, life, love, and healing to these women."

I also continued to pray for God's guidance with the Mr. E situation. Much to my disappointment, in the weeks since E's visit to Tennessee, he seemed to be growing distant. It was beginning to feel like "Two Years Earlier: the Remix." Though we still spoke every few days, he seemed to be becoming more and more disengaged and cool in our conversations, and his text messages and e-mails eventually all but stopped. He was also floundering a bit after the loss of the election and the end of his campaign management run. He seemed unsure about what to do with himself and his career. Each time we spoke, I could sense him growing increasingly restless. And I knew what happened when Mr. E got restless. He changed jobs, changed cities, changed girl-friends, changed lives. I sensed something big was coming but had no idea what it might be.

Until a few weeks later when he called me up to tell me he had just accepted a job in Seattle.

"Seattle?" I asked in shock.

"Yeah," he replied with no real emotion. "There's a reporter position out there that a friend recommended me for, so I'm headed out there next week. I can't keep sticking around Boone. There's nothing for me here now that the election is over."

"What about your family? Aren't they going to be sad to see you go?" I knew they must be heartbroken at the thought of E running amuck on the other side of the country after he had been living so close to them and doing so well for the past two years.

"They understand," he said in a clipped voice.

"Well, I'm happy for you if you're happy," I said. "But you don't really sound all that overjoyed to me."

"I'm happy, Mandy."

"Well, can I ask . . ." I hesitated for a moment. "Can I ask where this leaves us? I mean, Boone is six hours away, but Seattle . . ." I trailed off.

"I don't know," he responded flatly.

"You don't know?" I asked incredulously. "Are we really back here again?"

"What do you want from me, Mandy?"

"What do I want from you? I want you to go back to being that sweet, open, loving guy from a few weeks ago. Where did he go?"

"I've never lied to you about who I am," Mr. E replied. "You've always known that I'm not really the guy to settle down."

I couldn't believe what I was hearing. I felt blindsided. After everything we had been through, after he had finally opened himself up to me and started to let me in, after I had laid my heart on the line for him, we were back to square one?

I honestly don't know why I was so shocked. This was typical behavior for someone who only allows himself to get so close to someone else before he hides behind physical or emotional distance—or in really special cases, both.

"You know what?" I responded. "I have to go. I wish you the best in Seattle. I really do."

With that, I disconnected the call.

In the past, I would have mourned the ending of yet another chapter of Mr. E, marking it perhaps with the type of angst-filled gestures that I'm famous for: writing his name on a big red balloon and releasing it into the sky; driving past all our old spots with Taylor Swift blasting at top volume; deleting him from my Facebook page in an attempt to delete him from my life, then immediately regretting it.

But not this time.

This time something was different. Something had shifted. Something had changed.

Was it my increasing impatience with and lack of tolerance for his inability to commit to a relationship, a career path, or even a city? Was it my preoccupation with my own life and the addition of so many new dreams and goals that kept me from dwelling on the subtraction of his presence from my life? Or did I just assume that, like most of his dramatic exits, this one was only temporary, and before I knew it, the invisible rubber band that bound us together would snap him back to Tennessee and back by my side?

Or was the "something" that had changed . . . me?

There comes a moment in every relationship when taking up permanent residence in the gray area between what is and what isn't is no longer enough. When the need for clarity surpasses the need to make things work. When you start to realize that the constant limbo of an undefined relationship isn't as fun as it was when the music first started. When you have to seek your own closure, because the other person cannot or will not give it to you.

In the movie *The Thing Called Love,* the characters talk about an old wives' tale that goes something like this: if you want to render a relationship null and void, you must go back to the place where you first met the person and say, out loud, "I divorce you, I divorce you, I divorce you!"* Theoretically, this works even if, as in my case, you're not actually married to the person. What a concept. In the movie, Samantha Mathis's character "divorces" River Phoenix's character, and since the film takes place in Nashville, I felt it was a sign. A few nights after my phone call with Mr. E, as I was on the way to grab dinner with Alli and a couple of other girlfriends, I quite coincidentally (and ironically) drove by the place where I first met him. Inspiration struck.

---

* *The Thing Called Love,* directed by Peter Bogdonovich (Paramount Pictures, 1993).

After dinner, the four of us went back to the scene of the crime and even managed to sit in the same booth I was sitting in when I saw Mr. E for the first time. Giggling, we grabbed a napkin and wrote out a contract, stating that as of this day, the twenty-ninth of July, I was free of Mr. E. All three of my ladies stood gleefully in agreement with me and signed the contract with the kind of gusto that could only come from friends who knew how much this single woman needed to symbolically release the past, once and for all, and move forward into the next chapter of her life. Then, as loudly and proudly as I could say it, I repeated the magic words: "I divorce you, I divorce you, I divorce you!" That's the thing, you know. Until we are willing to close the book on what was, it's impossible to fully embrace what will be. Sometimes all we need is a push in the right direction by a few good friends to give us the courage we need to surrender our will to God and let Him take care of the rest. Maybe some would say the whole thing was silly, but as I looked around at the faces of my friends and heard the band, quite by chance, breaking into "Free Falling" by Tom Petty, I felt a little piece of my heart that had belonged to Mr. E for the past four years finally return to me.

And aren't we all free-falling just a little bit? We're free-falling into love, free-falling out of love, free-falling into a new career or a new city or a new life completely. Maybe at the end of the day, all we can do is cling to what completes us (like our best friends) and release what depletes us (like a guy who can't see the crown jewel standing right in front of him). Maybe when a romantic interest can't decide if he wants to love us or not, we have to take away his right to leave us stranded in relationship purgatory for even one more minute. After all, shouldn't there be a statute of limitations on how long a person gets to take deciding whether or not they want to love us and let us know, or gently let us go? Sometimes in life we have to create our own closure. Sometimes we have to decide when enough is enough and walk away. So whether you try a relationship fast; or have a bonfire with all the things that remind you of that person like Monica, Rachel, and Phoebe once did on one of my favorite episodes of *Friends*; or whether you, as I did, go in search of the end by going back to the place where it all began; I urge you to find a way to peacefully close the door on your past so you can walk away with your head held high and with no regrets. Because at the end of the day, sometimes it takes opening a door to get to a new place.

And sometimes it takes closing one.

———

It was the beginning of August, and my glorious summer was drawing to a close. Alli was leaving to go back to school, Mr. E had just left to move to Seattle, and my lease at my apartment in Murfreesboro was expiring. It seemed that everything was ending to make way for a new season.

In a way, I was kind of relieved to give up the apartment in Murfreesboro. Though I loved the community itself, it was where I had lived with Steven, and it was time to close that chapter once and for all. Plus, as I tended to do about once a year, I was getting an itch to move back to Nashville.

So that's why, in August 2010, I moved back in with Crawford; though since the last time I had lived with him, he had acquired a cat, two gerbils, and a bird, plus you toss in Jeeves, and we were ready for our own bizarre, much furrier version of *The Brady Bunch*.

Other than my expiring lease and my desire to be back in Nashville and closer to work, another big reason I was moving back in with Crawford was to help see him through what was possibly the most difficult time of his life. It was a season of growth and pain and change and uncertainty for him, when circumstances beyond his control had broken his heart but never his spirit. His ex-wife was planning to move and take their seven-year-old son with her. And did I mention she only announced this after Crawford showed up at her house to pick up their son one day to discover her entire house, even the goldfish, packed?

"What are you going to do?" I had asked him that night after he came over in a daze from another day of prepping for a custody battle he was hoping desperately to avoid. It was Friday night, which meant our signature chocolate and caramel candy bars were present and accounted for, and we were going about our usual routine of watching movies and eating everything that wasn't nailed down.

"I'm going to fight it," he said without hesitation, with a resolve and a fire in his eyes that I had never seen before.

"Really?" I asked incredulously, not doing a very good job of hiding the surprise on my face. If you meet Crawford, you'll pretty quickly discover that he tends to be more of a lover than a fighter, with his temperament hovering somewhere near that of a Muppet Baby. He had let his ex push him around for years now, all to avoid an inevitable confrontation, much to my great frustration. But now fate and circumstance had put him in a position where he could not back down, and I have to say, his new and improved and somewhat Chuck Norris–like disposition was a welcome change.

"I have to," he said softly, looking pained yet determined. "It's my son. I have to fight for him."

And I knew he meant it. There is nothing Crawford wouldn't do for his precious son, Adam. His relationship with him was like the kind you see in movies—the kind of father-son bond that all kids dream of but few actually realize. He spoke to Adam on his level, teaching him about the world, about God, about movies and art and books. He was firm when he needed to be, but he never disciplined him without explaining to him exactly what he had done wrong and why he was in trouble. As a result, you can sometimes carry on a conversation with Adam for hours before remembering you are shooting the breeze with a seven-year-old child. He is brilliant and outgoing, with a sunny disposition and a personality that never knew a stranger. He loves life and exudes happiness and light. And now he might have to go away, to a new state, a new home, a new life—far away from Crawford and everything he had ever known in Tennessee. The thought of having to stand by helplessly and watch Crawford lose custody of his son terrified me. I am a woman of action who likes to formulate a plan of attack for every situation, and this time my hands were tied. There was nothing I could do for my friend but be there for him.

And so I was. Literally. I had packed up my apartment, put my furniture in storage, and moved back into my old bedroom in Crawford's tiny stone cottage. My full-length mirror was still waiting for me in the closet. My shoe rack was still hanging on the back of the door. It was eerie. I had to pinch myself a few times to make sure that it was, in fact, 2010; and that I hadn't fallen asleep like Victoria Principal did in the hit eighties show *Dallas* and woken up back in 2008, with the entire past two years having just been a dream. (And Patrick Duffy in my shower. Now *that* would have been creepy.)

A couple of weeks after I moved back in, Crawford started the process of the long, trying, uncertain custody battle.

One day he came home from work and crumpled onto the kitchen floor in a heap of sobs. The case didn't look good, he said. The mother almost always gets primary custody, especially when she has been the child's main caregiver for his entire life. It was going to take a miracle to make any judge see that uprooting Adam from the only city and home he'd ever known was not in his best interest, even if it did mean keeping him with his mother. Plus, his ex was raking him over the coals, portraying him as a liar, a cad, and a womanizer—which was so ridiculous, it was beyond laughable. I mean, Crawford is attractive and has a lot going for him, but he's truly one of those rare gems of a man who treats women like ladies and not playthings. He's respectful, he opens car doors, he doesn't play games; basically, Mr. Bean is a bigger womanizer than he is.

Another day he was so distraught over the circumstances he was up against, and so worn down by the battle he was facing, that I came home to find him lying flat on his back, in the middle of the living room floor, staring at the ceiling without expression. His sadness was palpable, and he was completely oblivious to the messiness of the floor he was lying on or our cats sniffing curiously around him, or even me staring down at him with concern. Without even thinking about it, I lay down next to him, in my dressy work clothes, flat on my back, staring at the ceiling right along with him, in the only way I knew to show him my camaraderie and support. We must have stayed there for twenty minutes or more, not saying a word, just staring at that ceiling as though it had all the answers to the mysteries of the universe. Finally I reached over and took his hand, and together we stood, ready to face the world again.

There are times in life when you aren't going to be able to do anything to help your friends except be there. It will be frustrating, especially when you'll want so badly to hunt down the idiot or idiots who broke your friend's heart and break their jaws. But as we get older, life stops being as simple and the bullies aren't as easy to spot as they once were on the playground. So what do you do if you're a woman of action—someone who defends the defenseless, loyally battles to the death for the underdog, and doesn't let anyone mess with the people you love? The answer is nothing. In this situation I was rendered helpless. There was nothing I could offer Crawford to make it any better—except my presence.

Here's a little nugget I've learned in life about the secret to being a good friend: when words won't suffice, lend an ear. When you can't march into a courtroom or a conference room or a classroom and lay the smack down, lend your shoulder to cry on. When you don't have money for expensive presents, offer your simple presence. And when you don't know what else to do for someone, pray for him or her. It does matter. It is enough. It will be remembered for years to come.

One day as the uncertainty dragged on and the outlook of the impending court case was growing bleaker and bleaker, a Bible verse popped into my head that I knew was for Crawford. Second Chronicles 20:17 says, "You will not have to fight this battle. Take up your positions; stand firm and see the deliverance the LORD will give you, Judah and Jerusalem. Do not be afraid; do not be discouraged. Go out to face them tomorrow, and the LORD will be with you."

I e-mailed the scripture to Crawford excitedly. "This is for you!" I wrote. "I don't know exactly how it's going to play out, but something is telling me that you won't even have to step foot into a courtroom. God's got this! Crazy, I know, but this verse popped into my head and I just knew immediately that it was for you."

I didn't know it at the time, but he clung to that scripture throughout the entire ordeal, repeating it, claiming it, believing it, and ultimately, realizing it.

Armed with that scripture, my beautiful friend, who would sooner walk through fire than face confrontation, met the battle of his life head-on, face set, eyes flashing, chin up—and he never backed down. He never lost faith in himself, and he never lost faith in God.

Several months later new information came to light at the last minute, completely unexpectedly and the *day before* the case was set to go to trial, which tipped the scales in Crawford's favor and awarded him primary custody of his precious little boy. He never even had to step one foot into a courtroom. I won't go into a lot of detail except to say that his goodness, honesty, and all-encompassing faith won the battle for him without him ever even having to step onto the battlefield. Just as the scripture laid on my heart so many months before had predicted, this was one battle that was not Crawford's to fight. All he had to do was show up big and let faith do the rest. And it did.

He came into my room late one Monday afternoon, where I sat holding my breath and hoping for the best, yet fearing the worst. I wanted so badly to believe that the scales of justice had tipped in Crawford's favor, but logic dictated that the court would side with the mother, as most custody cases do. Most custody cases, it would appear, except this one. Crawford pulled a manila folder out of his backpack and held it suspended in front of me. He stopped at the end of my bed and fanned the paperwork in front of me dramatically as I sat with my mouth dropped open, already knowing by the triumphant look in his eyes what he was going to say. Still, we faced off silently for a few moments, him smiling like the Cheshire cat, my eyes starting to fill with tears before the words even left his lips.

"I am holding in my hands the paperwork that awards me primary custody of Adam."

Instantly, the tears spilled over, the yelps of joy, disbelief, and sheer wonder now coming from both of us as I leapt off of my bed and pulled Crawford into an ecstatic hug. I clung to him, sobbing both for him and with him as the realization that the long months of pain my friend had endured were now over. Just like that. He had emerged from the darkest storm of his life, and victory, restoration, and sunshine were waiting for him on the other side.

We danced around the room like crazy people for a few minutes, giggling, hugging, cheering, sobbing, not believing it was really true yet knowing somehow that the culmination of all the months of heartache, prayer, and struggle had brought us here to this moment, together. Life knew what it was doing when it tossed us, seemingly unwittingly, back together under one roof. I needed someone to love me unconditionally, encourage me, and be patient and kind and motivating as I continued to balance my dream with my job. Crawford needed someone to get feisty, sassy, and in his face; to kick his butt into chasing victory instead of settling for defeat. (And I was definitely the girl for the job.)

A week later Crawford, his parents, and some other friends, and I got together to celebrate, and as his mom hugged me tight, she whispered in my ear, "He needed you, you know. He couldn't have done any of it without you."

The truth is, I needed him too. Without him and his

unwavering belief in me over the years, I might have never learned to believe in myself.

As most gloriously happy events do, this story has a flip side of sadness, as very rapidly the night approached that would be our last official night together in our house as roommates. Now a full-time single dad, Crawford was going to live with his parents as he adjusted to life as a single parent, juggling life, work, and responsibilities with soccer, homework, and birthday parties.

When I got home from work the day after he moved out, the silence of our house was deafening.

A few months before, we had sat and mused about the day when his situation would be resolved and he would be able to move on with the rest of his life. We laughed, planned, and wondered what that mysterious future would look like. Now it was here, and my partner in crime was not. We would likely never be roommates again. And though I was so incredibly happy for him and his new beginning, I was still deeply sad to see the credits roll on our ending. Yes, we will always be best friends, and that will never change, but living through some of the most defining moments of your life with another person is the kind of thing that will never come again. I look back on all of it now—the tears, the fears, the laughter, the fights, the prayers, the dreams—and marvel at the beauty of it all.

For a moment, we were becoming who we were going to be—together. Then we woke up one morning and *were* the people we were going to be—apart.

That's what friendship is all about, you know. The pulling, pushing, challenging, healing, praying, feeling, loving, and moving on.

I would urge you, as someone who found myself sitting on

the other side of a good-bye I wasn't quite ready for: Don't wait until you're faced with someone's absence to acknowledge the importance of their presence. Love them *now*. Realize that the flaws, irritations, bad habits, and imperfections are all a part of what makes them, and you, unique, special, and rare to this universe. Realize that some moments are worth staying up late and missing out on sleep for. Some messes are worth overlooking. Some road trips do need to be taken, right then and there. In ten years, you're not going to remember that time you got in trouble with your boss for calling in sick for three days in a row, but you *will* remember that spontaneous road trip to the beach when you stayed up all night and ate nothing but McDonald's and Krispy Kreme for three days and struck out on the open road with nothing but a tank of gas, twenty dollars in your pocket, and your best friend by your side.

As for me, sitting there gazing at the packed boxes, the newspaper, and the packing tape littering the floor where Crawford and I had once lain side by side gathering the strength to stand and take on the world, I knew that a defining season of my life was over. It was time to move on to the next chapter of my own life—a chapter that hadn't been written yet. Just a few months before, I marveled at how it seemed as though history was repeating itself, and I was reliving two years ago all over again. If that was indeed the case, and I got a chance over the course of those crazy, tragic, sometimes almost magical six months to reboot my past, I'd like to think I was a little better friend, and a little better person the second time around.

Chapter 18

Flying Solo, Flying Free

I stayed at Crawford's for about a month after he moved out. I needed the time to look for a place of my own, finally settling on an adorable basement apartment in a home in Brentwood, a suburb of Nashville, that was in a fantastic neighborhood and had all utilities included. I felt like I had hit pay dirt. The neighborhood was nestled in the hills and was very woodsy. Every morning when I would drive into work, I would catch glimpses of ducks, deer, and squirrels, and once even a flock of turkeys crossed the road right in front of my car! It was very charming, and I felt like I was living in a Disney movie coming to life.

It was February 2011 by that point, and 2011 would prove to be one of the most exciting years of my writing career. February first marked the one-year anniversary of The Single Woman. I could hardly believe it had already been a year. I had set a goal on my vision board to hit two hundred thousand Twitter followers by the time the one-year anniversary rolled around, and a little after midnight on the first, we hit the mark. Two hundred thousand Twitter followers! I gave thanks to God for the incredible first year of The Single Woman, and I could hardly wait to see what the next year would bring.

I had started meeting with a web team a few months earlier to design an official website for The Single Woman, since I felt like the brand was outgrowing the *Examiner*, and it was time for a change to my own platform. We decided it would be fitting to launch the new site at midnight on Valentine's Day. A few weeks before the launch, we scheduled a photo shoot with an incredible local photographer to shoot some fun, sassy, "official" pictures for the website. My web team went above and beyond to help coordinate the shoot, locating the photographer and even finding a local hair and makeup artist to come in and beautify me for the shoot. You can imagine my shock and horror when I was told the name of said makeup artist less than twenty-four hours before the shoot.

It was Anna. As in, the girl Steven had disappeared with for a full twenty-four hours that fateful night almost two yeras earlier. The girl I always assumed he cheated on me with. The same girl with whom his cheating ways had caused him to flunk the now infamous lie detector test. She had apparently moved to Nashville and was now running a quite successful hair and makeup business. Good for her. I had moved on with my life and wished her no ill will. But did I want her designing my hair and makeup for something as important as my first official photo shoot as The Single Woman?

Absolutely not.

"Um . . . ," I stuttered when my web guy told me her name. "I'm not so sure about this." I went on to explain the whole bizarre situation to him in a nutshell.

"Oh wow," he replied. "Oh wow. Well, it's so late in the game now, I'm not sure we'd be able to find anyone else. Are you sure she'd even know who *you* are? I mean, just because you know her name doesn't mean she knows yours. Right?"

Being a woman, I instantly knew the answer to that question (*of course* she would know who I was), but my web team had worked so hard to put this shoot together, I couldn't bring myself to throw a wrench in the plans. I told my web guy not to worry about it—we would proceed with the shoot as planned. Then I prayed to God that He would not allow this woman to transform me into Bozo the Clown.

The next night I arrived at the location for the shoot in a bundle of nerves. The minute I came face-to-face with Anna, it was like a giant pink elephant had entered the room. It was so glaringly obvious that we both knew who the other one was, but we didn't acknowledge the awkwardness of the situation. We just carried on like we were complete strangers. As she went to work on my hair and makeup, I almost started to bring it up a few times, just to let her know that I was okay with the situation, but then I would think, *Well, what if she actually* doesn't *know who I am, and I bring it up, and it turns into a huge fiasco?* So I kept my mouth closed, holding my breath and praying silently that when I looked into the mirror after our session, I wouldn't look like something from the *Rocky Horror Picture Show.*

Much to my relief, Anna did a beautiful job on my hair and makeup. The shoot went great, and the photos couldn't have turned out better. But more importantly, I got to see the other side of a situation that had caused me months of pain and heartache and self-doubt. I got to actually meet the girl with whom my ex had allegedly cheated on me. And not just meet her, but get to know her a little. Hear her stories. See her passion for her work. Get a glimpse inside her life. How often in life does that happen?

Though I went into that shoot firmly expecting to hate her, I was surprised to find that I didn't at all. In fact, under different circumstances, we even might have been friends.

Though I'm not condoning her actions or Steven's actions in any way if they really did participate in clandestine behavior on that fateful, long-ago night, I did find a way to forgive Anna for her part in the whole painful episode. I didn't know what had led her to get involved with Steven or what her motivation might have been, but I did witness her class and professionalism in the way she handled herself in what could have been a very embarrassing situation. And I was finally able to let the weight of any unforgivingness, bitterness, and anger I might still have buried in my heart against Steven fall away, silently thanking God for His infinite wisdom, divine appointments, and full-circle moments.

———

The launch of my official website and the continued growth of The Single Woman had me thinking about the next steps I needed to take to make writing and sharing my message of positivity for single women a full-time career. I knew in my heart that I was going to one day write a book; I just didn't know when or how that dream was going to become a reality. I decided to put together a book proposal and start sending it around to various literary agents and publishing houses. I had heard rumors about how impressive a built-in platform is to publishers looking to sign new authors, and I knew beyond a shadow of a doubt I had a platform.

Much to my surprise, all of the twenty to thirty query letters I sent out received big, fat rejections. It seemed no one was buying what I was selling. I didn't take the nos personally, however, as I knew that every no was pushing me one step closer to a yes. I even saved all the rejection letters and e-mails so I could look back on them someday and smile. "I will be a *New York Times* best-selling author," I added to my vision board. I knew when it was God's perfect timing, I would find the right publisher.

In the meantime, other big things were happening for me. In spring 2011, I was named a "Woman of Influence" by the *Nashville Business Journal,* and a couple of months later the *Huffington Post* dubbed me a "Twitter Powerhouse." I also received a mention in *Forbes* magazine, where one columnist drew a comparison between me and Facebook founder Mark Zuckerberg! I could hardly believe the doors God's favor was opening.

I had also found a church I really liked in Brentwood, and I quickly got involved in a life group that focused on social media outreach—both the church's and social media in general. One night at life group we brainstormed a promotional video to introduce a segment at church that week, and then decided to shoot the video right there on the spot! It was one of the few times I was able to put my producer hat back on since leaving CMT, and though I now knew beyond a shadow of a doubt that TV production was not my ultimate destiny, I loved how God allowed me to take detours into the land of TV at least once a year, for no other reason, I am convinced, than to see me smile. A month or so later I was invited to speak at church during a service focused on the power of social media in the kingdom of God. I was honored to get to share my full testimony for the first time ever publicly; and I knew in my gut that God was telling me it wouldn't be the last.

By the time summer 2011 rolled around, I decided it was time to invest some good, old-fashioned QT and attention into one of the most important relationships in my life: the one with myself.

How often do we go through life pouring every ounce of our time, passion, talents, treasures, and blood, sweat, and tears into everything else and everyone else in our lives except *us*? I considered myself a happily single, empowered, and evolved woman, so why was I so neglectful about self-care? I decided there was no time like the present to try something new, something different, something revolutionary: I would date myself!

My first act of really getting to know me was to set some boundaries. If this was going to be a monogamous, committed relationship, I needed to take myself off the market. I did so by embarking upon a thirty-day "love cleanse," something the likes of which I had tried in the past but didn't really take all that seriously. This time would be different. I would cleanse myself of the residue from relationships past and journey to the center of myself to a place of peace that could only be found by entering alone. It was time to declare myself free of the ghosts of relationships past, once and for all.

If you choose to fast from dating or do a love cleanse of your own, how you go about it is really a personal decision. I completely abstained from dating, texting, e-mailing, tweeting, Facebooking, calling, flirting, stressing, or obsessing with or about the opposite sex. This is much easier said than done, but I've found that when you make a commitment to focus on yourself and your personal growth, it makes not dwelling on your male counterparts a whole lot easier.

The ground began to shift beneath me almost as soon as I embarked upon my love cleanse, with the powerful energetic waves of my decision to lay down love for thirty days sending out what I can only imagine was a distress call to the guys I had dated over the past few years: "Warning! We interrupt your regularly scheduled flirting to instruct you to reach out to Mandy this instant! Do it *now!*" I heard from ex-loves right and left. Out of the blue they began to contact me, as though their primal instincts sounded an alarm to try and hunt what was no longer on the market: my heart. It got to the point where it was almost amusing.

A more important development over the course of my thirty-day love cleanse was that I entered into a new place of understanding and patience and love for *me*—for the often wrong, often imperfect, often uncertain person whose heart had lost many battles with love, but refused to lose the war. At the end of the day, the love cleanse didn't magically take away my feelings for Mr. E as I had hoped it would, but it did help me find the courage to look those feelings in the eye and tell them that from here on out, I would be the one in charge—and I didn't have to allow my emotions to rule the day. I realized I may never be in complete control of my heart, but the power to have complete control of my emotions was mine. I could be grateful for the chips and cracks in my heart left by past loves, because that's how new love would find its way in. And I could go bravely and confidently into the world, daring love to find me, because at last, I had found myself. And that was perhaps the greatest lesson of all.

The next hurdle I decided to overcome on my journey of dating myself was my fear of having dinner or going to a movie alone. I had always wanted to try solo dining and movie going, but had never quite worked up the nerve. What was at the heart of this fear? I was determined to find out.

I quickly learned I wasn't alone in my hesitancy. Google the phrase *dining alone,* and the first page of results is all articles about "How to handle the traumatic experience of dining alone" and "How to survive dinner—party of one." So much drama over something that should be so simple! I realized that if I was going to be able to speak authentically on the subject of "loving your single life" to my readers, I needed to walk the talk and learn to love all aspects of my single life, including something that challenged me a little—like going out to dinner or to a movie or enjoying a sunny day on the patio at Starbucks without the armor of my girlfriends.

So I began to venture out.

I first went to brunch alone one Sunday afternoon at a popular brunch spot in Nashville's Hillsboro Village. I requested a seat on the crowded patio, and the hostess escorted me to a table in the dead center of the room, right in the middle of all the action. At first it felt a little awkward, and I felt a little exposed, naked even. The natural instinct is to sit staring into your phone the entire time so as to avoid the curious stares of the people around you, but I felt like hiding behind my phone was no different from hiding behind my friends. So even though it was hard, I kept my phone in my purse. And within a few minutes, the initial weirdness started to pass, and I actually started to enjoy myself. The sun felt wonderful, there was a nice afternoon breeze blowing, and the food was delicious. What was not to love?

The poor servers, however, didn't seem to know how to handle my solo status, and I think even felt a little sorry for me. I'm pretty sure they thought I was being stood up. Every five minutes I would have a waiter or waitress at my table: "Is there anything I can get for you? Are you still doing okay? Can I bring you a dessert menu?" And although the service there was always great, I had never received that much attention in the past while dining in a group. It was interesting to watch how other people reacted to my aloneness, like it was something to pity or fear. When did spending quality time with oneself become a bad thing in our culture?

Having successfully conquered the dining-alone portion of my personal challenge, I decided it was time to try going to a movie alone. This initially didn't seem quite as intimidating as eating at a crowded restaurant alone, but when I entered the theater and realized just how much of a couple's activity going to a movie really is, my heart sank a little. I would certainly stick out like a sore thumb here.

I needn't have worried. Even though by the time I got settled into my seat with a giant box of Junior Mints and a Coke Zero, I was feeling relaxed, content, and eager to get this party of one started, another lady who was also seeing the movie alone spotted me and decided to plop down right next to me and jabber through the entire film. It was funny; I had gone into the theater almost dreading the idea of sitting through a movie alone, and now I wanted nothing more than to be left alone! I almost think God sat that lady next to me on purpose that day, to show me one of the great silver linings of flying solo—not having to listen to someone chatter incessantly for two hours straight! A week or so later I had to do a redo since my first effort at seeing a movie alone turned into a joint venture with me and Mrs. Chatterbox, and I actually found that I enjoyed going to a movie by myself as much or more than I did having company. I'm such a movie geek that sitting in a darkened, quiet theater with my feet kicked up and not a care in the world is the ultimate form of relaxation for me, almost like getting a massage. And I don't want anyone else lying next to me interjecting comments and opinions while I'm getting a massage, so why would seeing a movie be any different? Though I still don't do much dining alone, I am proud to say that these days I regularly take solo trips to the movies and love nothing more than kicking back at Starbucks armed with nothing more than a good book and a Frappuccino.

So, having successfully made it to the end of my love cleanse and having overcome my issues with solo outings, I decided I would devote the rest of my summer of dating me to just having some good, old-fashioned fun. And I didn't have to look any further than my own Tennessee backyard! I traveled to Memphis with a girlfriend to tour Graceland for the second time in my life, just because. I attended a couple of nights of the CMA Music Festival in downtown Nashville and had an absolute blast. Living in Nashville, it's easy to take incredible musical events like that for granted, but sitting outside under the stars on a hot July night listening to one great act after another reminded me of why it's so cool to live in Music City, USA.

I also hit the open road a few times on spontaneous road trips. New Kids on the Block were touring that summer, and I indulged myself by hitting four of their tour stops, without apologies. After all, I was answering to no one but myself, so why shouldn't I spend a little time reminiscing about my first loves?

I highly recommend setting aside a season of time to focus on yourself and get back to the basics of you, whatever that process might look like for you. It doesn't have to emulate mine. It needs to be true to who you are. My Summer of No Regrets 2010 had been amazing, but it had been all about someone else: Mr. E. My Summer of Me 2011 was about getting to know *me*, falling in love with *me*, learning to make *me* happy. And because I took time to get my foundation in check, I now felt healthier and happier and readier than ever to start testing that foundation. I knew that no matter what, never again would my proverbial house be in danger of being blown down by the Big Bad Wolf of heartbreak, because I had learned to stand alone without fear. Armed with that knowledge, I was ready to open the door of my heart with confidence, knowing that for perhaps the first time ever, I was ready for whoever walked through it.

———

Fall 2011 dawned brightly and happily for me. For the first time in almost five years, I felt *free*. I felt like I had truly let go and moved on from the past. From Steven, from my multitude of bad dates over the years, and especially from Mr. E. I wasn't thinking about him anymore; I wasn't crying over him anymore; I felt like I had finally unchained myself from him and his memory for the first and the last time. I shared this in a long phone conversation with my friend Jennifer one night, going on and on about how footloose and fancy-free I felt to have finally laid my Mr. E ghost to rest and moved on with my life. She was sad and a little weepy over her ex, her own version of Mr. E, and I assured her unequivocally that better days and greener pastures were ahead.

"You *will* get there!" I encouraged her. "And it's amazing! If I can get there, anyone can! I'm finally over him! And it's so incredible!"

As is typical in Boy Land, me throwing it out there into the universe that I was "finally over him" meant that I set off an internal alarm somewhere in Mr. E's psyche, immediately prompting him to call me.

What is it they say? The minute you get over someone is the very minute they come back around? How do they know? How do they *always* know?

The very next night after my "free-as-a-bird" conversation with Jennifer, Mr. E called for the first time in many months.

I happened to be taking a nap with the ringer off when he called. When I woke up to discover one missed call and saw his name flashing across my phone screen, I promptly dropped the phone, flicked it away from me as far to the edge of the bed as it could get without falling off, and covered it with my quilt.

One night about two weeks later, just as I was getting the initial phone call out of my head, I was on the way over to a girlfriend's house, phone in hand. As I was navigating my way there via GPS, suddenly the screen lit up. There it was. His name again. And I was powerless to make it stop. Short of tossing my BlackBerry out the window, I didn't know what else to do but hit the send button. So I did, and just like that, Mr. E was back in my life again.

I know the typical response to this is, "*What?* How could you allow him back *into* your life after you spent so much time trying to get him *out of* your life?"

For the naysayers out there, I'd like to say this: you can't always follow *The Rules* or the *He's Just Not That Into You* checklists or even the advice of the most renowned love gurus when it comes to matters of the heart.[*] I mean, come on—even the Millionaire Matchmaker, Patti Stanger, found herself *un*matched and single. Love isn't black and white, and you can't always simplify it by trying to make it a black-and-white issue. The bottom line was this: I still loved Mr. E. I had loved him for five long years. It wasn't a

---

[*] Ellen Fein and Sherrie Schneider, *The Rules* series (New York: Grand Central Publishing, 1995); Greg Behrendt and Liz Tuccillo, *He's Just Not That Into You* (New York: Simon & Schuster, 2004).

dark, tortured love; I wasn't a masochist; I wasn't attracted to him because he was a bad boy or someone I couldn't have. I just loved him, purely and simply, for his heart and for the person I knew him to be, despite his flaws. I had prayed about these feelings. I had asked God to take away these feelings. I had let Mr. E go and had gone about my merry way. And he had come back. The Single Woman's message centers around following your heart and soul above all else, and I can't even count the number of times I've tweeted about letting things go and seeing if they come back to you. I'm a firm believer that if God, in His infinite wisdom, gives you another shot at love, you should take it. I'd rather put my heart on the line, risk everything, and walk away with nothing than play it safe and not do what every fiber of my heart was telling me to do—which was to give this man another chance.

So I did.

What can I say? I wasn't following logic. I was following my heart.

I wasn't standing out here on this limb alone. And this time, it seemed, it wasn't one-sided love.

This time he had raised the stakes.

He "missed me." He "needed me in his life." And, for the first time in five years, *he loved me.*

Yes, one September day he said those three words I thought I'd sooner see pigs fly through the streets of downtown Nashville than ever hear him utter.

"When I called you earlier, Mandy, and I left you that voice mail, there was something I wanted to say. But, no, I can't."

"What?" I asked cluelessly, completely oblivious about just how hard my world was about to be rocked.

"I wanted to say . . . uh . . . no, I can't say it."

"*What?*" I asked again, now growing a little impatient.

"I can't believe I'm having so much trouble saying this to you," he said. "This is silly!"

"*What?*" I exclaimed, by now past the point of frustration. "And you should know if you don't just say it, I'm hanging up."

"Okay, okay. Here goes. When I was leaving you a voice mail earlier, I wanted to say . . . well, I wanted to tell you . . . that I love you."

Silence.

I couldn't find my voice.

"I like saying that to you," he said with a smile in his voice.

Still, I said nothing. I couldn't speak. Was I hallucinating? Had I heard correctly? Did the man who was so petrified of the L-word that he put an entire country between us every time we got too close just tell me that *he loves me*?!

"Are you there?" he asked.

"Yes. Yes!" I said, finally locating my vocal chords. "I'm still here."

"Well, what do you have to say about *that*?"

"I don't know what to say about that," I stammered. "That was about the last thing in the world I ever expected to hear you say."

He laughed affectionately. "And that's *why* I love you," he said, leaving me once again shaking my head, still having trouble believing that the moment I had wished for, hoped for, prayed for, for so long had finally dropped into my lap, and completely out of nowhere.

"Well," I said, smiling now too. "Not that I haven't made it abundantly clear over the last several hundred years or so, but . . . I love you too."

"I like the way it sounds, hearing you say that," he responded.

"I do too," I said, thinking that something about this moment, unlike all the moments of uncertainty before, felt so right. So real. So special. It was as though we were finally in the same place at the same time; and though we couldn't have been any farther apart physically, with him on the opposite side of the country in Seattle, I had never felt so close to him.

From that day forward, we started talking on the phone every few days, sometimes saying those three words to each other, sometimes not.

We started to talk more about the future than we ever had before. For the first time ever, he expressed to me how he wanted to get married and have kids, and the person he pictured experiencing all of this with was me. "You're the light at the end of the tunnel for me, Mandy," he said. "You feel like coming home."

And, as fate would have it, the last weekend in September, just two weeks after I redid my vision board, pasting a picture of the Statue of Liberty on it with the declaration: "I will travel to New York City," the opportunity for me to travel to New York City presented itself. On the very same weekend that Mr. E would be in NYC on business. His newspaper was sending him there to conduct an important interview for an upcoming story.

There were other reasons for me to be in New York that weekend, but since Mr. E lived in Seattle and I myself hadn't traveled to New York City in six years, the whole thing seemed like much more than just a coincidence at work.

It felt like a defining moment in our relationship.

It felt like it was finally time. Time to step up to the plate. Time to be completely spontaneous and take a chance. Time to stop playing it so safe in my life for once, and not just go out on a limb but dance on it.

It felt like now or never.

It was a very spur-of-the-moment, spontaneous trip. My friend Whitney and I planned it in about three days. It seemed that fate was aligning to work out every last detail, down to the place we would stay (with Whitney's aunt, in her fabulous apartment on Lexington Avenue, for free).

The night before the trip, however, I started to get cold feet. I started to doubt myself. I started to give in a little to the fear that I was, once again, the one going the distance and making it happen with Mr. E, while he wasn't really being required to make much of an effort to see me at all. These were all thoughts I expressed to him in the late-night hours before Whitney and I were to set out on our adventure.

"I don't know," I told him. "I just feel like I need to see more from you. I need to not just *hear* you say that you love me. I need to actually *see* it in action."

"You need me to prove my love to you, is what you're saying?" he asked.

"Well, yes," I said. "I mean, it's been five years. I feel like it's time for the grand gesture. Basically, if you were Matthew McConaughey and I was Kate Hudson, you would be chasing me to the airport right now."

He laughed. "I hear what you're saying. You need the grand gesture. I get it. And I can do that."

The confidence in his voice took me by surprise a bit; I can't lie. He was actually ready for this. He was calm, cool, collected, and seemed completely ready to step up and take my breath away. Which left just one final question.

"I need to ask you something," I said seriously. "And I need you to answer me straight, with a yes or a no. No deflecting, no avoiding, no placating me—just a yes-or-no answer. Can you do that?"

"Yes," he said, just as seriously.

I took a deep breath.

"I know you say you love me, and obviously I love you too, both as a friend and as more . . ."

"Yes?"

"But"—I paused—"are you . . . *in* love with me?"

It was a bold question, I knew. And the answer had the potential either to break my heart or usher in a new start—a new chapter in the saga of me and Mr. E that had never been explored. But I had to know, either way. I had to know before I took the leap and ventured all the way to New York that he was going to be there to catch me, not just with words but with actions.

And then . . .

"I would have to say, *yes*," he replied, a big smile in his voice. "Now what do you think about that?"

At three the next morning, I left for New York City. I didn't know exactly what was ahead of me, but I knew in my heart what I was leaving behind me: Fear. Safety. Security. Everything that had come before.

And I didn't look back.

Chapter 19

Destination: New York City

$\mathcal{W}$hitney and I left for New York at 3:00 a.m. on a Thursday. Our complicated travel plan was the result of (1) my extreme distaste for flying and (2) the fact that we planned a trip to New York in about three days' notice and spur-of-the-moment air travel was insanely expensive. Whitney and I drove to Washington, DC, and then hopped a commuter bus into the city, making for about a seventeen-hour travel day.

We were a little past Baltimore when my phone rang. It was Mr. E. Butterflies had been swooping around in my stomach all day, so the sight of that familiar name calling lit up not just my phone's screen but my heart.

"Hey! Where are you?" the voice that never failed to make me weak in the knees asked.

"Probably about three hours away," I answered. "What's up?"

"Okay, so, I've made you a salon appointment for tomorrow at a really upscale salon," he replied. "I thought you would want to look like a princess for tomorrow night."

My heart started beating faster.

"O-kaaay. Wow! I'm pretty stoked to go to an NYC salon! And what happens tomorrow night?"

He chuckled.

"I can't tell you. It's a surprise. But. Prepare. For. Your. Mind. To. Be. Blown." He spaced out his words for emphasis, as though it was needed. My mind was already blown, and I hadn't even seen him yet.

"Oh my gosh! Wow. Wow. Okay, I'm excited! Call you when I get there?"

"Sounds good! Can't wait to see you!"

"Me too!" I said, unable to keep the big, goofy grin from spreading across my face as I tossed my phone back into my purse.

Whitney's smile matched mine as I conveyed the conversation to her.

"I'm so excited for you! He's finally stepping up for you!" she said. "What do you think your surprise could be?"

"I have no idea," I replied. "He asked me for locations where Mr. Big and Carrie went on *Sex and the City*, and the only date of theirs that I could remember was the one where they rode in the carriage through Central Park. Maybe he's planning to do that?"

Whitney and I giggled and chattered our way through the rest of the bus ride, wondering what was awaiting us in the city. And we didn't have long before we would find out. In no time at all, we were crossing the giant bridge into New York, the city lights glittering all around us, our exhaustion from the full day of travel forgotten as we both bounced in our seats with excitement.

The next hour flew by in a flurry of arriving at Whitney's aunt's fabulous apartment, freshening up after our long day, and figuring out our plan of attack for the evening. Whitney was going one way, and I was going the other. We hadn't realized it, but we wouldn't see much of each other from this point forward in the trip. She was meeting her friends and I was meeting Mr. E, and though we arrived in the city together, we would be like two ships passing for the rest of the trip.

Which brings me to an interesting point.

When it comes to traveling, I tend to be a bit on the cautious side. Though I have a bit of a free spirit, because of my struggles with panic attacks, I haven't had nearly as much of an opportunity to explore that side of myself as I would like. In other words, until this trip, the idea of wandering around New York City alone would have seemed like a foreign concept to me—even a little scary. But I wanted to step out of my comfort zone, and step out of my comfort zone I did, more during those three days in New York than ever before in my life.

Starting with meeting up with Mr. E. He was rushing around to meet a deadline on the story he was working on so he could devote the next twenty-four hours to me. I asked him for an address of a diner near his apartment so I could wait for him there. (Obviously I didn't really want to have a cab deposit me in front of a dark apartment building at eleven at night in New York City. Taking risks, I was ready to do. Taking stupid risks, I was not.)

Mr. E directed me to go somewhere called the Neptune Diner, so I innocently told the driver the address, expecting a short cab ride since Mr. E had told me the apartment where Whitney and I were staying on Lexington Avenue was just "a couple of train stops down" from his place.

Twenty minutes, thirty dollars, and a jaunt across the Queensboro Bridge later (did I mention my phobia of bridges?), the cabbie attempted to drop me off on a dark street corner in Queens, no Neptune Diner in sight.

I tapped out a frantic text message to Mr. E.

"Are you in Queens and neglected to tell me, or is my cab driver attempting to kidnap me?"

He wrote back, "I'm in Queens." (Information that would have been nice to know before I spent my life savings on a cab to a different borough.)

"Umm . . ." I cleared my throat, trying to figure out how to convey to my cab driver that I would *not* be exiting his cab until the words *Neptune Diner* were blazing down on me in neon lighting. "I'm sorry, sir, but I'm from Tennessee. I don't get out of cars on dark street corners even there, let alone in New York City. Is there any way we can find Neptune Diner?" I repeated the address again, and the frustrated cabbie gestured that we were, in fact, at 3105 Astoria Blvd.

I stared harder into the dark, seeing nothing but a couple of bags of garbage and two alley cats looking as if they were either about to fight or mate passionately. Either way, this was clearly *not* the Neptune Diner.

The next fifteen minutes were spent with me GPSing the irritated NYC cab driver around Astoria, while he was probably ruing the day I ever got into the back of his cab, and I was wondering when Ashton Kutcher was going to jump out from behind a bush, yelling that I had been "Punk'd!" (And, honestly, don't even get me started on the fact that a clueless girl from Tennessee was having to direct a streetwise cabbie from the city around the streets of New York.)

Then, suddenly, there it was, looming above me, as beautiful as the North Star must have been to the three wise men (okay, that's probably a *tad* overdramatic), the Neptune Diner! I was ready to kiss my cabbie in relief, but he peeled off the moment my boots hit the pavement, probably heading back to headquarters to turn in his keys and go into early retirement.

Nevertheless, I was there! Somehow, some way, I was sitting in a diner in Queens, packed with New Yorkers even at 11:30 at night, surrounded by strangers, waiting on the boy I hadn't seen in almost a year and a half but had loved for as long as I could remember. My heart beats faster just writing these words as I recall how nervous and excited I was, waiting for my prince to swoop in and sweep me off my feet. After all, it *was* almost midnight, and though I was wearing black boots instead of glass slippers, never had I felt more like Cinderella.

Every time the diner door would open, I would glance up from my menu, eyeing the door in search of that familiar face. A few minutes went by, a few more, then a text:

"Don't order food! I have a surprise for you."

A couple of minutes later the diner door swung open, and there he was.

He came galloping through the door in his usual cloud of excitement, vitality, and energy, his golden hair and skin lighting up the room and causing several waitresses to stop mid-order and stare. He had a Cheshire-cat grin on his face when his eyes met mine, and as cheesy as it might sound, for a moment, everything else fell away.

Then he was by my side, swooping me up into his arms, and everything else was forgotten: the year and a half of distance, the seventeen hours of travel, the crazy cab ride, the numerous bridges and tunnels and miles I had journeyed to be here with him in this moment.

None of it mattered. None of it mattered a bit.

I was in a city of over eight million people where I knew

exactly two, in a strange diner, and in a funny little borough I had never actually been to before, but somehow, I was home.

That's how I found myself on a breezy September night in New York City being pulled along excitedly by Mr. E as he grabbed my hand eagerly and hauled me out of the Neptune Diner and into the next chapter of my life. We were both as joyful as children as we walked along, arm in arm, talking a mile a minute as we tried to catch up on a year and a half's worth of absence in the space of five minutes.

A few minutes later we were passing through a small, wrought-iron gate and climbing the stairs to the Queens apartment that Mr. E called home when he was in NYC on a story. A delicious-looking feast of chicken and vegetables awaited us, two glasses of wine already poured. He had enlisted his roommate's help with preparing a beautiful dinner for us. My stomach rumbled in hunger as we sat down to eat, but the butterflies flapping around and E's smile across the table made it hard to concentrate on my food. Something about this night felt different. I soon discovered why.

"So I was talking to my parents about you earlier," Mr. E said with a curious look on his face. Half mischievous, half trepidatious—like he had a secret that he wasn't sure he wanted to tell.

"Oh, your parents! I love them! What about?" I asked.

"Well." He paused. "I wanted to tell them about my surprise for you and get their advice."

"And? What did they say?"

He looked at me seriously. "They said I shouldn't do it unless I'm really, really sure."

My heart flipped over in my chest. "Oh?" I asked. "Well, whatever it is, are you sure?"

"Mandy, you know how busy I am with work right now," he began.

"Yes," I agreed. Having been in his life for five years, I knew how single-minded he could be when it came to his career. Everything else tended to fall away in the presence of his extreme tunnel vision.

"And I'm going to be really, really busy through the rest of the winter. They've been giving me more and more responsibilities at work, and I'm really starting to climb the ladder. I probably won't even get to go home for Christmas," he continued.

"Okay?" I said, not sure where this was leading.

"Things probably aren't going to slow down for me at all until the spring. I really won't have time for much of anything besides work," he went on. "And you know how my life is going to be. I'm going to always be moving around, never staying in the same place very long."

As a former news writer, I understood, perhaps better than anybody, what the life of someone in the news world was like. But why did it sound like he was breaking up with me?

He grabbed both my hands suddenly, looking at me very intently. "You said you would marry me tomorrow if I asked. Knowing how hectic and unsettled my life is going to be, is that still true?"

I awoke with a start, momentarily confused by my surroundings. One glance out the window at the fire escapes across the way and the city skyline in the distance reminded me of where I was; and the strange, intense conversation that had gone on with Mr. E until the wee hours of the morning ran through my mind.

Mr. E's talk of marriage had shocked me. The M-word had never really been a part of his vocabulary before, and I had to wonder what it all meant.

Still, I was in the city I loved and adored, with the man I loved and adored, and though I was going on about three hours of sleep, the sunlight filtering through the window brought joy to my heart and a smile to my face.

I couldn't find Whitney anywhere in the apartment, so I assumed she had already left for the day with her friends. My hair appointment was at two; it was already eleven thirty, so after meeting up with Mr. E at Dunkin' Donuts for a chocolate donut with sprinkles (me), and coffee (him), we headed toward the subway. This was only my second subway ride in my entire life, and I think fate must have been conspiring to make this the perfect day, because a musical quartet boarded the train behind us and immediately broke into a roof-raising rendition of "My Girl."

A couple of hours later I arrived for my first-ever NYC fancy salon experience. They rolled out the red carpet for us, and Mr. E made sure I was fussed over, with two or three stylists at my beck and call. When I walked out an hour and a half later, I truly did feel like Cinderella on her way to the ball, and we spent the afternoon walking hand in hand through the streets of New York, the promise of my big "surprise" still lingering in the air for later. I felt like I was walking through the pages of my own fairy tale come to life. But, like every fairy tale, there was a plot twist up ahead that I never in a million years saw coming.

Mr. E's phone rang around 5:00 p.m., and he looked at me with a knowing smile. He chatted with whoever was on the other end for a few minutes, then turned to me with a wink. "Did you know that today is Rosh Hashanah? As in, Jewish New Year?" he asked me.

"Um, no," I replied in confusion. "But what does that have to do with anything?"

"My friend we're going to go see is Jewish, so he's off work today for the holiday," Mr. E explained.

"Oh! Okay, cool. Are we just going to his place to hang out?" I asked.

Mr. E laughed. "You could say that."

We made our way to a fancy apartment building a few blocks away from Times Square. A few minutes later we were standing on the street corner with who I can only describe as the most authentic New Yorker I have ever seen. Short and stocky, with his hair pulled back into a brief ponytail, Mr. E's friend also had a *Sopranos*-worthy Jersey accent. (We'll call him Tony.)

"How you doin', dahlin?" Tony asked. "Ready to go look at some stuff?"

I looked over at Mr. E in confusion. He just grinned.

"Yeah—sure?"

We walked several blocks in the typical New York hustle that natives favor, quickly and briskly with little conversation, headed for destinations unknown. I had to struggle to keep up in my not-so-street-friendly four-inch wedges. Mr. E and Tony walked a little ahead of me, their heads together, conspiring about something that I wasn't within earshot to hear.

Then, suddenly, we were at a glass door of what looked like the back of a business. Mr. E kept looking back at me with a grin the size of Texas. I still had absolutely no idea where we were or what we were doing, but I continued to follow along as we wound our way through a back hallway, up an elevator, and into what I was guessing were Tony's offices.

"Even though it's Rosh Hashanah today, I talked Tony into

opening up his store just for us," Mr. E explained, taking my hand and leading me to a chair in front of Tony's desk. I noticed Tony behind him, unlocking a large safe. This was starting to get really weird. The only time I had seen something like this was in the grand proposal scene in *Sweet Home*—

Wait a minute.

"And in case you haven't figured it out yet," Mr. E continued, "he sells engagement rings."

"*What?!*" I exclaimed in shock and disbelief as Tony brought out ring after ring for my review. Eight carats, one carat, five carats, princess cut, teardrop, canary yellow, pink, platinum, silver, gold, Titanic-sized boulders—they were all there, sitting in front of me, just waiting for me to place on my unpolished finger. Yes, my lack of a proper manicure to try on engagement rings caused me much anxiety that day, but how was a girl to know that a guy who treats commitment like it's a communicable disease was going to do a complete 360 and . . . propose?

Yet there was E, sitting there with a huge grin on his face, very much looking like the cat who swallowed the canary-yellow diamond. "Try them on," he said, pulling out his phone and snapping a picture of the stunned look on my face.

I had so many questions. My head was spinning, but I wasn't sure if it was from my confusion or the array of bling laid out before me. With shaking hands, I tried on one ring, then another, then another, as Mr. E snapped photo after photo. He noted the ones that I liked the best, taking careful pictures, even texting Crawford a shot of me holding up my ring-laden hand. Finally I reached the end and looked over at him with questions in my eyes, wondering what could be coming next.

"Let me go out and talk to Tony for a moment," he said. "I'll be right back."

He left the room, and I could hear him and Tony out in the hall, whispering back and forth. I scooped up my BlackBerry and tapped out a frantic text message to Alli: "Alli, we're at a diamond store, looking at engagement rings. *This* is my surprise!"

She responded within seconds. "What does this mean?! Did he *propose*?"

I was just starting to text back when Mr. E and Tony came back into the room.

"Hey, there's a great rooftop restaurant near here," Tony said. "You guys should check it out. Awesome view of the city."

Mr. E looked at me. "Do you wanna go there and talk about everything?"

I hadn't seen a money exchange or a ring hand over, so I was more confused than ever.

"Yes, that's a good idea," I replied. It looked like it was going to be a beautiful evening.

"Let's go then."

We said good-bye to Tony and walked almost silently the few blocks to the bar. It was a very New York rooftop lounge, overlooking the city and filled with young professionals who were dressed to impress and obviously there for after-work mingling. We found a seat near the ledge so I could gaze out at the lights surrounding us. It was then that my feelings of elation from the past two days started to settle into something very close to sadness. I had just experienced one of the most important moments in a woman's life, hadn't I? Yet I had walked away without a ring on my finger. What did it all mean?

I turned to him and posed the question, "What does this all mean?" I asked directly. "I mean, it was so exciting, and I appreciate immensely that you went to all the trouble that you did to make this day special, but I'm not sure I understand."

"Mandy, I wanted to see how it felt to look at rings with you," he explained. "I needed to know if it felt right."

"And . . . ?"

"I liked it," he said with a smile. "I think it felt right."

"You think?" I paused. "So, does this mean . . . we're in a relationship?" I asked hesitantly. We had never really been "in a relationship," at least not one that warranted a Facebook status update, so this would be a really huge, really welcome change for us.

He looked away without responding. I waited. He wouldn't meet my gaze. His silence said everything that his words wouldn't.

"Does it mean we're in a relationship?" I asked again. "Like boyfriend, girlfriend?"

"Mandy, I see what we are as so far beyond boyfriend and girlfriend," he finally responded, shifting in his seat. "Can't we just leave things as they are until I put that ring on your finger?"

I looked at him in astonishment. "Wait a minute." I set down my drink. "Wait a minute. You mean you're telling me you want to be my husband, but you still don't want to be my *boyfriend*?"

"Mandy, you told me to make the grand gesture. I made the grand gesture! Why is this not enough for you?"

I sat back in my seat, the realization finally hitting me that after everything we had been through, absolutely nothing between us had changed.

"Why is this not enough for me? Because I deserve more than someone who's going to show me a fancy ring. I deserve someone who's going to actually put it on my finger! Do you know what this feels like? This is the moment that every girl dreams about her entire life. It feels like you just handed me the most beautifully wrapped package in the entire world, and I opened the box, and it's empty!"

He just sat there in silence, as though he couldn't comprehend what I was saying or why I was frustrated.

"I'm just not sure I understand what we're supposed to do until March if we're not committed to each other. I know you're going to be busy, and we might not get to see each other, and you can't promise me anything till then—I get it. But am I supposed to go into hibernation? What am I supposed to do if another guy asks me out?"

Still, he sat there. Never has so much been said without saying a word.

I tried another approach. "Okay, well, why don't we just call it a night and figure everything out tomorrow?"

Finally he seemed to snap out of his haze. "Mandy, I can't hang out with you tomorrow. I have interviews all day."

"On a Saturday?"

"Well, you know how it is. The news doesn't stop on the weekends."

"Okay. I understand if you can't spend all day long with me, but you're telling me you have no time whatsoever to spare for me tomorrow? Not even an hour?" We hadn't seen each other in a year and a half, and we had just looked at engagement rings together, and he was telling me that twenty-four hours was all he had to give?

"Yes, that's what I'm telling you."

I couldn't believe it. Gone was the sweet, open, romantic guy from the night before—even from an hour ago. It was as though that invisible wall had dropped down between us again, and he had frozen me out of his heart and his life like he had done so many times before when things got too intense.

As we left the rooftop, it began to rain. First little sprinkles and then suddenly big, fat, heavy drops, like the ones that were threatening to fall from my eyes. I didn't have an umbrella, and I didn't care. My salon-styled hair that had just hours earlier been so shiny and perfectly curled started to droop around my face— the perfect metaphor for how I was feeling. Mr. E and I didn't even walk together. Instead, we walked in a single-file line; two people who had been on the same page for perhaps the first time ever, now like two strangers reading completely different books.

We made our way to Grand Central Station, as Mr. E wanted to show it to me. He knew that since I was such a movie buff, and since so many films had been shot there, I would get a kick out of seeing it. The gesture meant something to me, but the irony of finding ourselves in the place where so many final scenes of movies have played out—the guy always chasing the girl to catch her and tell her his true feelings before she gets on the train and speeds out of his life forever—was almost too much for me to bear.

It was late, almost midnight by that time, and surprisingly, Grand Central Station was fairly quiet, none of the usual hustle and bustle that you see in the movies. A few people wandered here and there, but we were largely alone. We sat on the empty marble steps and shared a hot chocolate and a divinely rich éclair—a moment that in another life could have been very romantic; but for me, it fell flat. I was starting to realize that as beautiful as our moments together could be, it felt as if it was all a smoke screen. Just like the movies, our love was one-dimensional. There was a lot of glitter but very little gold.

"You're never gonna be that guy at the end of the movie who chases me, are you?" I asked him quietly.

He just sat and stared straight ahead, a sad look on his face, a brick wall surrounding his heart.

His silence told me all I needed to know. No answer is very

much an answer if you're willing to listen with your heart instead of your ears.

It was so late and stormy at that point, we just went back to his place for the night, and I lay awake on the couch, never sleeping, silent teardrops falling on my pillow. He stayed up all night too, watching movies in his room. I guess the nice little ninety-minute version of life and romance was easier for him to deal with than the real thing. In the movies, the beginning of the relationship is usually the end of the movie, and he was too scared to ever take a chance and see what happens after the screen fades to black.

He walked me to the subway the next morning, a distant look in his eyes, his mind already far away from me and onto his next project for work. He explained to me in great detail which stop I needed to get off at and tucked money into my pocket for a cab once I got off the subway that would take me the rest of the way to Whitney's aunt's apartment. He gave me a big hug, a quick kiss, and then it was time to say good-bye.

"So this is it?" I asked, a tear sliding down my cheek. "This is really how we're ending things? This is breaking my heart."

He looked at me, pulled me into one more hug, and held on for a long moment. "I do love you, Mandy. I'm just . . . confused. I need some time to think." With that, he pulled away, quickly swiped his subway card for me, and gave me a little nudge through the gate.

"You need the N train. If you don't see it, ask someone where it is."

With that, he disappeared into the crowd, taking my heart with him.

That was the last time I ever saw him. But as with most "lasts" in my life, I didn't know it at the time.

I boarded my first-ever solo subway ride (after I asked some-one which one the N train was), replaying the events of the past two days in my head. I couldn't believe we had come so far, both geographically and emotionally, only to go our separate ways again. How many times could two people lose each other?

But we hadn't really lost each other. Technically, he had given me up. And without even so much as a fight! A man who truly wants to commit to a woman doesn't almost put a ring on her finger. He actually does it! And I deserved more than an almost proposal. I deserved a real one. I suddenly realized that Mr. E's grand gesture wasn't so grand after all, and that made me realize that perhaps his big feelings for me were really quite small.

Somewhere on that N train between Queens and Manhattan, I found my gumption again. A different girl emerged from that subway than the one who had traveled across the Queensboro Bridge just forty-eight hours before. One with a heart that was a little more battered, a little more bruised, but also a little more brave.

I was dozing in the car on the way back to Tennessee when a thought startled me awake.

What if I had let fear stop me from going to New York?

The adventure I had been on for the past few days had taken me far away from everything I knew, but it had brought me home to myself. I was a girl who just a few short years earlier could scarcely even leave my driveway without having a panic attack. And now here I was riding subways, hailing cabs, hopping buses to big cities, and traveling essentially alone, and I was doing it all without an ounce of fear. Had I never followed my heart to the Big Apple, I might not have realized how brave, bold, and independent I can be. I might never have known I can navigate a big city all by myself. And I might never have grasped how vital it is to follow your intuition wherever it guides you, even if it happens to guide you far outside your comfort zone and ultimately far away from the one person you thought you'd always love.

If my three days in New York taught me anything, it's that in life, we often go in search of one thing and end up finding something so much better. Something unexpected. Something we never knew we wanted but now we couldn't imagine our lives without. Going in search of Mr. E's heart had led me to my own. A vital piece of me that had been long ago swept away in the chaos surrounding my departure from CMT and the resulting months of anxiety, depression, and fear was finally reclaimed during those three days in New York.

And then it hit me.

I had opened myself up to fearless love, and fearless life showed up instead.

And that was enough for me.

When I returned home from New York—by the way, I had been awake for forty-two hours straight by the time my head hit the pillow back in Nashville—I didn't hear from Mr. E for eight days.

Eight days.

When I searched the headlines in New York City and determined that he hadn't fallen off a skyscraper or been plowed over by a rogue taxi, I called him.

"Are your fingers broken?" I asked.

"No."

"Was your voice box damaged?"

"No."

"Were you abducted by aliens? Lost at sea? Entered a monastery and took a vow of silence?"

"No. No. And no."

"So what you're telling me is that you were choosing, every day, for *eight days*, not to call me? After you took me to look at engagement rings?"

"I guess so."

Needless to say, I told him in no uncertain terms what I thought of his behavior and hung up the phone. Then, just in case he didn't get it, I fired off an e-mail, telling him everything I had needed to say to him for the past five years. I held nothing back. Nothing.

We didn't speak again for nearly three months.

Then, on Christmas Day 2011, a little over five years to the day that I met him, my phone rang. It was him.

We talked for about forty-five minutes and managed to come to a place of peace with each other. Though I knew in my heart that we would never be together, I also knew, in the history books of our relationship, I wanted the last page to be one of forgiveness and healing, not anger and resentment. In his own weird way, I think Mr. E did love me, and he did try to make the grand gesture. It just wasn't grand enough.

That was the last time I spoke to Mr. E. I'm not sure where he is now or what he's doing. Whatever it is, wherever it is, I wish him nothing but happiness.

Here's the thing about that person you think you'll love, long for, and pine for forever: one day you'll wake up and you won't anymore. You just won't. It might take a week, or it might take a year, or, as in my case, it might take six or seven years and a *lot* of hard-earned lessons. But one day you will wake up and be free of him. Just like that, the heartache, the tears, and the unrequited love will have vanished, and in its place will be just a memory—one that you'll even take out every now and again on a rainy day and smile at.

And as for my Hollywood ending?

Maybe Prince Charming would find me someday; maybe he wouldn't. Heck, maybe he got lost somewhere along the way. Or maybe he, like me, had a few more miles to travel before he settled down.

Those three days in New York taught me that this whole Happily Ever After thing, it happens one moment at a time, one unforgettable adventure at a time. And it might not look the way you thought it would. The person you thought you'd spend forever with might really just be a stop along the way. And maybe when you step back and look at the bigger picture, you'll see that loving that person, even if he wasn't your forever, taught you lessons that will last a lifetime. Maybe you'll even begin to see how that person challenged you, stretched you, inspired you, and made you a better person. And maybe, just maybe, someday you'll get to write a book and tell him thank you for being a chapter in your story—or even a few chapters—because without his colorful era in your life, however short or long it may have been, you wouldn't be the woman you are today.

A few weeks after I returned home from New York, I was contacted by Thomas Nelson Publishers for the first time. We wound up meeting to discuss the potential of me writing the very book you are now holding in your hands, only a couple of weeks after I spoke to Mr. E for the last time. Coincidence? I think not. It took me surrendering the life that wasn't meant for me to embrace the life that was. Pretty much everything major that has happened in my career happened post-Mr. E. I believe God brings people into our lives to teach us the lessons we most need to learn, and then once we've learned the lessons, I think He sits back and watches to see if we will be obedient enough to let those people go or if we will cling to them out of stubbornness, even though their presence in our lives is no longer fruitful. Everything that happens next is a result of how we respond to that test.

Mr. E helped prepare me for my destiny, but he wasn't my destiny. I had to sacrifice the lesser for the greater, the short-term for the long run, the smaller piece for the bigger picture.

And looking back on six years of memories, laughter, heartbreak, tears, kisses, magic, adventure, and romance, I knew I wouldn't change a thing. Not a bit of it. Including the end.

Because if the hellos that followed my good-bye to Mr. E have taught me anything, it is this: I had to surrender Mr. E so I could step into everything I was meant to be.

Chapter 20

Destination: Me

$\mathcal{L}$ike He always does when I'm feeling lost and beaten down, and I've forgotten who I am, God came along and reminded me.

A few weeks after I returned home from New York, I received a text from my friend Mastin Kipp, whose online help had been so formative in the early days of The Single Woman. "You're about to get a call that's going to change your life," it said.

Mastin had mentioned to me in passing that he had met with Oprah's team a few times to discuss the possibility of getting involved in her *Oprah's Lifeclass* events, and he told me he had passed along my information to them as "someone to watch." Still, I had no idea what his cryptic text could mean. How thrilling! And what proof that it truly is darkest before the dawn.

The call Mastin hinted at in his text came a few days later.

I was sitting at my desk at work one morning when the phone rang. It was a Chicago area code, which set my pulse racing. Chicago . . . Harpo . . . Oprah. Taking a deep breath, I answered.

It was a member of Oprah's team, Maya, inviting me to be an official member of Oprah's VIP press corps as she traveled to St. Louis and New York to film her show *Oprah's Lifeclass* live on location. Only eight bloggers from across the world were being invited to participate. I was one of them.

All I could see in my mind as Maya explained the VIP press corps to me and what it entailed was my eleven-year-old self rushing home every day and fighting my sister over the remote to watch my inspiration, Oprah, on TV. I saw a flash of myself fresh out of college, refusing to give up my dream of working in local news in Nashville, because that's where Oprah got her start. Then I saw myself, just a few weeks earlier, with hope in my heart, scrawling across my vision board: "I will meet Oprah."

"Mandy, are you there?" the voice on the other line said.

"Yes! Yes, I'm here," I replied, shaking away the memories. "I'm sorry. I guess I'm just in shock!"

Maya laughed. "So do you want to participate? Can we officially add you to the list of our VIP bloggers?"

"Count me in."

———

A few weeks later I struck out for St. Louis Alli and Jennifer in tow.

Being invited to this event put me in a league of people that was far beyond what I ever imagined for myself as a small-town girl from Murfreesboro, Tennessee. I had given God complete control of The Single Woman, prayed that He would be the one to take it to the next level, and asked for opportunities for my message to shine from a public platform; I just never dreamed one of the public platforms He would thrust me onto would be Oprah's! I could scarcely comprehend the sheer magnitude of the gift of being there in that moment, with those people, to play my small role in adding a little inspiration to the world and helping make it a better place.

I was a bundle of nerves and jitters as I left my friends for the day and strolled into the rather opulent and impressive Peabody Opera House in downtown St. Louis to meet the Oprah Winfrey Network team and my fellow bloggers.

I was the first one there, as the other bloggers were all delayed at the airport. That's always a bit of an overwhelming thing, to be tossed into unfamiliar waters without the comfort of fellow swimmers treading water beside you. I felt anxious, overwhelmed, and vastly out of my comfort zone. Vulnerable, unsure, inadequate even. I mean, this was *Oprah*. The most iconic and inspiring figure of our time, and the woman I had sworn I was going to meet since I was knee-high to a grasshopper, as my mom would say.

A few steps into the venue, though, I was greeted by a quote on a big, colorful placard: "The whole point of being alive is to evolve into the whole person you were intended to be."[*] It's one of my favorite Oprah quotes. It instantly calmed my nerves. Then, the very still, small voice of God spoke to the very depths of my heart: *I've got you. Trust Me.* And just like that, I let go of my fears and my anxiety and allowed myself to fall into the safety net of His embrace. It was in that moment that I realized what the wonderful folks at OWN must have seen in me, and in the words that poured forth from my heart onto my blog: I was a work in progress. I had not "arrived." I was still in the midst of the journey, and as messy, battle-scarred, and imperfect as my journey might be, it was enough for Oprah. Even greater than that, it was enough for God.

And that made it enough for me.

---

[*] Biography.com, "Oprah Winfrey," accessed August 19, 2013, http://www.biography.com/people/oprah-winfrey-9534419/.

About an hour later, the rest of the team arrived, chattering loudly and excitedly, everyone introducing themselves to one another all at once. I was thrilled to finally meet Mastin face-to-face and to get to give him a huge hug of gratitude for everything he had done to help further my message, and even to help bring me there to *Oprah's Lifeclass*.

Everyone there was fun, creative, and eclectic, and the energy was wonderful. There was a mom blogger, a couple of entertainment bloggers, and three inspirational bloggers, myself included. The great thing about the VIP blogging program was that we were all there to blog and tweet about our individual *Oprah's Lifeclass* experiences from our own perspectives. That's what made it so genius. Obviously a mom blogger would have a very different vantage point from a TV blogger, and so on. We would all glean our own lessons and wisdom from the experience and pass it on in our own unique ways. Between all of us, we had a total following of somewhere around three million people across the globe. It was a brilliantly inventive and groundbreaking method of sharing *Oprah's Lifeclass* message with the world.

The OWN staff gave us the grand tour of the backstage area, and we were able to actually witness several brainstorming sessions as they happened among Oprah's production staff and social media team. We had a front-row seat to all the action, and my inner TV production nerd was overjoyed. Once again, God had found a way to resurrect my TV dreams in a far bigger and more thrilling way than anything I could have ever made happen for myself. And seeing how kind, warm, and welcoming Oprah's staff was—even in the midst of chaos, deadlines, and last-minute planning—restored my faith in a business that

I had long ago deemed cutthroat. My own TV career had come to such an abrupt, unexpected, and hurtful end, I had more or less assumed since then that all TV people were ruthless, cold, and only out to advance themselves and their own careers. It was an assumption that was completely blown out of the water by witnessing the inner workings of the OWN team. Even when they didn't know we were watching, the spirit of teamwork, support, and cohesiveness was on full display. I humbly realized in that moment the importance of not writing people off or placing them in boxes of your own limited thinking. Just because one TV executive, friend, or love interest hurts you doesn't mean they all will. This experience was turning into life class for me in more ways than one.

The next morning we all had breakfast with Iyanla Vanzant. She was someone I quoted often on The Single Woman Twitter page, and I was delighted to learn she was just as colorful, spirited, and feisty in person as I hoped she would be. All through breakfast I just kept looking around the table thinking to myself, *How did I get here?* I was sitting alongside a personal hero of mine who had jumped off the Twitter page on which I so often quoted her and into my reality. I could feel God smiling down on me the entire day. It was amazing how quickly and powerfully your dreams can become reality when you hand them over to Him.

I had made it through part one of my *Oprah's Lifeclass* adventure, and I still had part two to go, looking bigger, brighter, and shinier to me than even the brilliant orange sun that beamed down on Alli, Jennifer, and me that day as we giggled and snapped photos in front of the St. Louis Arch.

Next up: the Big Apple.

––––––

Precisely six months to the day after I traveled to New York City to see Mr. E, I returned to the city for round two of *Oprah's Lifeclass*. I couldn't help but reflect upon the last time I traveled to the Big Apple and what different circumstances surrounded the trip. I didn't even feel like the same girl this time around. As much as I had learned about myself on the last trip, it had been about chasing love, chasing an illusion, chasing Mr. E; and this time I was here for no other reason than to chase my dreams. Unlike Mr. E, it seemed my dreams were actually within reach. I was so grateful to God in that moment that He doesn't allow us to catch everything and everyone we chase. Imagine if He did. Think back on your own life, and remember some of the fruitless goals, relationships, friendships, and careers you've chased but haven't caught. Then imagine what your life might have been like had you actually caught them. Chances are, when you finally surrendered the chase, slowed down, and stopped running, the thing that really was meant for you showed up and caught *you*. Had I realized my temporary goal of catching Mr. E, I might have forfeited my lifelong dream of working with Oprah. Remember that the next time the object of your desire dances just beyond your reach. It might be best to drop your arms and let whatever it is dance away.

For this trip, I had brought my parents with me. The *Oprah's Lifeclass* taping was at Radio City Music Hall, and I was thrilled to get to share the experience with my mom and dad. We arrived a day early so we could have a little time to enjoy the city, and we took full advantage, hitting Times Square, touring the 9/11 memorial site, and doing a little shopping (my idea, not my parents'). The pinnacle of the day came for me when I managed to track down Carrie Bradshaw's brownstone as it was featured in *Sex and the City*. I stood there on the street, staring up at it in awe. Though my message was far more PG-rated than Carrie's, I felt a kinship to the fictional character through our love of writing, shoes, and unavailable men. And how could I not draw the obvious parallel between Carrie and her ever-elusive Mr. Big, and me and my ever-elusive Mr. E? As I sat on the steps of her iconic building, my mind drifted to one of my favorite episodes of the show when Carrie had finally moved on from Mr. Big with someone new, and he couldn't stand it. He started calling frantically, pleading with her to see him, finally showing up in front of her apartment. But he was too late. Carrie was moving to Paris, and she was finally ready to leave Mr. Big in her rearview mirror. I could picture her turning to him on the sidewalk, the same sidewalk that stretched in front of me now, saying firmly, "You can drive down this street all you want, because I don't live here anymore!" before disappearing down the street.[*] I smiled, thinking of my time here six months ago with Mr. E, thinking of the disappointment of being shown engagement rings but not receiving a proposal, thinking of all the years I had spent on the dead-end road that was our relationship. And thinking of how I had finally learned to love myself enough to walk away. Then I stood, facing my fictional counterpart's door, and said aloud to the ghost of Mr. E that darted all around me: "You can drive down the road not taken all you want, because *I don't live there anymore.*"

Then I turned, feeling a feisty, unbreakable spirit rise up in me as I disappeared down the street and into the rest of my life.

———

[*] Darren Star, Michael Patrick King, and Candace Bushnell, "An American Girl in Paris: Part One," *Sex and the City,* season 6, episode 20, directed by Timothy Van Patten, aired Februrary 15, 2004 (Home Box Office (HBO), 1994).

The blogging team was reunited the next morning at Radio City Music Hall, and it was wonderful to see everyone again. We learned that we would be meeting with Tony Robbins and Deepak Chopra that morning, then, a little later in the day, with fellow blogger Perez Hilton. All three gentlemen were on the panel that day and wanted the opportunity to meet with us and answer our questions. Once again I was blown away to be in the company of such greatness, Mr. Robbins and Mr. Chopra especially. Both men had even left gifts for us in our dressing room (our dressing room area was the same one used by the Rockettes)—a copy of his new book from Deepak, an iPod touch from Tony.

The morning went by in a whirlwind as we were escorted in to meet Tony, Deepak, and then Perez. Tony was just as intense and passionate as I imagined he would be. Deepak was incredibly humble, gentle, and kind, and Perez lived up to my expectations and beyond with his wildly outspoken, slightly eccentric personality. Though a lot of people have criticized Perez over the years (myself included), I actually had to admire his willingness to speak out on such a public platform about how he was working to "change his energy" and transform the tone of his often catty and abrasive blog into something a little kinder and gentler. Regardless of whether I agreed with his tactics or not, it took bravery to sit in front of thousands of people and admit how wrong you had been and ask for forgiveness, and I admired him for it.

After a busy and hectic morning, I think all the bloggers were looking forward to a chance to kick back in our dressing room for a few minutes and rest. Instead, following our meeting with Perez, we were ushered in to a small room to receive some very important news.

We were going to meet Oprah.

Though we had been told in advance that we "might" get a chance to see Oprah or speak to her in passing at some point during the *Oprah's Lifeclass* process, Oprah had instead requested a thirty-minute meet and greet with the blogging team so she could sit down with us and hear a little bit of each of our stories.

The culmination of the past thirty years of my life, every step of my journey, every fear, heartbreak, disappointment, victory, and defeat—it all came into focus. It had all been leading me here, to this moment, to realize one of my biggest dreams of meeting one of my biggest inspirations.

As we made our way through the backstage area of Radio City Music Hall, down one long hallway after another, my heart was nearly pounding out of my chest. *So this is what a dream come true feels like*, I was thinking.

We walked through several long hallways, down a couple of staircases, through a back door to an outside area before we wove our way back into a different part of the building, no one making a sound. Everyone, I think, was lost in their own thoughts about what the experience meant to them. Finally we made our way to a closed-off room, guarded by a giant bodyguard, where Oprah was finishing up a media interview. Still no one made a peep. I think we were all too busy soaking in the moment that truly felt like one of the biggest of our lives to bother with idle chatter. I felt close to tears as I imagined what my eleven-year-old self would do if she could see me in this moment. I pictured that little girl who loved to read and loved to write and dreamed of being a journalist someday, a little girl who faithfully watched the Oprah show every day after school and dreamed of what it would be like to host her own show and inspire people and change lives. What would that little girl say if she could see me now? Had she known all along?

I had met famous people before, but never the person who had inspired so much of the very direction that my life path had taken, and I had no idea what to say to her. So I reached out and silently took God's hand, asking Him to usher me through the next few moments. As He always does, He calmed my nerves, quieted my anxious thoughts, and spoke words of comfort and encouragement into my heart. *I am bigger than this moment*, I felt Him whisper in that still, small voice. *Your destiny is bigger than this moment. I designed this moment to remind you of that. Keep hold of My hand, and there will be no position of favor too high for you to realize.*

Then, suddenly, it was time.

The OWN team ushered us all into the room, where we sat in a semicircle facing a solitary chair holding none other than— *ta-da!*—Oprah herself. It was a setting as intimate as a dinner table with friends. Was this *really* happening?!

Within five minutes, I truly felt like I was sitting there chatting with someone I had known my entire life. And I guess, in a way, I was. As amazing as I always thought Oprah would be, she surpassed that and then some. She was so down-to-earth, so funny, so warm, so centered, and so sure of herself. At one point, her team motioned that it was time for her to go, and she said, "But we're not done talking yet!" And there she stayed, for ten to fifteen more minutes, probably edging into her next appointment in her insanely busy schedule in order to carve out time for a group of writers who would have been happy with even just five minutes of her time.

Though I only got to speak to Oprah briefly that day, I was able to tell her how special it was to me to be sitting there with her.

"Meeting you has been a goal on my vision board for many years," I admitted shyly.

She smiled broadly. "Was I wearing this?" she joked, gesturing to her purple blouse. The entire room broke out in laughter. It was a priceless moment.

Before we left the room, we all got to take photos with her. As I started to leave after our photo was snapped, she called behind me, "You know, there's a Twitter page called The Single Woman."

I turned back to her, grinning from ear to ear.

"That's me!"

"Oh wow. Good for you!" she replied in her Oprah cheerleader voice, giving me two big thumbs-up.

Oprah knew who I was. My biggest hero knew who I was.

I was in New York City at Radio City Music Hall, meeting some of the biggest voices of inspiration, healing, and hope in the world, working with some of the most dynamic and talented bloggers in the country, having been invited there by Oprah's team to be a part of a VIP blogging program that would open doors to me in the future that before I would have likely only pounded on fruitlessly. And to top it all off, Oprah herself knew who I was. Better yet, she knew what I was building with The Single Woman. I was Oprah-approved.

But even better than that, I was God-approved.

This I know to be true, friends: your life, your path, your journey—it isn't going to look like everyone else's. And that's okay. Mine hasn't. I planned to be married with children by now. Instead, I'm single and giving birth to books instead of babies. And while I haven't yet realized my dream of someday getting married, I've realized other dreams. Amazing dreams. I've traveled to cities I love, met my biggest heroes, become a published author, been on television, walked red carpets, and prayed with and for single women who live in parts of the world my toes have never touched. I've looked high and low for love and haven't found it, but you know what? Along the way I found myself.

We paint an idea of what our lives are *going* to look like and are *supposed* to be like in our minds, and the reality very rarely matches up with the fantasy. You lose the job. You lose the love. You get sidetracked. You get discouraged. You get blindsided by bad news. You get beat up by life. You lose your way, and you lose your career, and you lose your faith. And you wonder if you'll ever get your Happy Ending or if you're destined to wander this planet alone.

But what you can't see at the time is this:

You lose the job because it wasn't your destination, but merely a stop along the way. God knows that you were never meant for a cubicle even though you don't yet realize it. You lose the love because to cling to it would hold you back from everything else you're meant to experience. Your arms are now free to grab on to life. You get sidetracked because God knows the only way to get you off the stubborn path you're on is to allow you to run smack dab into a detour. You get discouraged because you're human, and fallible, and sometimes you need those down moments to rest, regroup, and prepare for the up moments. You get blindsided by bad news and beat up by life because this is life and bad things happen, but the beautiful flip side of your present struggle is that it prepares you for your future success. You lose everything you think is so vital to your very existence because God longs for you not just to see but to truly grasp that all you really need in this life is Him. You wander the planet alone for a longer time than you would have liked because you have a destiny that's so special, and so important, and so far beyond anything you could have ever imagined for yourself, a relationship before its time would only distract you from fulfilling it.

And somewhere along the way, amidst all the loss, tears, triumph, tragedy, joy, pain, laughter, transformation, restoration, lessons, love, and life, you realize that the true meaning of it all isn't to settle for merely a Happy Ending, but to hold out for a Happy Everything.

Epilogue

$\mathcal{L}$ife after *Oprah's Lifeclass* finds me still very much a student in the class of life.

The whole experience of working with Oprah truly did usher in a new era of my life. A couple of months after I returned from New York, I signed my first book deal. And a couple of months after that, I turned in my notice at my day job. The three-year struggle to balance my dream and my job was over. I was a full-time writer. (My vision board had certainly had a very successful few months!)

As I look back over the many mishaps and miracles I've encountered on the road to my own unorthodox and often wildly colorful version of Happily Ever After, it seems the hand of God on my life has been there every step of the way, bringing some of my biggest dreams to life right in front of me. Because I'm perfect? No. Because I'm willing to share my weaknesses and imperfections to help others overcome theirs.

So would I whisper hints of the future in younger Mandy's ear if I could talk to that girl now?

I don't think so.

If I could talk to her now, I'd simply let her know that she's

266

going to face some tough times ahead. She's going to be hurt and get her heart broken more than a few times. She's not always going to get the job, or the guy, or her way. She's going to stray far from the path a few times, and disappoint God, her family, and herself more than a few times. But as the prophecy spoken over her at age twenty would reveal, I would remind her: "God has never been, nor will He ever be, very far from you."

And after sharing a few giggles with her about the fact that while we once thought we'd be married with kids by age twenty-five, we're thirty-four and still single, I'd tell her this:

> There is a bigger plan at work here. What now seems wrong, unfair, and ridiculous will all make sense later. The colorful characters in your life will one day be colorful characters in your story, and the lessons learned from each broken heart you endure will help heal thousands more.
>
> So take chances, take leaps of faith, bet on yourself, kiss the boy, go out on more limbs. Even if things go horribly awry (and they sometimes will), at least you'll be left with a fabulous memory instead of a painful regret.

Then I'd give her a great big hug and tell her to throw down her expectations, throw up her hands, and enjoy the ride. Because it's not going to turn out the way she thought it would.

It's going to turn out so much better.

———

I've never made it back to Vegas. Who knows if I ever will? Every step of my journey is in God's hands, and where He leads, I will follow. The one thing I do know for certain is this: If and when I do make it to Las Vegas someday, my luggage can join me if it feels so inclined.

But my baggage is staying behind.

Acknowledgments

To my family: Dad, Mom, Cher, Kevin, Emma, Livi, and Nanny—Thank you for your unwavering support, love, prayers, and belief in me. You've always known my head was just a little bit more in the clouds than everyone else, and instead of trying to talk me down, you give me a boost. I would not be the woman I am without you.

To my lifelong friend, Alli—Thank you for being my "person." I am so blessed to have you in my life. Here's to many more crazy adventures and dreams coming true!

To my friend, Mastin Kipp—For believing in me, inspiring me, and yes, even challenging me—thank you.

To Dodinsky—I don't know where I'd be without you as my guide on this crazy journey of a writer! I know you don't like to be called my "mentor," so I will simply call you my friend. For a million reasons, THANK YOU. The only thing more beautiful than your message is your heart.

To my church friends and family at both Cross Point and Oasis—I am in awe of your endless love, support, encouragement, and prayers. I could not be more blessed to walk amongst two of the greatest church bodies in the city of Nashville.

To Jennifer Deshler—How thankful I am that you "discovered" me on that long-ago day. You took my dream and made it a reality. I am honored to call you a colleague and a friend.

To Amanda Shanks—For creating the logo that launched a brand. Your talent and heart and creativity inspire me more than you will ever know. I could say a million thank you's, and it still wouldn't be enough!

To Stephanie Yeagar—Providence crossed our paths on Twitter because we were simply meant to be friends! You are a social media genius and a master at building relationships. For everything you've done to help, plan, encourage, connect, promote, strategize, the list goes on and on and on—THANK YOU.

To my entire wonderful team at Thomas Nelson: Joel Miller, Brian Hampton, Kristen Parrish, Chad Cannon, Katy Boatman, Belinda Bass, Katherine Rowley, Julie Allen, Debbie Eicholtz, Mallory Perkins, Ramona Wilkes, and Emily Lineberger, as well as videographer Caleb Rexius—Thank you for believing in me and my story. What an adventure this has been. Who knew that by NOT getting to Vegas, I would arrive at my destiny instead? You all have been the most amazing "traveling companions" on this journey that I could ask for. For not yelling at me when I missed a deadline, to honoring the book title I first dreamed up over a decade ago, to helping me fend off crazed geese while shooting promotional videos in the park—thank you. Me AND my luggage would be lost without you.

And finally, to my 550,000+ readers and followers across the world—YOU are why I do what I do. It has been my great honor to speak into your lives over the past few years. I hope this book inspires all of you as much as you've inspired me . . . and reminds you that on the road to Happily Ever After, sometimes the journey is even more beautiful, colorful, and magical than the destination.

About the Author

Blogger turned hit author, Mandy Hale is affectionately known around the world as The Single Woman. With a heart to inspire single women to live their best lives and to never ever settle, Mandy cuts to the heart of the matter with her inspirational, straight-talking, witty, and often wildly humorous take on the life of a modern single woman.

A contributor to Glamour.com, Mandy was also invited by Oprah in 2012 to cover her "Lifeclass: The Tour" events in St. Louis and New York City as part of OWN's "VIP Press Corps." That same year, she was featured at the Women of Faith conference in Hartford, Connecticut. She has been named a "Twitter Powerhouse" by the *Huffington Post*, a "Woman of Influence" by the *Nashville Business Journal*, and a "Single in the City" by *Nashville* Lifestyles magazine. She has been featured in *Forbes*, the *Christian Post*, the *Huffington Post*, as well as on the *700 Club*. With more than one million readers from around the world, Mandy has made a name for herself as the voice of empowerment and sassiness for single women everywhere.

Mandy's first book, *The Single Woman: Life, Love, & a Dash of Sass*, was released in August 2013 and has gone on to garner rave reviews.

Connect with Mandy online at:

www.TheSingleWoman.net

www.Twitter.com/TheSingleWoman

www.Facebook.com/TheSingleWoman

www.Instagram.com/TheSingleWoman